S0-ADC-330

Our Daily Bread

2012
DEVOTIONAL
COLLECTION

DISCOVERY HOUSE
PUBLISHERS®

Feeding the Soul with the Word of God

© 2009, 2011 by RBC Ministries
All rights reserved.

Discovery House Publishers is affiliated with
RBC Ministries, Grand Rapids, Michigan.

Discovery House books are distributed to the trade exclusively by
Barbour Publishing, Inc., Uhrichsville, Ohio.

Requests for permission to quote from this book should be directed to:
Permissions Department, Discovery House Publishers, P.O. Box 3566,
Grand Rapids, MI 49501, or contact us by e-mail at
permissionsdept@dhp.org

All Scripture quotations, unless otherwise indicated, are taken from the
New King James Version. Copyright © 1982 by Thomas Nelson, Inc.
Used by permission. All rights reserved.

ISBN: 978-1-57293-511-2

Printed in Italy

First printing August 2011

Quiet Time with God

Before God can work through us, He must work in us. That's why we must keep on growing in our relationship with Him. And there is no better way to nurture that relationship than to spend time daily with Him, reading the Bible, reflecting on what it has to say for our life, and spending time in prayer. This year's worth of daily readings selected from the popular *Our Daily Bread* devotional encourages this daily discipline with short devotional readings for each day of the year. Each devotional is based on a Scripture passage and developed around a relevant story or illustration that illuminates the truth of God's Word.

> Many followers of Christ find that a daily time of Bible reading and prayer is essential in their walk of faith. This "quiet time" is a disconnection from external distractions in order to connect with God. The "green pastures" and "still waters" of Psalm 23:2 are more than an idyllic country scene. They speak of our communion with God whereby He restores our souls and leads us in His paths (v. 3). —David C. McCasland

Keeping a daily appointment with God is a vital part of the Christian life. The more time we spend with God—reading His Word, conversing with Him in prayer, meditating on thoughts from His Word—the better we get to know Him and the more our lives begin to reflect His image and His truth.

We hope that this yearly devotional drawn from the pages of *Our Daily Bread* will help you keep those daily appointments and give you spiritual guidance along your way.

Live It!

READ: Ezekiel 33:30–33

You are to them as a very lovely song . . . they hear your words, but they do not do them. —EZEKIEL 33:32

Each year, one of my goals is to read the entire Bible. While listing it among my New Year's resolutions, I noticed a bookmark on my desk. On one side was a brief appeal for people to take in foster children. On the other side were these words referring to that appeal: "Don't read it. Live it. Real children. Real stories. Real life." The people who produced the bookmark knew how easily we absorb information without acting on it. They wanted people to respond.

Regular intake of God's Word is a worthy practice, but it's not an end in itself. The prophet Ezekiel spoke to an audience who loved to listen but refused to act. The Lord said to Ezekiel: "Indeed you are to them as a very lovely song of one who has a pleasant voice and can play well on an instrument; for they hear your words, but they do not do them" (33:32).

Jesus said: "Whoever hears these sayings of Mine, and does them, I will liken him to a wise man who built his house on the rock" (Matthew 7:24).

How will each of us read the Bible this year? Will we read it quickly to achieve the goal of getting through it? Or will we read it with the aim of doing what it says?

Don't just read it. Live it!

—DM

The Bible gives us all we need
To live our lives for God each day;
But it won't help if we don't read
Then follow what its pages say. —Sper

The value of the Bible consists not only in knowing it but obeying it.

Don't Waste Your Breath

READ: Genesis 2:1–7

Let everything that has breath praise the Lord.
—PSALM 150:6

If I were to scoop up a handful of dirt and blow into it, all I would get is a dirty face. When God did it, He got a living, breathing human being capable of thinking, feeling, dreaming, loving, reproducing, and living forever.

As one of these human beings, I speak of "catching" my breath, "holding" my breath, or "saving" my breath, but these are idioms of language. I cannot save my breath for use at a later time. If I don't use the one I have now, I'll lose it, and I may even lose consciousness.

When God breathed into Adam, He gave more than life; He gave a reason to live: Worship! As the psalmist said, "Let everything that has breath praise the Lord" (Psalm 150:6).

This means that we waste our breath when we use it for something that doesn't honor the one in whom "we live and move and have our being" (Acts 17:28).

Although we cannot blow life into a handful of dirt, we can use our breath to speak words of comfort, to sing songs of praise, and to run to help the sick and oppressed. When we use our breath to honor our Creator with our unique combination of talents, abilities, and opportunities, we will never be wasting it.

—JAL

Breathe on me, Breath of God,
Fill me with life anew,
That I may love what Thou dost love,
And do what Thou wouldst do. —Hatch

All that I am and have I owe to Jesus.

Eating as Worship

READ: Genesis 2:8–17

Have you found honey? Eat only as much as you need.
—PROVERBS 25:16

When you walk into the bookstore and see a table filled with books on dieting, you know it must be January. After several weeks of overeating all kinds of holiday foods, people in many cultures turn their attention to not eating.

Food plays an important role in Scripture. God uses it not only to bless us but also to teach us. Our misuse of food keeps us from knowing God in ways He wants to be known.

In the Old Testament, God gave instructions to Adam as to what to eat and what not to eat (Genesis 2:16–17). Later He gave the Israelites manna to convince them that He was God and to test them to find out if they believed Him (Exodus 16:12; Deuteronomy 8:16). In the New Testament, the apostle Paul stated the proper attitude for everything we do, including eating: "Whether you eat or drink, . . . do all to the glory of God" (1 Corinthians 10:31).

When we think of food as a friend that comforts us or an enemy that makes us fat, we miss the wonder of receiving with gratitude a splendid gift from God. Obsessive eating or not eating indicates that we are focused on the gift rather than on the giver, which is a form of idolatry.

When eating becomes a true act of worship, we will no longer worship food.
—JAL

You alone are worthy, Lord,
To be worshiped and adored;
We to You our tribute bring
As our hearts rejoice and sing. —Hess

When food becomes our god, our appetite
for the Bread of Life is diminished.

Living Deceptively

READ: 2 Timothy 3:10–17

You have known the Holy Scriptures, which are able to make you wise for salvation through faith which is in Christ Jesus. —2 TIMOTHY 3:15

The year 2007 was labeled the "Year of Living Deceptively" for South Korea, because of the country's numerous scandals involving fake academics and corrupt politicians. A survey of 340 professors selected the Chinese phrase "ja-gi-gi-in" (deceiving yourself and others) to sum up the year.

It should not surprise us to hear of deception like that. The apostle Paul wrote in 2 Timothy 3:13, "Evil men and impostors will grow worse and worse, deceiving and being deceived." To deceive is to make others believe falsehood as truth and accept wrong as right.

Our defense against deception is to know God's Word, for "all Scripture is given by inspiration of God, and is profitable for doctrine, for reproof, for correction, for instruction in righteousness" (v. 16). *Correction* is to set right what is wrong, and *instruction* is to make known what is right. God's Word not only makes us aware of wrongs, it also prompts and teaches us to do what is right.

Is your New Year's resolution to walk rightly before God and others and to be "thoroughly equipped for every good work" (v. 17)? Then read and apply God's Word, asking the Lord to make you a person of integrity.

—AL

> *When reading God's Word, take special care*
> *To find the rich treasures hidden there;*
> *Give thought to each truth, each precept hear,*
> *Then practice it well with godly fear.* —Anonymous

The more we meditate on Scripture, the more readily we'll detect error.

A Lot to Remember

READ: Proverbs 10:11–21

He who restrains his lips is wise. —PROVERBS 10:19

Thanks a lot," the man behind the postal counter said to the person in front of me. The clerk, Jon, had seen me in line and was hoping I would overhear him. When it was my turn, I said hello to Jon, who had been a student of mine when I taught high school in the 1980s.

"Did you notice what I said to her?" Jon asked. "I told her, 'Thanks a lot.'" Sensing that I was missing his point, he explained, "Remember what you told us about the term *a lot*? You said *a lot* was a piece of land, not a phrase to use instead of *much*."

Astounding! An English lesson from a quarter-century before had stuck with Jon through all those years. That speaks clearly to us of the importance of what we say to others. It also confirms one of my favorite lines by poet Emily Dickinson:

> *A word is dead*
> *When it is said,*
> *Some say.*
> *I say it just*
> *Begins to live*
> *That day.*

The words we say may have long-term consequences. Our comments, our compliments, and even our harsh criticisms may stick with the hearer for decades.

No wonder Scripture says, "He who restrains his lips is wise" (Proverbs 10:19). The words we speak today live on. Let's make sure they come from "the tongue of the righteous" (v. 20).   —DB

THINKING IT OVER

How can I be more thoughtful today in what I say?

The tongue is a small organ that creates either discord or harmony.

Faith of a Child

READ: Matthew 18:1–5

Unless you are converted and become as little children, you will by no means enter the kingdom of heaven. —MATTHEW 18:3

One Sunday I heard Mike talk about his relationship with his two fathers—the one who raised him as a child, and his Father in heaven.

First he described his childhood trust of his earthly father as "simple and uncomplicated." He expected his dad to fix broken things and to give advice. He dreaded displeasing him, however, because he often forgot that his father's love and forgiveness always followed.

Mike continued, "Some years ago I made a mess of things and hurt a lot of people. Because of my guilt, I ended a happy, simple relationship with my heavenly Father. I forgot that I could ask Him to fix what I had broken and seek His advice."

Years passed. Eventually Mike became desperate for God, yet he wondered what to do. His pastor said simply, "Say you're sorry to God, and mean it!"

Instead, Mike asked complicated questions, like: "How does this work?" and "What if . . . ?"

Finally his pastor prayed, "Please, God, give Mike the faith of a child!"

Mike later testified joyfully, "The Lord did!"

Mike found closeness with his heavenly Father. The key for him and for us is to practice the simple and uncomplicated faith of a child. —JY

> *Have you noticed that the childlike faith*
> *Of a little girl or boy*
> *Has so often shown to older folks*
> *How to know salvation's joy?* —Branon

Faith shines brightest in a childlike heart.

The Innocent Man

READ: Genesis 18:22–33

Shall not the Judge of all the earth do right? —GENESIS 18:25

John Grisham is well known for his courtroom novels—fast-paced tales of lawyers and victims, authorities and wrongdoers. However, his book *The Innocent Man* is not fiction. It is a real-life story of injustice. It tells of the brutal murder of a young woman and the two men who, though innocent, were convicted and sentenced to death for the crime. Only with the advent of DNA testing were they proven innocent and spared from execution after seventeen years of suffering wrongly. At long last, justice prevailed.

Everyone desires justice. But we must recognize that our human frailty makes it challenging to mete out true justice. And we can be bent toward revenge, making a casualty out of the pursuit of it.

It's helpful to remember that perfect justice can be found only in God. Abraham described the God of justice with the rhetorical question, "Shall not the Judge of all the earth do right?" (Genesis 18:25). The answer is yes. His courtroom is the one and only place where we can be certain that justice will prevail.

In a world filled with injustice, we can take the wrongs done to us, submit them to the Judge of all the earth, and trust Him for ultimate justice. —BC

The best of judges on this earth
Aren't always right or fair;
But God, the Righteous Judge of all,
Wrongs no one in His care. —Egner

Life is not always fair, but God is always faithful.

The King

READ: Revelation 17:9–14

These will make war with the Lamb, and the Lamb will overcome them, for He is Lord of lords and King of kings. —REVELATION 17:14

It might be surprising how many people around the world know that today is Elvis Presley's birthday. His enduring popularity spans generations and cultures. More than thirty years after his death, sales of Presley's music, memorabilia, and licensing agreements generate millions of dollars in annual income. Once dubbed "The King of Rock and Roll," Elvis is often called simply, "The King."

Whether the "kings" of this world are celebrities, athletes, crowned heads, or tycoons, they come and go. Their influence may be immense and their followers fanatically loyal, but it doesn't last forever.

The Bible, however, refers to Jesus Christ as the eternal King. Revelation 17 speaks prophetically of earthly kings who will fight to establish their authority at the end of the ages. Biblical scholars have debated the identities of these kings, but there is no mistake about the one they cannot overpower: "These will make war with the Lamb, and the Lamb will overcome them, for He is Lord of lords and King of kings; and those who are with Him are called, chosen, and faithful" (Revelation 17:14).

Jesus Christ the Lord is King, and He will reign forever.　—DM

> *The King of kings and Lord of lords,*
> *Who reigns today within our heart,*
> *Will one day bring His peace on earth—*
> *A kingdom that will not depart.* —Sper

There is no greater privilege than to be a subject of the King of kings.

To Judge or Not to Judge

READ: Matthew 7:1–21

Judge not, that you be not judged. —Matthew 7:1

What better way to tell people to mind their own business than to quote Jesus? People who seldom read the Bible are quick to quote Matthew 7:1 when they want to silence someone whose opinion they don't like. "Judge not, that you be not judged" seems like the perfect response.

In context, however, the passage indicates that we are indeed to judge; we're just supposed to avoid *faulty* judgments. Furthermore, our judgments are to begin with self: "First remove the plank from your own eye, and then you will see clearly to remove the speck from your brother's eye," Jesus said (v. 5). He then said, "Beware of false prophets" (v. 15). This too requires judging—we need to be able to discern truth from falsehood.

Jesus used the metaphor of fruit to give us the proper criteria for judging: "By their fruits you will know them" (v. 20). We are to judge people (including ourselves) by the quality of the fruit they produce. This fruit cannot be judged by earthly values, such as how good we look (v. 15). It must be judged by heavenly values—the fruit of the Spirit produced within us—love, joy, peace (Galatians 5:22).

Our tendency is to judge by appearance. But God judges by what we produce, and so should we.   —JAL

> They truly lead who lead by love
> And humbly serve the Lord;
> Their lives will bear the Spirit's fruit
> And magnify His Word. —D. DeHaan

Be slow to judge others and quick to judge yourself.

The Old and the New

READ: Galatians 5:16–23

If anyone is in Christ, he is a new creation; old things have passed away; behold, all things have become new. —2 CORINTHIANS 5:17

Typical resolutions in January are to lose weight, exercise more, spend less time at work and more time with family—maybe even stop chatting on the cell phone while driving.

It's not surprising that we want to change the things in our lives that we're unhappy about, even though most New Year's resolutions are kept for no more than three weeks. But what if you were to ask God what He wants you to change, improve, or begin this year? He might tell you to:

- Demonstrate more of the fruit of the Spirit in your life, which is "love, joy, peace, longsuffering, kindness, goodness, faithfulness, gentleness, self-control" (Galatians 5:22–23).
- "Love your enemies, bless those who curse you, do good to those who hate you, and pray for those who . . . persecute you" (Matthew 5:44).
- "Go into all the world and preach the gospel to every creature" (Mark 16:15).
- "Be content with such things as you have" (Hebrews 13:5).
- "Walk according to His commandments" (2 John 1:6).

As believers and new creations, we can be free from old patterns and failures. We must ask God to help us live each day in the power of the Holy Spirit. Then we can shed the old and embrace the new (2 Corinthians 5:17).

—CHK

How can we live to please the Lord?
By knowing what He says to do
And trusting in the Spirit's strength
To make us into someone new. —Sper

Resolutions are easier to keep when you rely on God.

That's Awesome!

READ: Psalm 66:1–12

Come and see the works of God; He is awesome in His doing toward the sons of men. —PSALM 66:5

The word *awesome* is tossed around a lot these days. Talk about cars, movies, songs, or food, and somebody will say, "That's awesome!"

But if we call earth-side stuff awesome and then call God awesome, we diminish how truly awesome He is. A friend of mine has a rule in her house—the word *awesome* is reserved only for God.

Trivializing God is no trivial matter. He is far more than a companion who will fit into our "buddy system" or a divine ATM responding to our impulses. Until we are stunned by the awesomeness of God, we will be way too impressed with ourselves and lose the joy of the privilege of belonging to an awesome God.

A look at the Psalms puts it all in perspective. One psalmist declares, "For the Lord Most High is awesome; He is a great King over all the earth" (47:2). And another psalm commands: "Say to God, 'How awesome are Your works!' . . . Come and see the works of God; He is awesome in His doing toward the sons of men" (66:3, 5).

What could be more awesome than the love that compelled Jesus to go to the cross for us? Put Him in His proper place as the only one who is truly awesome, and praise God for His awesome work in your life!

—JS

Holy, Holy, Holy! All the saints adore Thee,
Casting down their golden crowns around the glassy sea;
Cherubim and seraphim falling down before Thee,
Which wert and art and evermore shalt be. —Heber

If you're too impressed with yourself, take a closer look at God's awesomeness.

Beyond Help?

READ: Luke 23:33–43

Jesus said to him, "Assuredly, I say to you, today you will be with Me in Paradise." —LUKE 23:43

A 110-year-old Israeli Bedouin shepherd was admitted to a Beersheba hospital while experiencing a heart attack. In spite of his age, doctors worked hard to save him. The man was thought to be the oldest heart patient ever to be treated successfully with anticlotting drugs. A hospital spokesperson reported that the Bedouin returned to his tent in the Negev Desert to tend his goats.

The care given to this 110-year-old man faintly echoes the way Jesus responded to those people we consider beyond help. His ability and willingness to go beyond social barriers to help lepers and social outcasts went far beyond the normal expectations of what a good person would do.

Even in the agony of His own suffering, Jesus reached out to a dying man everyone else regarded as beyond help. The man was a criminal, condemned to die, and only hours from entering a lost eternity. In that moment, Jesus responded to the man's cry for help and said, "Today you will be with Me in Paradise" (Luke 23:43).

Do you know someone who seems beyond help today? Perhaps you think *you* are without hope. The God of the Bible specializes in giving help to those regarded as so old, so guilty, or so weak as to be beyond help.   —MD

Jesus seeks the lowly ones
When others do not care;
His lovingkindness and His help
He longs with them to share. —D. DeHaan

God's strength is best seen in our weakness.

Your Name Is Safe

READ: Revelation 2:12–17

I will give him a white stone, and on the stone a new name written which no one knows except him who receives it. —REVELATION 2:17

There's an old saying, "Sticks and stones may break my bones, but words can never hurt me." It isn't true. Words can hurt us most of all.

In my case the hurtful word was "Skinny-bones," a name I was given in the fourth grade. I chuckle now when I think of it—no one would call me "Skinny-bones" these days. But back then the name wounded me. It became the way I thought of myself.

My father and mother, however, had the grace and wisdom to have given me another name, David—a name that means "beloved" in Hebrew. Despite the taunts I received on the schoolyard, I knew I was loved at home.

Perhaps you were one of those children whom people called names: "Dummy," "Idiot, "Fatso," or some other cruel epithet. Perhaps people still call you names or use your given name with contempt. But take comfort in this: I believe that God will one day give you a new name, a term of endearment known only by your heavenly Father and you (Revelation 2:17). And His voice will convey tenderness, love, and acceptance because your name is dear to Him.

As a little child once put it, "When someone loves you, the way they say your name is different. Your name is safe in their mouth."

You—and your name—are safe with God.   —DR

> *The Father knows your name—but more than that,*
> *He knows your heart and all you think and do;*
> *With Him your name is safe—that will not change—*
> *But one day He will write your name anew.* —Hess

Your name is precious to God.

On the Wing

READ: Matthew 10:27–31

Do not fear therefore; you are of more value than many sparrows. —MATTHEW 10:31

In his book *On the Wing*, Alan Tennant chronicles his efforts to track the migration of the peregrine falcon. Valued for their beauty, swiftness, and power, these amazing birds of prey were favorite hunting companions of emperors and nobility. Sadly, the wide use of the pesticide DDT in the 1950s interfered with their reproductive cycle and placed them on the endangered species list.

Interested in the recovery of this species, Tennant attached transmitters to a select number of falcons to track their migration patterns. But when he and his pilot flew their Cessna behind the birds, they repeatedly lost signal from the transmitters. Despite their advanced technology, they were not always able to track the birds they wanted to help.

It's good to know that the God who cares for us never loses track of us. In fact, Jesus said that not even one sparrow "falls to the ground apart from [God's] will. . . . Do not fear therefore; you are of more value than many sparrows" (Matthew 10:29–31).

When we face difficult circumstances, fear may cause us to wonder if God is aware of our situation. Jesus' teaching assures us that God cares deeply and is in control. His tracking of our lives will never fail.
—DF

I would tell the Lord my longings,
Roll on Him my every care;
Cast upon Him all my burdens,
Burdens that I cannot bear. —*Weigle*

If God cares for birds, will He not care for His children?

It's in God's Word

READ: Psalm 119:25–32

*I will run the course of Your commandments, for
You shall enlarge my heart.* —PSALM 119:32

As optimistic as I am (I can find a bright side to just about everything), I also know that life can be a dark and lonely place.

I've talked to teenagers who have a parent whose anger makes just going home after school a dreaded trip.

I've known people who can't escape the curtain of depression.

I've spent considerable time with others who, like my wife and me, are enduring life with the sudden death of a child.

I've seen what relentless poverty can do to people all over the world.

Despite knowing that these scenarios exist, I don't despair. I know that hope is available in Jesus, that guidance comes through the Spirit, and that knowledge and power are found in God's Word.

The words of Psalm 119 give us encouragement. When our soul "clings to the dust," we can be revived according to God's Word (v. 25). When our soul is full of sorrow, we can be strengthened by His Word (v. 28). When we are threatened by deceit, we can follow the truth of His Word (vv. 29–30). Our heart can be set free by God's commands (v. 32).

Are life's demands overwhelming you? If so, you can find hope, guidance, and knowledge to help. It's in God's Word.   —DB

If your soul is parched and thirsty
And you feel weighed down by care,
Go to God's Word for refreshment—
You'll find strength and comfort there. —Sper

A well-read Bible makes a well-fed soul.

Impossible?

READ: Matthew 5:38–42

You have heard that it was said, "An eye for an eye and a tooth for a tooth." But I tell you not to resist an evil person. —MATTHEW 5:38–39

When Nobel Chairman Gunnar John delivered his presentation speech for Martin Luther King's 1964 Peace Prize, he quoted Jesus: "Whosoever shall smite thee on thy right cheek, turn to him the other also" (Matthew 5:39). As Mr. John noted: "It was not because he led a racial minority in their struggle for equality that Martin Luther King achieved fame. . . . [His] name will endure for the way in which he has waged his struggle."

In 1955, King had led a year-long, peaceful boycott to protest segregation on buses. He paid a high price. His home was bombed, and he was assaulted and arrested. He never retaliated. Eventually he was murdered.

How contrary Dr. King's peaceful example stands to my fleshly nature! I want justice now. I want retribution. I want others to pay for their wrongdoing, especially when it's directed at me. What I do *not* want is to turn the other cheek and invite them to take another swing.

Haddon Robinson comments on the lofty standards Jesus set forth in the Sermon on the Mount (Matthew 5–7), calling them "goals . . . not impossible ideals. [Jesus] wants His disciples to strive toward these goals to master a new kind of life."

Amid the injustices of life, may we have the courage, faith, and strength to turn the other cheek. —TG

> *So send I you to hearts made hard by hatred,*
> *To eyes made blind because they will not see,*
> *To spend—though it be blood—to spend and spare not—*
> *So send I you to taste of Calvary.* —Clarkson

It takes true strength to refuse to retaliate.

Brotherhood of the Sea

READ: Ephesians 2:14–22

Now, therefore, you are . . . fellow citizens with the saints. —EPHESIANS 2:19

On August 8, 2005, the world learned of the dramatic rescue of seven Russian sailors trapped in a small sub entangled in a fishing net. The men had survived three cold, dark days on the bottom of the ocean and had less than six hours of oxygen left. Meanwhile, up above, a frantic, unified rescue effort by Russian, Japanese, British, and American personnel was underway. Finally, the sub was freed. The Russian Defense Minister praised the operation, saying, "We have seen in deeds, not in words, what the brotherhood of the sea means."

The book of Ephesians talks about the unity of believers in Jesus by referring to the oneness of "the household of God" (2:19). The Gentiles, who were once "aliens" and "strangers" (v. 12), had now been "brought near by the blood of Christ" (v. 13), uniting them with their Jewish brothers and sisters. This unity is to permeate the efforts of the Christian community today.

Believers in Jesus are commissioned to undertake the most important rescue effort. People are dying without Christ. Praise God that united mission efforts are bringing hope, salvation, education, and relief to desperate people around the world. That's what the brotherhood of Christ is all about. —DE

In Christ there is no East or West,
In Him no South or North,
But one great fellowship of love
Throughout the whole wide earth. —Oxenham

A healthy church is the best witness to a hurting world.

Wonderfully Made

READS: Psalm 139:7–16

*I will praise You, for I am fearfully and
wonderfully made.* —PSALM 139:14

A conversation in George MacDonald's book *David Elginbrod* speaks
to those who wonder, at times, why God has made them the way
they are—and who wish they were someone else.

Lady Emily muses, "I wish I were you, Margaret."

Margaret answers, "If I were you, my lady, I would rather be what
God chose to make me than the most glorious creature that I could
think of. For to have been thought about—born in God's thoughts—
and then made by God, is the dearest, grandest, most precious thing
in all thinking."

MacDonald may have had Psalm 139:17 in mind: "How precious . . . are Your thoughts to me, O God!" In this psalm, David is
thinking about his conception, and vividly describes God's thoughts
as He wove him together in his mother's womb, creating a unique and
special individual to be the object of His love.

It's a comforting thought to know that we're not a terrible mistake,
but a very special creation, "born in God's thoughts." David could stand
before a mirror and say in all honesty and humility, "I am fearfully and
wonderfully made; marvelous are Your works" (v. 14).

You are a designer original! As such, you are dear, grand, and precious
to God.

—DR

Of all creation's treasures rare,
Not one compares in worth with man;
In God's own image he was made
To fill a place in His great plan. —D. DeHaan

You are one of a kind—designed to glorify God as only you can.

A Sin by Any Other Name

READ: Genesis 39:1–9

*How then can I do this great wickedness,
and sin against God?* —GENESIS 39:9

Joseph found himself in a difficult position one day when his master's wife attempted to seduce him. How tantalizing this woman must have been to a healthy young man! And it must have occurred to Joseph how fearsome her wrath would be when he spurned her advances. Yet he flatly resisted her.

Joseph's moral convictions stemmed from his clear view of sin and his reverence for God. He said to her, "How then can I do this great wickedness, and sin against God?" (Genesis 39:9).

Today, it is popular to call sin by more acceptable names. But using euphemisms for offenses against God will only weaken our resistance and trivialize sin's harmfulness to us.

To Joseph, sin was not just "an error of judgment." Nor was it a mere "slip of the tongue" or an "indiscretion" in a "moment of weakness." Joseph saw sin for what it was—a serious offense against the Lord—and he did not play down the gravity of the offense.

God's moral standards are absolute. It is only when we see sin as something abhorrent to the Lord that we will be motivated to make right moral judgments.

Calling sin by a softer name will change neither its offensiveness to God nor its cost to us.
—CPH

> *Was it for crimes that I have done*
> *He groaned upon the tree?*
> *Amazing pity! Grace unknown!*
> *And love beyond degree!* —Watts

There's no excuse for excusing sin.

Protocol

READ: James 1:1–8

Let him ask in faith, with no doubting, for he who doubts is like a wave of the sea driven and tossed by the wind. —JAMES 1:6

If you were invited to a meeting at the White House with the President of the United States, regardless of your opinion of him or her, you would probably go. Upon entering the White House, a protocol officer would meet you and outline the proper procedures for meeting the President. Suffice it to say, it would be unacceptable to let loose with a burst of undignified familiarity or negative criticism as you shook hands.

So it should come as no surprise that God's Word makes it clear that there is a protocol for entering the presence of God. Hebrews 11:6 outlines one aspect of appropriate interaction: "He who comes to God must believe that He is, and that He is a rewarder of those who diligently seek Him." God wants us to be fully devoted to Him—and He takes it personally when our hearts are filled with criticism, unbelief, and doubt.

James tells us that when we ask God for wisdom, the key to His response is whether or not we are asking "in faith" (1:6). God is pleased when we approach Him with unwavering faith.

So leave your doubt at the door and follow the protocol: Approach God with a heart of faith, and He will be pleased to provide all the wisdom you need.

—JS

> *God, give me the faith of a little child!*
> *A faith that will look to Thee—*
> *That never will falter and never fail,*
> *But follow Thee trustingly.* —Showerman

Exchange the dissatisfaction of doubt for the fulfillment of faith in God.

The Perfect Sentence

READ: Exodus 3:13–18

Who is like You, O Lord, among the gods? Who is like You, glorious in holiness, fearful in praises, doing wonders? —EXODUS 15:11

As a young girl writing in my diary, my secret ambition was to compose the perfect sentence. I wondered what it would look and sound like. Perhaps it would include a strong verb and colorful adjectives.

My pursuit of the perfect sentence will never be satisfied, but I have found a statement of perfection in Exodus 3:14. When the Lord God called Moses from the burning bush, He told him that he had been chosen to bring His people out of bondage in Egypt (v. 10). Moses, who was anxious about this responsibility, wondered what to say if the Israelites doubted him and asked who he was representing.

The Lord replied, "I AM WHO I AM" (v. 14). By using His unique name, He offered Moses a glimpse of the nature of His eternal existence in one sentence. You might say it's a statement of perfection!

Bible commentator G. Bush writes this about God's description of himself: "He, in distinction from all others, is the one only true God, the God who really is. . . . The eternal, self-existent, and immutable Being; the only being who can say that He always will be what He always has been."

God says, "I AM WHO I AM." He and His name are perfect. In reverence we are to bow before Him. —AC

Looking for perfection? Look to Jesus.

The God of Victory

READ: 2 Corinthians 2:14–17

*Do not be overcome by evil, but overcome
evil with good.* —ROMANS 12:21

In Greek mythology, Nike was the goddess of victory. Nike fought on the side of the Olympian gods, gaining a victory over the mighty Titans. As a result, she became a symbol of winning. But Nike's alleged powers were not just limited to warfare. She also became a favorite goddess of athletes who wanted to win in competitive sports. The Romans adopted her into their worship and gave her the Latin name Victoria.

In the Greco-Roman world where Paul taught, victory was highly valued. So when he expressed Christian truth, he used words his audience could understand. In his letters, he described Christ as the one who leads us in a military procession of triumph (2 Corinthians 2:14–17) and compared the Christian life to someone training for the ancient Olympic games (1 Corinthians 9:24–27).

Paul also used the word for victory in reference to our struggles with those who intentionally hurt us. "Overcome [be a victor over] evil with good" (Romans 12:21). This may mean returning kindness for spite or respectfully setting limits on evil behavior. In either case, an attitude of love cannot be generated in our own strength. But in Christ we have divine power that ancient pagans could only hope for. Jesus Christ is the genuine God of victory. —DF

*Through trials we learn to overcome,
Through Christ our victories are won;
Come lay your burdens at His feet
And find this inner peace so sweet.* —Halsey

God will give us the victory when we join Him in the fight.

Supersize It

READ: Isaiah 6:1–10

In the year that King Uzziah died, I saw the Lord sitting on a throne, high and lifted up, and the train of His robe filled the temple. —ISAIAH 6:1

After you placed your food order at a popular fast food restaurant, the cashiers used to ask that famous question: "Would you like to supersize that?" In essence, they were asking the customers if they wanted more of what they were already getting.

In a similar way, when we come into God's presence, I believe He asks us: "Would you like to enlarge your understanding of me today?"

Isaiah had one such experience with God. Through a painful event in his life, Isaiah saw the Lord "high and lifted up" (Isaiah 1). Through this encounter, God supersized Isaiah's understanding of His holiness. He saw God's complete moral excellence that unifies His attributes.

God also enlarged Isaiah's realization of his own sin (v. 5). This led to an expansion of his understanding of God's complete forgiveness and cleansing (vv. 6–7). Only when Isaiah understood the depth of his sin could he appreciate and accept forgiveness and cleansing from God. Finally, his encounter with God led to Isaiah's declaration of availability and commitment to reach out to others and to help them increase their understanding of God (vv. 8–9).

Let's ask God to supersize our understanding of His greatness today. —MW

Oh, I want to know You, blessed Lord,
Better than I've ever known before!
In Your Word I read of Your great purpose—
Help me understand it more and more. —Hess

Knowing about God is fascinating. Knowing God personally is life-changing.

Small Is Beautiful

READ: John 6:53–71

Who has despised the day of small things? —ZECHARIAH 4:10

Just the other day someone said of a friend, "This man is destined for a great ministry," by which he meant the man was headed for the big time—a high-profile church with a big budget.

It made me wonder: Why do we think that God's call is necessarily upwardly mobile? Why wouldn't He send His best workers to labor for a lifetime in some small place? Aren't there people in obscure places who need to be evangelized and taught? God is not willing that any perish.

Jesus cared about the individual as well as the masses. He taught large crowds if they appeared, but it never bothered Him that His audience grew smaller every day. Many left Him, John said (John 6:66), a fickle attrition that would have thrown most of us into high panic. Yet Jesus pressed on with those the Father gave Him.

We live in a culture where bigger is better, where size is the measure of success. It takes a strong person to resist that trend, especially if he or she is laboring in a small place.

But size is nothing; substance is everything. Whether you're pastoring a small church or leading a small Bible study or Sunday school class, serve them with all your heart. Pray, love, teach by word and example. Your little place is not a steppingstone to greatness. It is greatness.　　—DR

> *The Lord will give you help and strength*
> *For work He bids you do;*
> *To serve Him from a heart of love*
> *Is all He asks of you.* —Fasick

Little is much when God is in it.

Benediction Blessing

READ: Numbers 6:22–27

The Lord bless you and keep you. —NUMBERS 6:24

Our church introduced a new practice for the close of our traditional morning worship service. We turn to one another and sing the familiar Aaronic blessing that the Lord gave to Moses to give to Israel: "The Lord bless you and keep you; the Lord make His face shine upon you . . ." (Numbers 6:24–26). Our hearts are uplifted as we mutually catch the eye of a fellow believer and extend our blessing to him or her.

One Sunday, I noticed a heartwarming and special exchange that has now become a weekly event. In a pew near the front sat Oscar and Marian Carlson, faithful followers of Jesus Christ and devoted partners for the sixty-two years of their married life. When we began to sing, Oscar reached over and took Marian's hands in his. They sang the opening words of this special blessing to each other before looking to others. Everyone nearby sneaked a peek at the look of love and tenderness on their faces.

A benediction is not simply a ritualistic closing; it's a genuine prayerful wish for God's goodness to follow the other person. In offering it to one another, Oscar and Marian exemplify its warmest and deepest meaning. In blessing others, we express gratitude for what God has done for us through Christ's death (Hebrews 13:20–21).   —DE

> *Bless me, Lord, and make me a blessing;*
> *I'll gladly your message convey;*
> *Use me to help some poor needy soul,*
> *And make me a blessing today.* —*Anonymous*

God gives blessing to us so we can be a blessing to others.

Cod Liver Oil Coercion

READ: John 16:8–11

When the Helper comes, whom I shall send to you from the Father, the Spirit of truth who proceeds from the Father, He will testify of Me. —JOHN 15:26

A woman bought a bottle of cod liver oil to give to her dog so he could have a healthier and shinier coat. Every morning, she pried the dog's jaws open and forced the liquid down his throat. He struggled, but she persisted. *He doesn't know what's good for him!* she thought. Faithfully, each day she repeated the process.

One day, however, the bottle tipped over and she released her grip on the dog for just a moment to wipe up the mess. The dog sniffed at the fishy liquid and began lapping up what she had spilled. He actually loved the stuff. He had simply objected to being coerced!

Sometimes we use a similar method in telling others about Christ. Called buttonholing, it's an intense, in-your-face kind of confrontation. While earnestly desiring to share the gospel, we may end up repelling people instead. In our sincere but overly enthusiastic attempt, we create resistance.

We are called to share the good news, but we are not responsible for someone's acceptance or rejection of Christ. It's not our job to try to convict someone of sin. That's the Holy Spirit's responsibility (John 16:8).

As you tell others of Christ's sacrifice, be sensitive. Know when to slow down and let God and His Word do the convicting and drawing to himself.
—CHK

The Spirit's role is to convict
The world of all their sin
So they will seek forgiveness and
Be cleansed and changed within. —Sper

The Spirit convicts so that Christ might cleanse.

Prayer Circles

READ: Luke 18:9–14

Everyone who exalts himself will be humbled. —LUKE 18:14

Around the circle the sixth-grade girls went, taking turns praying for each other in the Bible-study group. "Father in heaven," Anna prayed, "please help Tonya not to be so boy-crazy."

Tonya added with a giggle, "And help Anna to stop acting so horrible in school and bothering other kids."

Then Talia prayed, "Lord, help Tonya to listen to her mother instead of always talking back."

Although the requests were real, the girls seemed to enjoy teasing their friends by pointing out their flaws in front of the others instead of caring about their need for God's help. Their group leader reminded them about the seriousness of talking to almighty God and the importance of evaluating their own hearts.

If we use prayer to point out the faults of others while ignoring our own, we're like the Pharisee in Jesus' parable. He prayed, "God, I thank You that I am not like other men—extortioners, unjust, adulterers, or even as this tax collector" (Luke 18:11). Instead, we're to be like the man who asked God to be merciful to him, "a sinner" (v. 13).

Let's be careful not to let our prayers become a listing of others' flaws. The kind of prayer God desires flows out of a humble evaluation of our own sinful hearts.   —AC

> *Lord, teach us how to pray aright,*
> *Oh, lead us in Your way;*
> *Humbly we bow in Your pure light;*
> *Lord, teach us how to pray.* —*Anonymous*

The highest form of prayer comes from the depths of a humble heart.

Murphy's Laws

READ: Exodus 20:1–17

You shall have no other gods before Me. —EXODUS 20:3

Murphy's Laws are observations about life that seem to have the weight of experience behind them. You've probably heard this one: "If anything can go wrong, it will." Here's another one: "You can't do just one thing; everything has its consequences."

My own experience seems to confirm many of Murphy's Laws, but it's that second one that I would hang on the wall as a motto. Wrong choices have their consequences. For example, if we choose to live for pleasure, that will affect our children, grandchildren, and great-grandchildren (Exodus 20:4–5). If we walk away from God, we may discover that our children have taken that trip with us. Later, even if we return to Him, they may not.

But there is also good news. Devotion to the Lord has its consequences too. Men and women who live in faith before God can have a strong influence on their children and their children's children. If they live a long life, they can witness the effect their faith has had on several generations. What satisfaction it brings to older people to see their posterity living for Christ!

Murphy and the Bible agree on this point: "Everything has its consequences."

—HR

If you sow seeds of wickedness,
Sin's harvest you will reap;
But scattered seeds of righteousness
Yield blessings you can keep. —Sper

People who follow Christ lead others in the right direction.

The Aging Process

READ: Psalm 71

Do not cast me off in the time of old age; do not forsake me when my strength fails. —PSALM 71:9

I was having breakfast with a friend who had recently celebrated his sixtieth birthday. We discussed the "trauma" of the number six being the first digit in his age and all that the age of sixty implies (retirement, social security, etc.). We also pondered the fact that he felt so much younger than such a "large" number would seem to indicate.

Then the conversation turned to the lessons, joys, and blessings he'd found in living those sixty years, and he said, "You know, it isn't really that bad. In fact, it's pretty exciting." The lessons of the past had brought a change in how he viewed the present.

Such is the aging process. We learn from our past in order to live in our present, a lesson reflected on by the psalmist: "For You are my hope, O Lord God; You are my trust from my youth" (71:5). He continued, "By You I have been upheld from birth; You are He who took me out of my mother's womb. My praise shall be continually of You" (v. 6).

As the psalmist looked back, he clearly saw the faithfulness of God. With confidence in that faithfulness, he could face the future and its uncertainties—and so can we.

May we say with the psalmist, "I will praise You—and Your faithfulness, O my God!" (v. 22). —BC

Great is Thy faithfulness, O God my Father!
There is no shadow of turning with Thee;
Thou changest not, Thy compassions they fail not;
As Thou hast been, Thou forever wilt be. —Chisholm

As the years add up, God's faithfulness keeps multiplying.

Planting Time

READ: Galatians 6:6–10

Do not be deceived, God is not mocked; for whatever a man sows, that he will also reap. —GALATIANS 6:7

Somewhere in the world right now a farmer is dropping seeds into the ground. Soon those seeds will begin to change the place where they were planted. The carefully prepared soil that appears barren today will become a field ready for harvest.

In the same way, New Year's resolutions can be seeds to alter the landscape of life for others and ourselves. This prayer of Saint Francis of Assisi is a powerful model of this longing to bring positive change in a hurting world:

Lord, make me an instrument of Your peace. Where there is hatred, let me sow love; where there is injury, pardon; where there is doubt, faith; where there is despair, hope; where there is darkness, light; and where there is sadness, joy.

A farmer who sows wheat is never surprised when wheat grows from the ground where it was planted. That's the universal law of sowing and reaping. Paul used it to illustrate a corresponding spiritual principle: "Do not be deceived, God is not mocked; for whatever a man sows, that he will also reap" (Galatians 6:7). Our sinful nature says, "Satisfy yourself," while the Spirit urges us to please God (v. 8).

Today is planting time. God has promised: "In due season we shall reap if we do not lose heart" (v. 9). —DM

> *Let's sow good deeds though life be grim*
> *And leave the harvest time with Him;*
> *Let's give and serve as to the Lord*
> *And look to Him for our reward.* —*Jarvis*

Sow today what you want to reap tomorrow.

A Breach in the Wall

READ: Nehemiah 4:7–18

All that is in the world—the lust of the flesh, the lust of the eyes, and the pride of life—is not of the Father. —1 JOHN 2:16

The 4,000-mile-long Great Wall of China was built to keep out invaders from the north. The first wall was constructed by Shi Huangdi, the first emperor of China, who lived between 259 and 210 BC. But in AD 1644 the Manchus broke through the Great Wall and overran China. They did this by bribing a general of the Ming Dynasty to open the gates.

During the reconstruction of ancient Jerusalem, Nehemiah understood the acute danger posed by those who opposed the rebuilding of the city's ruined walls. So he commanded constant vigilance. Half of the workers were to stand watch while half rebuilt the walls (Nehemiah 4:13–18).

As Christians, we must be vigilant that nothing breaches our spiritual defenses. Even the most mature believer can never afford to let down his guard.

The apostle John warns us of enemies from three quarters. He identifies them as "the lust of the flesh, the lust of the eyes, and the pride of life" (1 John 2:16). These enemies lure us away from God and His Word and leave a gap for the enemy to sneak in.

Let's be alert to what entices us today. A lapse opens the door to sin, which in turn may develop into a habit that overwhelms us. Don't permit a breach in the wall. —CPH

> *It may not be some heinous deed*
> *That chills our hearts and chokes the seed;*
> *It's often just a trifling toy*
> *That grabs our eye and steals our joy.* —Gustafson

The world is passing away, and the lust of it; but he who does the will of God abides forever. —1 John 2:17

God Is at Work

READ: Philippians 2:12–18

It is God who works in you both to will and to do for His good pleasure. —PHILIPPIANS 2:13

We always crave change in a new year. This is why on January 1 we start diets, exercise programs, and new hobbies. Of course, a month later we're usually back to our old bad habits. Maybe that's because we crave too big a change and do not have enough power and will to make the changes.

I wonder how many Jesus-followers have made commitments to change and grow spiritually but are experiencing frustration because they don't have the will and power to carry out those steps.

Paul addresses this issue in his letter to the Philippians. As he encouraged them to work out their salvation with fear and trembling (2:12), Paul said they would not be on their own. God himself would energize them to grow and carry out His tasks. The first area affected would be their desires. God was at work in them, giving them the desire to change and grow. He was also working to give them the power to make the actual changes (v. 13).

God has not left us alone in our struggles to attain spiritual growth. He helps us want to obey Him, and then He gives us the power to do what He wants. Ask Him to help you want to do His will.   —MW

Every day more like my Savior,
Every day my will resign,
Until at last Christ reigns supremely
In this grateful heart of mine. —Brandt

The power that compels us comes from the Spirit who indwells us.

Punxsutawney Phil

READ: 2 Peter 1:16–21

We have the prophetic word confirmed, which
you do well to heed. —2 PETER 1:19

Punxsutawney Phil is a groundhog that comes out of his burrow on Gobbler's Knob, Pennsylvania, each February 2 to predict the weather. According to legend, if Phil sees his shadow, there will be six more weeks of cold weather. If he doesn't see his shadow, spring will come early.

This is all humbug and good humor, of course. No one to my knowledge takes Phil's predictions seriously. Furthermore, he's unreliable—more often wrong than right, I'm told.

There is one, however, who is always right and whom we must take seriously. Peter writes of Him, "We have the prophetic word confirmed, which you do well to heed as a light that shines in a dark place, until the day dawns and the morning star rises in your hearts" (2 Peter 1:19).

Peter was thinking of that day on the Mount of Transfiguration with James and John when he saw Jesus standing with the two great prophets of the Old Testament, Moses and Elijah. In that august company of true prophets the Father pointed to the Son and said: "This is My beloved Son. Hear Him!" (Luke 9:35). Jesus' word is a "prophetic word" that is certain!

There is one who is never wrong and who will never lead us astray: our Lord Jesus. We must hear Him!   —DR

> *At the name of Jesus bowing,*
> *Falling prostrate at His feet,*
> *King of kings in heaven we'll crown Him*
> *When our journey is complete.* —Baxter

In a world full of speculation, only God's Word is certain.

Child's Play

READ: Matthew 18:1–11

Unless you are converted and become as little children, you will by no means enter the kingdom of heaven. —MATTHEW 18:3

After a surprise storm blanketed the Middle East with snow, a newspaper photo showed four armed men smiling as they built a snowman outside the battered walls of a military headquarters. The wintry weather also caused a protest to be canceled and delayed a debate over parliamentary matters of pressing importance. Men wearing long robes and women in traditional black dresses and headscarves were seen playing in the snow. There's something about snow that brings out the child in all of us.

And there's something about the gospel that beckons us to abandon our deep hostilities and feelings of self-importance in favor of a childlike humility and faith. When Jesus was asked, "Who then is greatest in the kingdom of heaven?" (Matthew 18:1), He called a little child to come to Him and said, "Unless you are converted and become as little children, you will by no means enter the kingdom of heaven" (v. 3).

It has been said that age diminishes our imagination, hopes, and possibilities. The older we get, the more easily we say, "That could never happen." But in a child's mind, God can do anything. A childlike faith filled with wonder and confidence in God unlocks the door to the kingdom of heaven. —DM

God, give me the faith of a little child!
A faith that will look to Thee—
That never will falter and never fail,
But follow Thee trustingly. —Showerman

Faith shines brightest in a childlike heart.

The Great Storyteller

READ: Luke 15:11–24

Jesus spoke to the multitude in parables; and without a parable He did not speak to them. —MATTHEW 13:34

In his book *Teacher Man*, Pulitzer Prize-winner Frank McCourt reflects on his thirty years as a teacher in New York City high schools. He used a variety of techniques in his English and creative writing classes, but one that seemed to surface again and again was the power of a compelling story to capture attention and encourage learning.

This method of instruction was used by the greatest teacher of all—the Lord Jesus Christ. The scholarly religious leader Nicodemus said to Jesus, "We know that You are a teacher come from God" (John 3:2). Yet when Jesus addressed the crowds that followed Him, He didn't quote from the tradition of the elders. Rather, He spoke with the homespun style of a storyteller.

The parables of Jesus endure because they showcase matters of the heart. Through the story of the Pharisee and tax collector (Luke 18), we learn about God's grace and forgiveness. And the story of the prodigal son (Luke 15) showcases God's love for repentant sinners.

The inspired parables of Jesus teach us about Him and the life He wants us to lead. We too can use our faith stories to point others to the ultimate storyteller and teacher, whose own life is the greatest story ever told.   —DF

> *Take control of my words today,*
> *May they tell of Your great love;*
> *And may the story of Your grace*
> *Turn some heart to You above.* —Sees

A good way to learn God's truth is to teach it to others.

The Search for Peace

READ: Philippians 4:4–12

The peace of God, which surpasses all understanding, will guard your hearts and minds. —PHILIPPIANS 4:7

At the height of their popularity, creativity, and wealth, the Beatles produced a controversial project called "The White Album." It signaled the breakup of the band by featuring pieces that were primarily individual in nature instead of collaborative.

It also revealed a growing disenchantment with all that their fame had produced. In his song "I'm So Tired," John Lennon expressed some of the emptiness of his "successful" and wealthy life when he wrote that he would give everything he had "for a little peace of mind." All that he had, all that he had accomplished, and all that he had become could not meet this simple, yet deep, personal need.

The world we live in cannot offer peace. It offers only poor options. Pleasure, power, and possessions are no substitute for peace of heart and mind.

Paul reminded the believers at Philippi, "The peace of God, which surpasses all understanding, will guard your hearts and minds through Christ Jesus" (Philippians 4:7). This is the peace God brings to those who have been reconciled to God by faith in His Son Jesus (Ephesians 2:14–16). It is a peace we are to share with a world that is desperate for it.

Peace—real peace—is found only in a relationship with Jesus. Have you received His peace?

—BC

FINDING REAL PEACE

Accept the reconciliation God offers by asking Him to forgive you. Believe that His Son Jesus died on the cross for your sins and was raised from the dead.

Peace I leave with you, My peace I give to you;
not as the world gives do I give to you. —Jesus

Rise Up!

READ: John 20:1–20

You, being dead in your trespasses, . . . He has made alive together with Him. —COLOSSIANS 2:13

On February 6, 1958, a chartered plane carrying most of the members of the English football (soccer) club Manchester United crashed on takeoff from Munich, Germany. With so many of their star players lost, some despaired over prospects for the club's survival. Yet today it is one of the best-known teams in the world. Fittingly, the man who rebuilt the team, Matt Busby, survived the crash himself.

Nearly 2,000 years ago, Jesus' arrest and subsequent crucifixion caused many of His followers to despair. The disciples themselves had lost hope. But their despondency evaporated on that first Easter morning when they found that the stone sealing the tomb had been moved aside (John 20:1). Jesus had risen!

Jesus soon appeared to Mary Magdalene (vv. 11–16) and then to His disciples, who had gathered behind locked doors (v. 19). His visit brought a remarkable change in them. As one version renders it, they were "overjoyed" (v. 20 NIV).

Perhaps your world has crashed around you. It may be a deeply personal loss, a tragedy in your family, or some other great trial. Jesus' resurrection proved that He is greater than the greatest obstacles. He can rebuild your life—as He did with His disciples—starting today. —CPH

He rose! And with Him hope arose, and life and light.
Men said, "Not Christ, but death, died yesternight."
And joy and truth and all things virtuous
Rose when He rose. —*Anonymous*

God can turn any difficulty into an opportunity.

Turkish Delight

READ: John 21:15–19

Your law is my delight. —PSALM 119:174

In C. S. Lewis's *The Lion, the Witch and the Wardrobe,* the White Witch needed to know only one thing about Edmund to get him to betray his siblings. By asking a few simple questions, the witch learned that Edmund's weakness was his love for a candy called Turkish Delight. The piece she gave to Edmund was more delicious than anything he had ever tasted. Soon Edmund could think only about "trying to shovel down as much Turkish Delight as he could, and the more he ate the more he wanted."

Each of us has a vulnerability like Edmund's that Satan is eager to exploit. It may be something addictive like drugs or alcohol, or it may be something seemingly harmless and perhaps even good like food, friendship, or work.

After His resurrection, Jesus asked Peter this personal and probing question: "Do you love Me more than these?" (John 21:15). Many have speculated as to what Jesus meant by the word "these," but it's probably better that we don't know. It allows each of us to personalize the question and ask ourselves, "What do I love more than Jesus?"

When Satan finds out what we love more than God, he knows how to manipulate us. But he loses his power over us when we delight in the Lord. —JAL

I love Thee, because Thou hast first loved me,
And purchased my pardon on Calvary's tree;
I love Thee for wearing the thorns on Thy brow;
If ever I loved Thee, my Jesus, 'tis now. —Featherstone

God takes delight in us—how can we help but delight in Him?

Breathless

READ: Psalm 8

Be exalted, O God, above the heavens; let Your glory be above all the earth. —PSALM 57:5

When was the last time something took your breath away because of its majesty?

I'm not talking about an electronic gadget or some special effects in a movie. I'm talking about a nighttime sky show such as an eclipse of the moon. Or walking outside on a starry night to see Orion or Pleiades—constellations mentioned thousands of years ago in Scripture (Amos 5:8) that are still glowing today for our enjoyment. I'm speaking of a bursting dawn that radiates with glorious colors to signal another sunrise. Or the sound and light show that accompanies God's way of watering the earth with food-producing rain (Job 36:27–33).

Have you stood by a fence and marveled at the power of a horse as it gallops gallantly through the field, mane flowing and hoofs pounding? (39:19–25). Or watched a soaring, swooping eagle drop from the sky because his God-designed vision has sighted supper from his mountain-peak nest? (39:27–30).

At creation, God gave man breath. Then he took man's breath away with the beauty, grandeur, and eloquence of a universe of marvels created by His own hand. Look around. Examine what God has done. Then, breathless, proclaim His majesty.   —DB

The wonder of creation speaks
To everyone in different ways;
But those who know and love the Lord
Can for His handiwork give praise. —Sper

All creation is an outstretched finger pointing toward God.

Something's Wrong with Harry

READ: 1 Peter 2:9–17

A merry heart makes a cheerful countenance. —PROVERBS 15:13

Every morning Harry, a Christian, walked into his office singing a song from the Rodgers & Hammerstein musical *Oklahoma:* "Oh, what a beautiful morning; oh, what a beautiful day! I got a beautiful feeling, everything's going my way!"

But one morning, he forgot to sing. Harry soon noticed that something was wrong at the office; everyone around him seemed on edge. When he finally asked a co-worker what was wrong, she replied, "You didn't sing this morning, and we thought you were upset!" Harry had become known for such a cheerful, positive spirit that his co-workers were sure something was wrong with him that morning.

Harry hadn't realized how closely people were watching him, and he resolved from then on *always* to come to work singing.

First Peter 2 reminds us that people are observing our lives (vv. 11–12). To be good representatives of Jesus Christ, Peter teaches, we're to be submissive to authority, to live an honorable life, to do good works, to honor all people, and to fear God (vv. 12–17).

The testimony of our lives can give us opportunities to share the good news of Jesus. So we might want to ask ourselves, "What do people see in me?"

—AC

> Help me to sing a joyful song
> For those bowed down with care,
> A song of hope and freedom
> For those in dark despair. —Andrews

Do others see Jesus in you?

What's for Dinner?

READ: Genesis 22:1–12

It came to pass . . . that God tested Abraham, and said to him, "Abraham!" And he said, "Here I am." —GENESIS 22:1

I can hardly imagine inviting special friends over for dinner and then throwing a few leftovers into the microwave to serve up to them. But if I were to do that, it would speak volumes about how I really feel about them.

Giving God the leftovers of our lives speaks volumes about His true worth to us. When God asked Abraham to give Isaac back to Him as an act of worship, Genesis 22:1 calls it a test—a test to see if there was anything in his life that he treasured more than God.

It's no different for us. There are times when God requires something really important to get His work done. He'll ask us to give up our natural instincts to seek revenge so that we can communicate His forgiving love by forgiving our enemies. He may call us to sacrifice portions of our time or money or comforts to advance His cause. Or He may require us to allow our sons and daughters to go to a far-off land to tell others about His saving love. The way we respond to what He requires says volumes about how we really feel about Him.

Anyone can offer the leftovers. Only those who love God more than anything else will serve up the very best for Him.   —JS

> *"Take up thy cross and follow Me,"*
> *I hear the blessed Savior call;*
> *How can I make a lesser sacrifice*
> *When Jesus gave His all?* —Ackley

No sacrifice we make is too great for the one who sacrificed His all.

Path to Humility

READ: Psalm 131

Humble yourselves in the sight of the Lord,
and He will lift you up. —JAMES 4:10

My friend declared, as he tried to keep a straight face, "I'm so proud of my humility!" That reminds me of the joke about a leader who was given an award for his humility. Because he accepted the award, it was taken back the following week!

David seemed to be making the same error when he said, "My heart is not haughty" (Psalm 131:1). When we understand the text, however, we know that he wasn't boasting about his humility. Rather, in response to the accusation of treason made by Saul's men, David stated that he didn't consider himself so important nor think of himself so highly as to have "lofty" eyes.

Instead, David learned to be like a "weaned child" in the Lord's arms (v. 2). Like a baby who is completely dependent on his parents, he waited on God for His protection while he was a fugitive under King Saul's pursuit. In his darkest hour, David realized his need and then advised his people: "Hope in the Lord from this time forth and forever" (v. 3).

The path to humility is twofold. It involves knowing who we are—having a proper self-esteem rather than thinking too highly of self. But most important, it requires knowing who God is—holding Him in highest esteem and trusting Him for His best in His time.   —AL

Humility's a slippery prize
That seldom can be won;
We're only humble in God's eyes
When serving like His Son. —Gustafson

When we think we're humble—we're not.

Learning from Lincoln

READ: Proverbs 3:1–8

In all your ways acknowledge Him, and
He shall direct your paths. —PROVERBS 3:6

The day before his 52nd birthday, Abraham Lincoln left Springfield, Illinois, to become President of the United States. With the threat of civil war looming, he said goodbye to the friends and neighbors who had come to see him off.

"I now leave," he told them, "not knowing when, or whether ever, I may return, with a task before me greater than that which rested upon Washington. Without the assistance of the Divine Being who ever attended him, I cannot succeed. With that assistance I cannot fail. Trusting in Him who can go with me, and remain with you, and be everywhere for good, let us confidently hope that all will yet be well. To His care commending you, as I hope in your prayers you will commend me, I bid you an affectionate farewell."

Lincoln's reliance on God for guidance and strength reflects the instruction of Solomon: "Trust in the Lord with all your heart, and lean not on your own understanding; in all your ways acknowledge Him, and He shall direct your paths" (Proverbs 3:5–6).

On this anniversary of Lincoln's birth, we celebrate his kindness, integrity, and courage. And we can also learn from him how to face a daunting future with confident hope in the Lord.   —DM

> *Into His hands I lay the fears that haunt me,*
> *The dread of future ills that may befall;*
> *Into His hands I lay the doubts that taunt me,*
> *And rest securely, trusting Him for all.* —Christiansen

Living without trust in God is like driving in the fog.

Enduring Love

READ: 1 Corinthians 13:1–8

[Love] bears all things, believes all things, hopes all things, endures all things. —1 CORINTHIANS 13:7

Like many people, I enjoy the Google homepage artwork that appears on special days and holidays. One Valentine's Day a few years ago, the artistic logo showed an older couple—a man with a cane and a white-haired woman—walking hand in hand as the woman held two heart-shaped balloons. It was a beautiful reminder that while our culture glorifies youthful romance, true love has many stages during our journey through life.

Paul's great essay in 1 Corinthians 13 celebrates the depth and tenacity of the love that carries us beyond self-interest and mere affection. "Love suffers long and is kind; love does not envy; love does not parade itself, is not puffed up; does not behave rudely, does not seek its own, is not provoked, thinks no evil; does not rejoice in iniquity, but rejoices in the truth; bears all things, believes all things, hopes all things, endures all things. Love never fails" (vv. 4–8).

Brian Wren has captured this reality in his moving hymn, "When Love Is Found":

> *When love is tried as loved ones change,*
> *Hold still to hope though all seems strange,*
> *Till ease returns, and love grows wise*
> *Through listening ears and opened eyes.*

When our commitments are tested in the fires of life, no matter what difficulties we face, may God grant us a greater experience of His enduring love and the grace to demonstrate it each day.   —DM

God's love is a fabric that never fades, no matter
how often it is washed in the waters of adversity.

Written in Red

READ: 1 John 4:7–19

God has sent His only begotten Son into the world,
that we might live through Him. —1 JOHN 4:9

My first Bible was printed mostly in black type, but some of its words were in red. It didn't take me long to discover that the ones in red had been spoken by Jesus.

More than one hundred years ago, a man named Louis Klopsch published the first "red-letter" Bible. As he thought about Jesus' words in Luke 22:20, "This cup is the new covenant in My blood, which is shed for you," he purposely used blood-red ink to call specific attention to His words.

The words of the Bible are priceless to us because they tell of the "love letter" God sent two thousand years ago in the Person of His Son (1 John 4:10).

Jesus' purpose in coming to earth as a man was to die, to be sacrificed, to give His life for ours. God's plan was written in red—written with "the precious blood of Christ, as of a lamb without blemish and without spot" (1 Peter 1:19).

Those of us who have accepted God's gift of love are called to be "letters" to those who don't know Him. We are epistles of Christ "written not with ink but by the Spirit of the living God" (2 Corinthians 3:3).

Long before a day in February was set aside to celebrate love, the world received a love letter—and that changed everything (John 3:16).

—CHK

If you'd like to know the love of God the Father,
Come to Him through Jesus Christ, His loving Son;
He'll forgive your sins and save your soul forever,
And you'll love forevermore this faithful One. —Felten

Nothing speaks more clearly of God's love than the cross of Jesus Christ.

Drift

READ: Hebrews 2:1–9

We must give the more earnest heed to the things
we have heard, lest we drift away. —HEBREWS 2:1

In the 1923 silent movie *Our Hospitality,* comedian and acrobat Buster Keaton performed a daring stunt near a waterfall. A retaining line, called a "holdback" cable, hidden in the water and attached to him, kept him from being carried over the falls.

During filming, the cable broke, and Keaton was swept toward the falls. He managed to grab an overhanging branch, which he clung to until the crew could rescue him. The dramatic scene appears in the finished film.

Drifting into unintended hazards can make for exciting film footage. In real life, however, dangers of this kind are usually marked with warning signs to prevent people from venturing into harm's way.

Similarly, the Bible has provided us with warning signs about drifting from the safety of God's Word. "Therefore we must give the more earnest heed to the things we have heard, lest we drift away" (Hebrews 2:1).

When we don't cling to God's Word through study and reflection, it's easy to drift. Like a swift stream, the attractions of this fallen world draw us toward sin. But as we meditate on Scripture and seek the Holy Spirit's guidance, we learn the reality of our spiritual anchor and are kept secure—even in the dangers of the world's current.   —DF

The Bible stands like a rock undaunted
'Mid the raging storms of time;
Its pages burn with the truth eternal,
And they glow with a light sublime. —Lillenas

The compass of God's Word will keep you from spiritual shipwreck.

The Answers

READ: 1 John 3:1–9

Beloved, now we are children of God. —1 JOHN 3:2

The story is told that the philosopher Arthur Schopenhauer (1788–1860) was sauntering through Berlin's famous Tiergarden one day, mentally probing the questions of origin and destiny that had been constantly perplexing him: *Who am I? Where am I going?*

A park-keeper, closely observing the shabbily dressed philosopher as he walked slowly with head bowed, suspected that Schopenhauer was a tramp. So he walked up to the philosopher and demanded, "Who are you? Where are you going?" With a pained expression, Schopenhauer replied, "I don't know. I wish somebody could tell me."

Are you ever perplexed by those same questions? *Who am I? Where am I going?* What a comfort it is to have God's authoritative answers in the Bible. Who are we? In 1 John 3, John calls his readers "children of God" (v. 2). We become His children by receiving Jesus as our Savior from sin (John 1:12). And where are we going? John 14:1–6 tells us that one day He will receive us into a home He is preparing in heaven.

Our Creator is not only the author of science and history, but He writes the story of every member of Adam's family—yours and mine. We can trust His answers. —VG

> Open my ears, that I may hear
> Voices of truth Thou sendest clear;
> And while the wave-notes fall on my ear,
> Everything false will disappear. —Scott

When you know Jesus, you know who you are and where you're going.

Perhaps Today

READ: Matthew 24:36–46

You also be ready, for the Son of Man is coming at an hour you do not expect. —MATTHEW 24:44

A few years ago I read an article saying that, on February 17, 2009, millions of TV sets in the United States would stop working unless they were able to receive digital signals. Notices appeared in electronics stores, and the government even offered a free $40 coupon toward the purchase of a converter box.

I suspect that most people took the necessary steps to make sure their TV set would work when they turned it on that day. We usually respond well to warnings tied to specific dates. Yet we often fail to prepare for an event that will come "some day."

When the disciples asked Jesus about the date of His return (Matthew 24:3), He told them that only God the Father knows: "But of that day and hour no one knows, not even the angels of heaven, but My Father only" (v. 36). Then He urged them to be prepared so that they would not be taken by surprise. "Therefore you also be ready, for the Son of Man is coming at an hour you do not expect" (v. 44).

We don't know when Jesus will return; He may come at any time. Dr. M. R. DeHaan, founder of RBC Ministries, kept a two-word motto in his office: "Perhaps Today."

When we make our daily plans, are we aware that Christ may return? Are we prepared to meet Him?　　　　　　　　—DM

> *The darkness deepens! Yes, but dawn is nearer!*
> *The Lord from heaven may soon be on His way;*
> *The "blessed hope" in these dark days grows dearer,*
> *Our Savior Christ will come—perhaps today!* —Smith

If Christ comes today, will you be ready to meet Him?

Making Melody

READ: Psalm 126

Speaking to one another in psalms and hymns and spiritual songs. —EPHESIANS 5:19

Do you know why bees hum? It's because they can't remember the words!

Ironically, that old joke reminds me of a serious story I read about a man awaiting heart bypass surgery. He was aware that people die during surgery. As he thought about all that could go wrong, he felt very much alone. Then an orderly walked into his room to take him to surgery. As the young man began to push his gurney along the corridor, the patient heard him humming an ancient Irish hymn, "Be Thou My Vision." It prompted the patient's memories of lush green fields and the ancient stone ruins of Ireland, the land of his birth. The hymn flooded his soul like a fresh breath of home. When the orderly finished with that song, he hummed Horatio Spafford's hymn, "It Is Well with My Soul."

When they stopped outside the surgical suite, the patient thanked the young orderly for the hymns. "God has used you this day to remove my fears and restore my soul."

"How so?" the orderly asked in surprise.

"Your 'hums' brought God to me," the man replied.

"The Lord has done great things for us" (Psalm 126:3). He has filled our heart with song. He may even use our "hums" to restore someone's soul. —DR

Be Thou my vision, O Lord of my heart—
Naught be all else to me, save that Thou art;
Thou my best thought, by day or by night—
Waking or sleeping, Thy presence my light. —*Irish hymn*

Praise flows freely from the choir of the redeemed.

Celebrate Winter

READ: Psalm 42

Why are you cast down, O my soul? . . . Hope in God, for I shall yet praise Him for the help of His countenance. —PSALM 42:5

I love living where there are four seasons. But even though I love settling down with a good book by a crackling fire when it's snowing, I must admit that my love for the seasons grows a little dim when the long gray days of winter drone on into February.

Yet regardless of the weather, there is always something special about winter: Christmas! Thankfully, long after the decorations are down, the reality of Christmas still lifts my spirits no matter what's happening.

If it weren't for the reality of Christ's birth, not only would winter be dark and dreary, but our hearts would be bleak and have nothing to hope for. No hope for the freedom from guilt and judgment. No hope of His reassuring and strengthening presence through dark and difficult times. No hope for a future secured in heaven.

In the winter of a troubled life, the psalmist asked, "Why are you cast down, O my soul?" The remedy was clear: "Hope in God, for I shall yet praise Him for the help of His countenance" (Psalm 42:5).

In C. S. Lewis's tales of Narnia, Mr. Tumnus complains that in Narnia it is "always winter and never Christmas." But for those of us who know the God who made the seasons, it is always Christmas in our hearts!

—JS

When our lives are heavy-laden,
Cold and bleak as winter long,
Stir the embers in our hearts, Lord;
Make Your flame burn bright and strong. —Kieda

Let the reality of Christmas chase away the blahs of winter.

Dying for Justice

READ: Deuteronomy 24:14–22

You shall remember that you were a slave in Egypt, and the Lord your God redeemed you from there. —DEUTERONOMY 24:18

When Presbyterian clergyman Elijah Lovejoy (1802–1837) left the pulpit, he returned to the printing presses in order to reach more people. After witnessing a lynching, Lovejoy committed to fighting the injustice of slavery. His life was threatened by hateful mobs, but this did not stop him: "If by compromise is meant that I should cease from my duty, I cannot make it. I fear God more than I fear man. Crush me if you will, but I shall die at my post." Four days after these words, he was killed at the hands of another angry mob.

Concern about justice for the oppressed is evident throughout Scripture. It was especially clear when God established the rules for His covenant people after they were released from Egyptian bondage (Deuteronomy 24:18–22). Moses emphasized concern for the underprivileged (Exodus 22:22–27; 23:6–9; Leviticus 19:9–10). Repeatedly the Israelites were reminded that they had been slaves in Egypt and should deal justly with the underprivileged in their community. They were to love strangers ("aliens") because God loves them, and they should remember that the Israelites had themselves been aliens in Egypt (Exodus 23:9; Leviticus 19:34; Deuteronomy 10:17–19).

God desires that His people affirm the supreme worth of every individual by fighting against injustice. —MW

> Open my eyes, Lord, to people around me,
> Help me to see them as You do above;
> Give me the wisdom and strength to take action
> So others may see the depth of Your love. —K. DeHaan

Standing for justice means fighting against injustice.

Is That You, Neighbor?

READ: Luke 6:27–36

And who is my neighbor? —LUKE 10:29

An English yachtsman sailing in the Caribbean, 4,000 miles from home, lost his mast in a storm. He had been adrift for two days, and his boat was taking water in twenty-foot waves, when his desperate SOS was picked up. According to Ananova news service, ninety minutes later he was rescued by the captain of a 116,000-ton superliner.

Only when he was pulled out of the water did the rescued sailor discover that the captain who had responded to his call for help was a neighbor from his Hampshire village of Warsash. The rescued man later asked, "What are the chances of being rescued in the middle of nowhere by your neighbor?"

Jesus saw neighbors in unlikely places. When an expert in Jewish law asked Him to define the neighbor we are to love, Jesus drew a big circle. He told the story of a merciful Samaritan to show that a neighbor is the friend, stranger, or enemy who needs the help we can give (Luke 10).

To distinguish ourselves as Jesus' people, we need to show kindness even to those who wish us harm (Luke 6:32–34). Only then will we reflect the heart of the one who, while we were still His enemies, paid the ultimate price to come to our rescue. —MD

> *How many lives shall I touch today?*
> *How many neighbors will pass my way?*
> *I can bless so many and help so much*
> *If I meet each one with a Christlike touch.* —Jones

Our love for Christ is only as real as our love for our neighbor.

Choosing the Hard Thing

READ: 2 Corinthians 4:5–18

We are hard-pressed on every side, yet not crushed; we are perplexed, but not in despair. —2 CORINTHIANS 4:8

On September 12, 1962, President John F. Kennedy delivered a speech at Rice University in Houston, Texas, about the difficult challenges facing the nation. He also shared his passion for the United States to place a man on the moon.

In balancing the needs of the people of his nation with the desire to conquer space, Kennedy said, "We choose to go to the moon in this decade. We choose to go to the moon and do the other things, not because they are easy but because they are hard." The nation responded. Seven years later, in July of 1969, Neil Armstrong took a "giant leap for mankind" by walking on the moon.

Today's world is filled with energy-saving devices that make life easier, but there is something to be said for embracing life's challenges. The apostle Paul found serving Christ hard, but he didn't see it as a cause for discouragement. He continued to focus on Christ, and wrote, "We are hard-pressed on every side, yet not crushed; we are perplexed, but not in despair" (2 Corinthians 4:8). Paul knew that "He who raised up the Lord Jesus will also raise us up with Jesus, and will present us with you" (v. 14). The goal was worth the pain.

By the grace of God, may we commit to serving Jesus—not just when it's easy, but when it's hard.　　　　　　　　　　　　—BC

Jesus gave His all to save us. Are we giving our all to serve Him?

Waiting for the Harvest

READ: Mark 4:26–29

First the blade, then the head, after that the full grain. . . . The harvest has come. —MARK 4:28–29

In the book *What's Gone Wrong with the Harvest?* James Engel and Wilbert Norton illustrate on a graph how people often go through a series of preconversion stages before stepping over the line of faith and receiving Jesus as their Savior.

When we hear individuals share their conversion experience, we may conclude that faith happened all at once. But their salvation frequently carries an extended back-story of spiritual pilgrimage before they made that decision. They needed time to reflect on the gospel. For them, coming to the Savior was a process.

This is similar to the process of farming: Months of waiting come to an end and workers stream into the fields to help with the harvest. One of our Lord's parables illustrates how faith—like a crop—needs time to develop. Responding to the gospel is like a seed that grows "first the blade, then the head, after that the full grain," until finally, "the harvest has come" (Mark 4:28–29).

Because people may need time and multiple exposures to the gospel before they are ready to make a decision, we need to be sensitive to where they are in their faith-journey. In the meantime, we can cultivate spiritual interest, pray for them, and wait for the harvest!   —DF

> *Have you thought of where you're going*
> *When this earthly life is past?*
> *Will the seed that you are sowing*
> *Bring a harvest that will last?* —*Jacobson*

We sow the seed; God produces the harvest.

Managing the Mess

READER: Ruth 1:15–22

Why do you call me Naomi, since the Lord has testified against me, and the Almighty has afflicted me? —RUTH 1:21

When we first meet Naomi in the Scriptures, her life is a mess. She and her husband had gone to Moab searching for food during a famine. While in that land, their two sons married Moabite women, and life was good—until Naomi's husband and sons died and she was stuck, widowed in a foreign land.

Though honest about her pain, Naomi obviously had a sense of who was in control: "The Lord has testified against me, and the Almighty has afflicted me" (Ruth 1:21).

The Hebrew word for "Almighty" (*Shaddai*) indicates God's sufficiency for any situation. The word "Lord" (*Yahweh*) refers to His faithfulness as the loving covenant-keeping God. I love how Naomi put these two names together. In the midst of her complaint, she never lost sight of the fact that her God was a capable and faithful God. And, sure enough, He proved His capability to deliver her and His faithfulness to care for her to the very end.

If there seems to be no way out of your despair, remember that Naomi's God is your God as well. And He specializes in managing our messes to good and glorious outcomes. Thankfully, He is both capable *and* faithful. So, when your life is a mess, remember who your God is! —JS

> *Be still, my soul: thy God doth undertake*
> *To guide the future as He has the past.*
> *Thy hope, thy confidence let nothing shake;*
> *All now mysterious shall be bright at last.* —*von Schlegel*

Stand back and watch the Lord manage your mess into a glorious outcome.

Okello's Story, Our Story

READ: Luke 5:12–16

[Jesus] put out His hand and touched [the leper]. —LUKE 5:13

My friend Roxanne has had some impressive jobs in her life. She has covered the Olympics as a reporter. She has worked in Washington, DC, for noted people and companies. For years, she has written articles about top Christian athletes. But none of those jobs can compare with what she is doing now: giving the love of Jesus to children in Uganda.

What are her days like? Consider the rainy Thursday when she walked the muddy pathway to a cancer ward. Once inside, she scooped up little Okello, whose arms bore sores from poor IV care and whose body raged with a high fever. She carried him to the office of the only cancer doctor in the building and stayed with him until he got help and his condition stabilized.

Jesus, our example, spent His entire ministry among the suffering, healing them and bringing them the good news of God's love (Luke 7:21–22).

How significant are the jobs we do? Sure, it's vital to make a living to support ourselves and our families. But is there something we can do to help relieve the suffering in our world of pain? We may not be able to move to Uganda like Roxanne, but we can all find ways to assist someone. In whose life will you make a difference? —DB

> *God uses us to show His love*
> *To people caught in life's despair;*
> *Our deeds of kindness open doors*
> *To talk of God and His great care.* —Sper

One measure of our likeness to Christ is our
sensitivity to the suffering of others.

A Sad Split

READ: Malachi 2:10–16

Let none deal treacherously with the wife of his youth. —MALACHI 2:15

The drama played out in a nest of bald eagles monitored by a webcam. A beloved eagle family, viewed by many via the Internet, was breaking up. After raising several offspring in previous seasons, the mother again laid new eggs in the spring. But then a young female invaded their happy home. When Dad started cavorting with her, Mom disappeared and the life in the abandoned eggs died.

In an Internet chat room, questions and accusations flew wildly. Everyone who loved the pair was distraught. Biologists warned the amateur eagle enthusiasts not to attribute human values to birds. But everyone did. We all wanted the original couple to reunite. Everyone seemed to "know" that the family unit is sacred.

As chat room members expressed their sadness, I wondered if they knew that God feels much the same way about human family breakups. I also wondered about myself: Why did I feel more sadness over the eagles than over the fractured human families in my community? Clearly, I need to revise my priorities.

In Malachi 2, we see God's view of marriage. It symbolizes His covenant with His people (v. 11). He takes it very seriously—and so should we. —JAL

--- THINKING IT OVER ---

In Malachi 2:11, what is "profaned" and how? How does Malachi 2:15 echo Genesis 2:24? Why is this important? (See Malachi 2:15–16.)

Put Christ first if you want your marriage to last.

Quiet Times

READ: Psalm 23:1–3; Mark 6:30–32

Be still, and know that I am God. —PSALM 46:10

My friend Mary told me that she had always valued the time she spent fishing with her dad. Not being a fishing aficionado myself, I was curious about what she found so enjoyable.

"I just like being with my dad," she said.

"So you just fish and talk?" I asked her.

"Oh, no, we don't really talk," she said. "We just fish."

It wasn't the conversation—it was the company.

Did you ever think about how much time we spend talking? In what we like to call our "quiet time" with God, we usually fill in any silence with our prayers. But do we ever practice just being "still"?

God said, "Be still, and know that I am God" (Psalm 46:10). When Jesus noticed that the disciples were so busy that they didn't even have time to eat, He told them, "Come aside by yourselves to a deserted place and rest a while" (Mark 6:31). When we leave the distractions of life behind, we can more easily rest and refocus on God.

Are you allowing quiet moments alone with God to be a part of your life? Do you desire for Him to restore your soul? (Psalm 23:1–3). Let Him teach you how to "be still." And listen when Jesus invites you: "Come aside with Me and rest a while." —CHK

The quiet times we spend with God
In solitude and prayer
Will strengthen and restore our souls
And help us sense His care. —Sper

Quiet times with God store up power for future emergencies.

Fever Pitch

READ: Matthew 22:34–40

You shall love your neighbor as yourself. —MATTHEW 22:39

In the movie *Fever Pitch,* Ben Wrightman is crazy about the Boston Red Sox baseball team. He rarely misses a game during the spring and summer months.

One winter, Ben falls in love with a young woman named Lindsey and wins her heart. Then spring rolls around, and she finds out that he's a different person during baseball season. He has no time for her unless she goes to the games with him.

When Lindsey ends her relationship with Ben because of his fanaticism, he talks with a young friend, who says, "You love the Sox. But tell me, have they ever loved you back?" Those words cause Ben to analyze his priorities and to give more time to the woman he loves, who loves him back.

We pour our lives into hobbies, pleasures, activities, work—many good things. But two things should always be thought about when making our choices. Jesus said, "You shall love the Lord your God with all your heart. . . . You shall love your neighbor as yourself" (Matthew 22:37, 39).

When it seems our life is getting out of balance, the question, "Has that hobby or activity or thing ever loved me back?" may help to keep us in check. Loving God and loving people are what really count.   —AC

> *Follow with reverent steps the great example*
> *Of Him whose holy work was doing good:*
> *So shall the wide earth seem our Father's temple,*
> *Each loving life a psalm of gratitude.* —Whittier

We show our love for God when we share His love with others.

Spray-On Mud

READ: 2 Timothy 3:1–9

Having a form of godliness but denying its power.
And from such people turn away! —2 TIMOTHY 3:5

A British company has developed a product called "Spray-On Mud" so city dwellers can give their expensive 4×4 vehicles the appearance of having been off-road for a day of hunting or fishing without ever leaving town. The mud is even filtered to remove stones and debris that might scratch the paint. According to the company, sales are going well.

There is something within each of us that values how we look on the outside more than who we are on the inside. It causes some people to pad their résumés or embellish their memoirs. But it has no place in our lives as followers of Jesus.

Paul warned Timothy about people in the church who had a form of godliness but denied its power. "They will maintain a façade of 'religion,' but their conduct will deny its validity. You must keep clear of people like this" (2 Timothy 3:5 Phillips). The inward reality of Christ is what counts, because it will produce the outward signs of faith.

Paul's authority to instruct the church about spiritual authenticity came through his suffering, not by "spraying on mud."

"I bear in my body the marks of the Lord Jesus," said the apostle (Galatians 6:17).

God calls us to authentic living today.

—DM

We fuss over form and we put on a face,
All the while showing God disrespect,
Not seeing how pride is eclipsing God's grace
That the light of Christ's life should reflect. —Gustafson

If you are true to God, you won't be false to others.

The Need for Nourishment

READ: Psalm 37:1–11

Trust in the Lord, and do good; dwell in the land,
and feed on His faithfulness. —PSALM 37:3

Our grandson Cameron was born six weeks prematurely. Undersized and in danger, he became a resident of the hospital's neonatal unit for about two weeks until he gained enough weight to go home. His biggest challenge was that, in the physical exercise of eating, he burned more calories than he was taking in. This obviously hindered his development. It seemed that the little guy took two steps backward for every step of progress he made.

No medicine or treatment could solve the problem; he just needed the strength-giving fortification of nourishment.

As followers of Christ, we are constantly finding our emotional and spiritual reserves drained by the challenges of life in a fallen world. In such times, we need nourishment to strengthen us. In Psalm 37, David encouraged us to strengthen our hearts by feeding our souls. He wrote, "Trust in the Lord, and do good; dwell in the land, and feed on His faithfulness" (v. 3).

When weakness afflicts us, the reassurance of God's never-ending faithfulness can enable us to carry on in His name. His faithful care is the nourishment we need, giving us, as the hymn "Great Is Thy Faithfulness" says, "strength for today, and bright hope for tomorrow." —BC

Pardon for sin and a peace that endureth,
Thine own dear presence to cheer and to guide;
Strength for today and bright hope for tomorrow,
Blessings all mine, with ten thousand beside! —Chisholm

Feed on God's faithfulness to find the strength you need.

Finding Our Calling

READ: Ephesians 4:1–16

I, therefore, the prisoner of the Lord, beseech you to walk worthy of the calling with which you were called. —EPHESIANS 4:1

A continuing struggle as we seek to follow Christ is trying to find our calling in life. While we often think in terms of occupation and location, perhaps a more important issue is one of character—the *being* that undergirds *doing*. "Lord, who do You want me to be?"

In Ephesians 4, Paul wrote, "I, therefore, the prisoner of the Lord, beseech you to walk worthy of the calling with which you were called" (v. 1). He followed this with three "be's," as one translation renders it: be humble, be gentle, be patient, "bearing with one another in love" (v. 2 NIV). Paul wrote this from prison, a difficult place where he continued to live out his calling from God.

Oswald Chambers said: "Consecration is not the giving over of the calling in life to God, but the separation from all other callings and the giving over of ourselves to God, letting His providence place us where He will—in business, or law, or science; in workshop, in politics, or in drudgery. We are to be there working according to the laws and principles of the Kingdom of God."

When we are the right people before God, we can do whatever task He sends, wherever He puts us. In so doing, we discover and affirm His calling for us.   —DM

> *You are called with a holy calling*
> *The light of the world to be;*
> *To lift up the lamp of the gospel*
> *That others the light may see.* —*Anonymous*

It's not what you do but who you are that's most important.

What Are We Holding on To?

READ: 1 Timothy 6:11–16

Fight the good fight of faith, lay hold on eternal life. —1 TIMOTHY 6:12

Tolkien's classic *The Lord of the Rings* trilogy came to life in recent years on film. In the second epic story, the hero, Frodo, reaches a point of despair and wearily confides to his friend, "I can't do this, Sam." As a good friend, Sam gives a rousing speech: "It's like in the great stories. . . . Full of darkness and danger they were. . . . Folk in those stories had lots of chances of turning back, only they didn't. They kept going. Because they were holding on to something." Which prompts Frodo to ask: "What are we holding on to, Sam?"

It's a significant question, one that we all need to ask ourselves. Living in a fallen, broken world, it's no wonder that sometimes we feel overwhelmed by the powers of darkness. When we are at the point of despair, ready to throw in the towel, we do well to follow Paul's advice to Timothy: "Fight the good fight of faith, lay hold on eternal life" (1 Timothy 6:12).

In life's battles, let's hold on to the fact that good will triumph over evil in the end, that one day we will see our master and leader face-to-face, and we will reign with Him forever. You can be part of this great story, knowing that if you have trusted Jesus for salvation you are guaranteed a victorious ending!　　　　　　　　　　　　　　　　　　—JS

> *Though weak and helpless in life's fray,*
> *God's mighty power shall be my stay;*
> *Without, within, He gives to me*
> *The strength to gain the victory.* —D. DeHaan

The trials of earth are small compared with the triumphs of heaven.

An Ocean of Ink

READ: Ephesians 3:14–19

To know the love of Christ which passes knowledge. —EPHESIANS 3:19

The words of the hymn "The Love of God" capture in word pictures the breathtaking magnitude of divine love:

Could we with ink the ocean fill,
And were the skies of parchment made,
Were every stalk on earth a quill,
And every man a scribe by trade,
To write the love of God above,
Would drain the ocean dry,
Nor could the scroll contain the whole,
Though stretched from sky to sky.

These marvelous lyrics echo Paul's response to the love of God. The apostle prayed that believers might "be able to comprehend with all the saints what is the width and length and depth and height—to know the love of Christ which passes knowledge" (Ephesians 3:18–19). In reflecting on these verses about God's love, some Bible scholars believe "width" refers to its worldwide embrace (John 3:16); "length," its existence through all ages (Ephesians 3:21); "depth," its profound wisdom (Romans 11:33); and "height," its victory over sin opening the way to heaven (Ephesians 4:8).

We are admonished to appreciate this amazing love. Yet as we expand our awareness of God's love, we soon realize that its full measure is beyond our understanding. Even if the ocean were filled with ink, using it to write about the love of God would drain it dry. —DF

God's love cannot be explained; it can only be experienced.

Idols in the Heart

READ: Ezekiel 14:1–8

Son of man, these men have set up their idols in their hearts. —EZEKIEL 14:3

When my husband and I first went out as missionaries, I recall being concerned about the growth of materialism in our society. It never crossed my mind that I myself could be materialistic. After all, hadn't we gone overseas with almost nothing? Weren't we choosing to live in a shabbily furnished, rundown apartment? I thought materialism couldn't touch us.

Nonetheless, feelings of discontent gradually began to take root in my heart. Before long I was craving nice things and secretly feeling resentful over not having them.

Then one day God's Spirit opened my eyes with a disturbing insight: Materialism isn't necessarily *having* things; it can also be *craving* them. There I stood, guilty of materialism! God had exposed my discontent for what it was—an idol in my heart. That day as I repented of this subtle sin, God recaptured my heart as His rightful throne. Needless to say, a deep contentment followed, based not on things but on Him.

In Ezekiel's day, God dealt thoroughly with this kind of secret idolatry. His throne on earth has always been in the hearts of His people. That's why we must rid our heart of anything that destroys our contentment with Him.

—JY

The dearest idol I have known,
Whate'er that idol be,
Help me to tear it from Thy throne
And worship only Thee. —Cowper

An idol is anything that takes the place of God.

You Are Not Forgotten

READ: Hebrews 11:24–40

God is not unjust to forget your work and labor of love
which you have showed toward His name, in that you
have ministered to the saints. —HEBREWS 6:10

When Britain's oldest man turned 111, vintage aircraft did a flyover, and the Band of the Royal Marines played "Happy Birthday." According to the *Daily Mirror,* Henry Allingham was amazed by all of the attention. Until six years earlier, he had for eighty-six years kept secret the horrific memories of what happened in the trenches of World War I. Only when tracked down by the World War I Veteran's Association did this old man, who had been shelled, bombed, and shot, receive honor for what he had endured in behalf of his country.

The story of the Bible gives us parallels to Henry's story. The Scriptures show that those who fight the battles of God often end up wounded, imprisoned, and even killed as a result of their service.

The cynic might observe such lives and conclude with a sigh that no good deed goes unpunished. But the author of Hebrews sees a bigger picture. He reminds us that everything and anything we have done in faith and love will one day be honored by God (6:10).

Are you discouraged today? Do you feel insignificant? Do you feel forgotten after trying to serve God? Be assured that God will not forget anything you have done in your service to Him or others.   —MD

Does the place you're called to labor
Seem so small and little known?
It is great if God is in it,
And He'll not forget His own. —Suffield

God remembers the good we forget.

God's Love and Ours

READ: Romans 5:1–11

While we were still sinners, Christ died for us. —ROMANS 5:8

Franklin Graham regrets it now, but in his youth he was wild and rebellious. One day he went roaring up to his dad's house on his Harley Davidson motorcycle to ask for some money. Dressed in his leathers, dusty and bearded, he burst into his father's living room—and walked right into a meeting of Billy's executive board.

Without hesitation, Billy Graham identified Franklin as his son. Then he proudly introduced him to every member of the board. Billy did not apologize for his son or show any shame or guilt. Franklin wrote later in his autobiography, *Rebel with a Cause,* that he never forgot the love and respect his father gave him that day, even during his rebellious years.

Our children don't have to earn our love. To withhold love for our own selfish purposes is to follow the enemy, not God. God's love for us is undeserved. We did nothing to earn it; no good in us merited it. "God demonstrates His own love toward us, in that while we were still sinners, Christ died for us" (Romans 5:8). In all our relationships, especially with our children, we must genuinely show that same kind of love.

We are called to treat our children, and all people, with love and respect. It helps to remember what we were when Christ died for us.

—DE

Help me, Lord, to show respect and love to others, always mindful of the fact that each of us is created in your image. May your love shine through my life and bring praise and honor to you. Amen.

God's love changes prodigal sons into precious saints.

The Time Will Come

READ: 2 Timothy 4:1–8

The time will come when they will not endure sound doctrine. —2 TIMOTHY 4:3

A *USA Today* article describes how parents today seek to initiate their children into a world of all faiths. Ema Drouillard, who runs a ceremony service, was asked by a couple to conduct a service for their baby, Greer. The mother said, "We just wanted a larger spirit to guide our daughter, but we didn't want to get specific. I wanted all her bases covered." The couple said, "We just do Christianity L-I-T-E" for Greer, who "believes in angels and fairies, leprechauns and Santa Claus." This illustrates the low value placed on scriptural truth that is so prevalent in our culture today.

The apostle Paul warned Timothy that a time would come when people would prefer "lite" spiritual meals and would not tolerate substantive teaching (2 Timothy 4:3–4). He predicted that false teaching would increase and be embraced by many because it caters to the needs of their flesh. They have a craving to be entertained and desire teaching that leaves them with good feelings about themselves. Paul instructed Timothy to combat this by teaching doctrines according to God's Word. The purpose of his instruction was to correct, rebuke, and encourage others (v. 2).

As believers we are called to teach and obey the Word of God, not to scratch the itches of our culture.　　　　　—MW

Lord, teach us from Your holy Word
All error to discern,
And by Your Spirit's light help us
From Satan's snares to turn. —Bosch

Stand on the Word of God and you won't fall into error.

You Can't Say That!

READ: Genesis 3:9–19

"Lord, what do You want me to do?" —ACTS 9:6

According to a career-building website, certain words should be avoided on the job. When someone in authority asks you to do a project, you shouldn't say, "Sure, no problem," if you don't mean it and aren't going to follow through. Otherwise, you'll become known as someone who doesn't keep his word. And don't say, "That's not my job," because you may need that person's help in the future.

And if your boss comes to you with a problem, careerbuilder.com suggests it's best not to blame someone else and say, "It's not my fault!"

That's the excuse Adam and Eve gave to God. They were told not to eat from the fruit on the tree of the knowledge of good and evil (Genesis 2:16–17). When they disobeyed and were confronted by God, Adam blamed God and Eve, and Eve blamed the serpent (3:9–19). They basically said, "It's not my fault!"

Perhaps there are things we should avoid saying to God about what He's told us to do or not to do. For example, He gives us specific instructions for Christlike behavior in 1 Corinthians 13, yet we may be tempted to say, "I just don't feel convicted about that," or, "That's not really my gift."

What is the Lord asking of you today? How will you respond? How about, "Yes, Lord!"   —AC

> *God wants complete obedience,*
> *Excuses will not do;*
> *His Word and Spirit show His will—*
> *Then we must follow through.* —Sper

The highest motive for obeying God is the desire to please Him.

For the Birds

READ: Hebrews 13:5–16

You shall not covet . . . anything that is your neighbor's. —EXODUS 20:17

The bird feeder attached to my office window is just beyond the reach of the squirrels. But one squirrel has made it his mission to get the seeds meant for the birds. Having seen his tiny neighbors nibbling noisily from the abundant supply, the squirrel is fixated on enjoying the same pleasure. He has tried coming at the feeder from every direction but without success. He clawed his way up the wooden window casing to within inches of the feeder but slid down the slippery glass. He climbed the thin branches of the forsythia bush. Then he reached so far that he fell to the ground.

The squirrel's tireless attempts to get what isn't meant to be his calls to mind a man and woman who reached for food that wasn't meant to be theirs. They too suffered a fall—a fall so severe that it hurt the whole human race. Because they were disobedient and helped themselves to food that God told them not to eat, He put them where they could no longer reach it. As a result of their disobedience, they and their descendants must now work hard to get what He originally had given as a gift—food (see Genesis 2–3).

May our desire to have what God has kept from us not keep us from enjoying what He has given to us (Hebrews 13:5). —JAL

THINKING IT THROUGH

What (or who) am I looking to for happiness? Is this wise? Or do I need to make some changes? How may I be content?

Godliness with contentment is great gain. —1 Timothy 6:6

Flying Machines

READ: Psalm 6

I am weary with my groaning; all night I make my bed swim; I drench my couch with my tears. —PSALM 6:6

Recording artist James Taylor exploded onto the music scene in early 1970 with the song "Fire and Rain." In it, he sang about the disappointments of life, describing them as "sweet dreams and flying machines in pieces on the ground." That was a reference to Taylor's original band Flying Machine, whose attempt at breaking into the recording industry had failed badly, causing him to wonder if his dreams of a musical career would ever come true. The reality of crushed expectations had taken their toll, leaving Taylor with a sense of loss and hopelessness.

The psalmist David also experienced hopeless despair as he struggled with his own failures, the attacks of others, and the disappointments of life. In Psalm 6:6 he said, "I am weary with my groaning; all night I make my bed swim; I drench my couch with my tears." The depth of his sorrow and loss drove him to heartache—but in that grief he turned to the God of all comfort. David's own crushed and broken dreams and expectations gave way to the assurance of God's care, prompting him to say, "The Lord has heard my supplication; the Lord will receive my prayer" (v. 9).

In our own seasons of disappointment, we too can find comfort in God, who cares for our broken hearts. —BC

Even in my darkest hour
The Lord will bless me with His power;
His loving grace will sure abound,
In His sweet care I shall be found. —Brandt

God's whisper of comfort quiets the noise of our trials.

Incomplete

READ: Philippians 1:3–11

He who has begun a good work in you will complete it until the day of Jesus Christ. —Philippians 1:6

When I was a little girl, my parents bought their first house. One afternoon, the family hopped into the car and drove to see where we soon would be living.

I couldn't believe it. The house had no windows or doors, and there was a strange odor. The basement was clearly visible through big gaps in the floor and we had to climb a ladder to get down there.

That night when I asked my mother why they wanted to live in a house like that, she explained that the builder wasn't finished with it yet. "Just wait and see," she said. "I think you'll like it when it's done."

Soon we began to see changes. The house got windows, then doors. The "funny smell" of new lumber faded. The holes in the floor were covered and a staircase was added. Walls were painted. Mom put up curtains at the windows and pictures on the walls. The incomplete house had been transformed. It had taken some time but finally it was finished.

As Christians, we need "finishing" too. Although the groundwork is laid at our conversion, the growing process continues throughout our life. As we obediently follow Jesus, "the author and finisher of our faith" (Hebrews 12:2), one day we too will be complete.   —CHK

God sees in us a masterpiece
That one day will be done;
His Spirit works throughout our lives
To make us like His Son. —Sper

Please be patient. God isn't finished with me yet!

To Be or Not To Be

READ: 2 Corinthians 1:3–11

We were burdened beyond measure . . . so that we despaired even of life. —2 Corinthians 1:8

When I was a child, kids on the playground jokingly quoted Shakespeare's famous line: "To be or not to be—that is the question!" But we really didn't understand what it meant. Later I learned that Shakespeare's character Hamlet, who speaks these lines, is a melancholy prince who learns that his uncle has killed his father and married his mother. The horror of this realization is so disturbing that he contemplates suicide. The question for him was: "to be" (to go on living) or "not to be" (to take his own life).

At times, life's pain can become so overwhelming that we are tempted to despair. The apostle Paul told the church at Corinth that his persecution in Asia was so intense he "despaired even of life" (2 Corinthians 1:8). Yet by shifting his focus to his life-sustaining God, he became resilient instead of overwhelmed, and learned "that we should not trust in ourselves but in God" (v. 9).

Trials can make life seem not worth living. Focusing on ourselves can lead to despair. But putting our trust in God gives us an entirely different perspective. As long as we live in this world, we can be certain that our all-sufficient God will sustain us. And as His followers, we will always have a divine purpose "to be." —DF

Lord, give us grace to trust You when
Life's burdens seem too much to bear;
Dispel the darkness with new hope
And help us rise above despair. —Sper

Trials make us think; thinking makes us wise;
wisdom gives us perspective and purpose.

Clearing Out the Clutter

READ: 1 Corinthians 6:12–20

Do you not know that your body is the temple of the Holy Spirit who is in you, whom you have from God, and you are not your own? —1 CORINTHIANS 6:19

My garage serves as "storage" for things that don't have a place in our home, and, frankly, there are times when I am ashamed to open the door. I don't want anyone to see the clutter. So, periodically, I set aside a workday to clean it up.

Our hearts and minds are a lot like that—they accumulate lots of clutter. As we rub shoulders with the world, inevitably, perhaps unknowingly, we pick up ungodly thoughts and attitudes. Thinking that life is all about "me." Demanding our rights. Reacting bitterly toward those who have hurt us. Before long, our hearts and minds are no longer clean and orderly. And while we think we can hide the mess, eventually it will show.

Paul pointedly asked, "Do you not know that your body is the temple of the Holy Spirit?" (1 Corinthians 6:19)—which makes me wonder if God often feels like He is living in our messy garage.

Perhaps it's time to set aside a spiritual workday and, with His help, get to work clearing out the clutter. Discard those thoughts of bitterness. Bag up and throw out the old patterns of sensual thoughts. Organize your attitudes. Fill your heart with the beauty of God's Word. Make it clean to the core, and then leave the door open for all to see!　　　　—JS

More like the Master I would ever be,
More of His meekness, more humility;
More zeal to labor, more courage to be true,
More consecration for work He bids me do. —*Gabriel*

Don't let the Spirit reside in a cluttered heart.
Take some time to clean it up today!

Reaching Up to Heaven

READ: Romans 8:18–27

The Spirit Himself makes intercession for us with groanings which cannot be uttered. —ROMANS 8:26

I see children reach up their hands to their mothers, eager to get their attention. It reminds me of my own efforts to reach up to God in prayer.

The early church stated that the work of the aged is to love and to pray. Of the two, I find love to be the most difficult, and prayer to be the most confusing. My infirmity lies in not knowing the exact thing for which I ought to pray. Should I pray that others will be delivered from their troubles—or that their troubles will go away? Or should I pray for courage to carry on through the difficulties that belabor them?

I'm comforted by Paul's words: "The Spirit also helps in our weaknesses" (Romans 8:26). Here the apostle uses a verb that means "to help by joining in an activity or effort." God's Spirit is joined to ours when we pray. He intercedes for us "with groanings which cannot be uttered." He is touched by our troubles; He sighs often as He prays. He cares for us deeply—more than we care for ourselves. Furthermore, He prays "according to the will of God" (v. 27). He knows the right words to say.

Therefore, I needn't worry about getting my request exactly right. I need only to hunger for God and to reach up, knowing that He cares.
—DR

O God, too weak and worn for words, I shrink
From trials that deeply wound, and yet to think
Your Holy Spirit helps me as I pray
And gives a voice to what I cannot say! —Gustafson

When praying, it's better to have a heart
without words than words without heart.

Thomas Time

READ: John 20:24–29

*Thomas answered and said to Him,
"My Lord and my God!"* —JOHN 20:28

A young adult was struggling with his faith. After growing up in a home where he was loved and nurtured in a godly way, he allowed bad decisions and circumstances to turn him away from the Lord. Although as a child he had claimed to know Jesus, he now struggled with unbelief.

One day while talking to him I said, "I know that you walked with the Lord for a long time, but right now you're not so sure about Jesus and faith. Can I suggest to you that you are in the 'Thomas Time' of your life?"

He knew that Thomas was one of Jesus' twelve apostles and that he had trusted Christ openly for several years. I reminded this young man that after Jesus' death, Thomas doubted that He had really risen from the tomb. But after eight days the Lord appeared to Thomas, showed him His scars, and told him to stop doubting and believe. Finally ready to abandon his doubts, Thomas said, "My Lord and my God!" (John 20:24–28).

I told this young man, "Jesus patiently waited, and Thomas came back. I think you will too. I'm praying that someday you will again say to Jesus, 'My Lord and my God!'"

Could you be in a "Thomas Time"—finding it hard to feel close to Jesus, perhaps even doubting Him? Jesus is waiting for you. Reach out for His nail-scarred hand.
—DB

*There can be times when our minds are in doubt,
Times when we ask what our faith is about;
But we can believe Him, we know that He cares—
Our God is real, as the Bible declares.* —Fitzhugh

A child of God is always welcomed home.

Take One Step

READ: Deuteronomy 30:15–20

*Love the Lord your God, . . . obey His voice,
and . . . cling to Him, for He is your life and the
length of your days.* —DEUTERONOMY 30:20

At a shopping mall in Coventry, England, researchers posted colorful signs along the steps of a staircase that said: "Taking the stairs protects your heart." Over a six-week period, the number of people who chose to walk up the stairs instead of riding the adjacent escalator more than doubled. The researchers say that every step counts, and that long-term behavior will change only if the signs are seen regularly.

The Bible is filled with "signs" urging us to obey the Lord and follow Him wholeheartedly. Just before the Lord's people entered the Promised Land, He said to them: "I have set before you today life and good, death and evil. . . . Therefore choose life, that both you and your descendants may live; that you may love the Lord your God, that you may obey His voice, and that you may cling to Him, for He is your life and the length of your days" (Deuteronomy 30:15, 19–20).

So often we hope our lives will change through a giant leap of faith, a profound decision, or a significant act of service. In reality, the only way we change is one step at a time, and every step counts.

Today, let's heed the signs and take a step of heartfelt obedience toward the Lord. —DM

> *It matters not the path on earth*
> *My feet are made to trod;*
> *It only matters how I live:*
> *Obedient to God.* —Clark

One small step of obedience is a giant step to blessing.

What's in a Name?

READ: Acts 11:19–26

*Walk worthy of the calling with which
you were called.* —EPHESIANS 4:1

My Chinese family name sets me apart from others with different family names. It also confers on me a family responsibility. I am a member of the Hia family. As a member of the family, I am expected to carry on the Hia line and uphold the honor of my ancestors.

Believers who have been saved by the atoning blood of Jesus Christ have a spiritual family name. We are called "Christians." In the New Testament, the name *Christian* was first given to the disciples in Antioch by those who noted their behavior (Acts 11:26). Two things defined these early believers. They talked about the good news of the Lord Jesus everywhere they went (v. 20). And they eagerly learned the Scriptures as Barnabas and Saul taught them for a whole year (v. 26).

The name *Christian* means an "adherent to Christ"—literally, one who "sticks" to Christ. Today many people call themselves Christians. But should they?

If you call yourself a Christian, does your life tell others who Jesus is? Are you hungry for God's Word? Do your actions bring honor or shame to Christ's name?

What's in a name? When the name is *Christian*, there is much indeed!

—CPH

> *Teach us that name to own,*
> *While waiting, Lord, for Thee,*
> *Unholiness and sin to shun,*
> *From all untruth to flee.* —Cecil

A Heart of Concern

READ: Philippians 2:1–11

Let each esteem others better than himself. Let each of you look out not only for his own interests, but also for the interests of others. —PHILIPPIANS 2:3–4

Jason Ray was a ray of joy on the University of North Carolina campus in Chapel Hill. He performed as Rameses (the school mascot) for three years, hauling his giant ram's head costume to sporting events one day and children's hospitals the next. Then, in March 2007, while with his team for a basketball tournament, Jason was struck by a car. His family watched and waited at the hospital, but the 21-year-old succumbed to his injuries and died.

His story doesn't end there, however. Jason had filed paperwork two years earlier to donate organs and tissue upon his death, and that act of concern saved the lives of four people and helped dozens of others. A young man in the prime of his life, with everything to live for, was concerned for the well-being of others and acted on that concern. Those individuals who were helped, as well as their families, are deeply grateful for this young man who thought of others.

Jason's act echoes the heart of Paul's words in Philippians 2, as he called believers to look beyond themselves and their own interests, and to look to the interests of others. A heart that turns outward to others will be a healthy heart indeed. —BC

Love thyself last. Look near, behold thy duty
To those who walk beside thee down life's road.
Make glad their days by little acts of beauty
And help them bear the burden of earth's load. —Wilcox

Looking to the needs of others honors Christ.

Never Too Old

READ: Genesis 18:1–15

Is anything too hard for the Lord? —GENESIS 18:14

The women of Brown Manor had raised their families and retired from their careers. Now they could no longer live on their own, so they came to Brown Manor as a sort of "last stop before heaven." They enjoyed each other's company but often struggled with feelings of uselessness. Sometimes they even questioned why God was so slow in taking them to heaven.

One of the women, who had spent years as a pianist, often played hymns on the Manor's piano. Other women joined her, and together they lifted their voices in praise to God.

One day, a government auditor was conducting a routine inspection during one of their spontaneous worship services. When he heard them sing "What Will You Do with Jesus?" the Spirit of God moved his heart. He recalled the song from his childhood and knew that he had chosen to leave Jesus behind. That day, God spoke to him again and gave him another chance to answer the question differently. And he did.

Like the women of Brown Manor, Sarah thought she was too old to be used by God (Genesis 18:11). But God gave her a child in her old age who was the ancestor of Jesus (21:1–3; Matthew 1:2, 17). Like Sarah and the women of Brown Manor, we're never too old for God to use us.

—JAL

The longer we live, the more that we know,
Old age is the time for wisdom to show;
Who knows how much good some word we might say
Could do for that one who has wandered away? —Bosch

God can use you at any age—if you are willing.

Crooked House

READ: Revelation 3:14–20

As many as I love, I rebuke and chasten. Therefore be zealous and repent. —REVELATION 3:19

When Robert Klose first moved into his 100-year-old house, its strange sounds were disconcerting. A carpenter told him the house was crooked. Klose admitted, "I could see it in the floors, the ceilings, the roofline, the door jambs, even the window frames. Drop a ball on the floor and it will roll away into oblivion." Seventeen years later, the house is still holding together and he has gotten used to it and even grown to love it.

In Revelation, Jesus confronted a church that had become accustomed to its crooked spirituality and had even grown to love its inconsistencies. Laodicea was a well-to-do city. Yet that very wealth led to its delusion of self-sufficiency. This had bled into the culture of the church and produced a crooked, "we don't need Jesus" type of spirituality. Therefore, Jesus rebuked these believers, calling them "lukewarm, . . . wretched, miserable, poor, blind, and naked" (3:16–17). He rebuked them because He loved them and still wanted an ever-deepening communion with them. So He gave them opportunity to repent (v. 19).

If self-sufficiency has skewed your fellowship with Jesus, you can straighten it through repentance and a renewal of intimate fellowship with Him.   —MW

Not to the world is the portion
Of fellowship sweet with God,
But to the humble believer
Who trusts in His faithful Word. —Anonymous

Repentance is God's way of making the crooked straight.

Casting Shadows

READ: 1 Corinthians 1:18–31

No flesh should glory in His presence. —1 CORINTHIANS 1:29

Legend has it that Michelangelo painted with a brush in one hand and a candle in the other to prevent his shadow from covering his masterpiece in progress.

That's the kind of attitude we should adopt if we are serious about wanting to display the masterpiece of God's glory on the canvas of our lives. Unfortunately, we tend to live in a way that draws attention to ourselves—our cars, our clothes, our careers, our position, our cleverness, our success. And when life is all about us, it's hard for people to see Jesus in us. Jesus saved us to be reflections of His glory (Romans 8:29), but when we live for ourselves, our shadow gets cast on the canvas of His presence in us.

When the believers in Corinth were feeling too full of themselves, Paul warned them "that no flesh should glory [boast] in His presence" (1 Corinthians 1:29), and reminded them of what Jeremiah said, "He who glories, let him glory in the Lord" (v. 31; Jeremiah 9:24).

Think of your life as a canvas on which a picture is being painted. What would you rather have people see: the masterpiece of the presence of Jesus or the shadow of your own profile? Don't get in the way of a great painting in progress. Live to let others see Jesus in you.   —JS

> *My life is a painting created by God,*
> *And as such I've nothing to boast;*
> *Reflecting the image of Christ to the world*
> *Is what I desire the most.* —Sper

A Christian's life is the canvas on which others can see Jesus.

Crazy Horse

READ: 1 Samuel 7:3–12

Samuel took a stone . . . and called its name Ebenezer,
saying, "Thus far the Lord has helped us." —1 SAMUEL 7:12

In 1876, the Sioux leader Crazy Horse joined forces with Sitting Bull to defeat General Custer and his army at Little Bighorn. Not long after that victory, though, starvation caused Crazy Horse to surrender to US troops. He was killed while trying to escape. Despite this sad conclusion to his life, he became a symbol of heroic leadership of a threatened people.

Today, in the Black Hills of South Dakota, Crazy Horse is commemorated with a monument being carved into a mountain—the Crazy Horse Memorial. When complete, it will be 641 feet long and 563 feet high. It will show Crazy Horse riding a galloping horse, pointing the way to his people.

Thousands of years ago, the prophet Samuel used a much smaller memorial stone in a significant way. In the midst of a crucial battle with the Philistines, Samuel called out to God on Israel's behalf, and the Lord answered his prayer (1 Samuel 7:10). In gratitude, Samuel set up a stone "and called its name Ebenezer, saying, 'Thus far the Lord has helped us'" (v. 12).

Samuel set an example for our spiritual journey. We too can use tangible reminders of God's faithfulness to help us worship and serve Him. It's good to remember "thus far the Lord has helped us." —DF

PUTTING IT INTO PRACTICE
- *Keep a spiritual journal and record God's blessings.*
- *Write answers to prayer in your journal.*
- *Tell a friend what God has done in your life.*

Gratitude is the memory of a glad heart.

Ordinary Days

READ: Luke 2:8–20

Behold, an angel of the Lord stood before them, and the glory of the Lord shone around them. —LUKE 2:9

Writer Anita Brechbill observed in *God's Revivalist* magazine that "Most often the Word of the Lord comes to a soul in the ordinary duties of life." She cites the examples of Zacharias performing his duties as a priest and the shepherds watching their flocks. They were at work as usual with no idea that they were about to receive a message from God.

Luke describes the ordinary days when these men received their message from God: "While [Zacharias] was serving as priest before God in the order of his division, . . . an angel of the Lord appeared to him" (1:8, 11). While the shepherds were "living out in the fields, keeping watch over their flock by night . . . an angel of the Lord stood before them, and the glory of the Lord shone around them" (2:8–9).

Oswald Chambers in *My Utmost for His Highest* said: "Jesus rarely comes where we expect Him; He appears where we least expect Him, and always in the most illogical situations. The only way a worker can keep true to God is by being ready for the Lord's surprise visits."

On this ordinary day, the Lord may have a word of encouragement, guidance, or instruction for us, if we're listening and ready to obey.

—DM

> *I wonder what I did for God today:*
> *How many times did I once pause and pray?*
> *But I must find and serve Him in these ways,*
> *For life is made of ordinary days.* —Macbeth

God speaks to those who are quiet before Him.

In All Kinds of Weather

READ: Acts 18:9–11

*Lo, I am with you always, even to the
end of the age.* —MATTHEW 28:20

When Jesus sent His disciples out, He gave them this promise: "I am with you always, even to the end of the age" (Matthew 28:20). Literally, the word *always* means "all the days," according to Greek scholars Jamieson, Fausset, and Brown.

Jesus didn't simply say "always," but "all the days." That takes into account all our various activities, the good and bad circumstances surrounding us, the varied responsibilities we have through the course of our days, the storm clouds and the sunshine.

Our Lord is present with us no matter what each day brings. It may be a day of joy or of sadness, of sickness or of health, of success or of failure. No matter what happens to us today, our Lord is walking beside us, strengthening us, loving us, filling us with faith, hope, and love. As He envelops us with quiet serenity and security, our foes, fears, afflictions, and doubts begin to recede. We can bear up in any setting and circumstance because we know the Lord is at hand, just as He told Paul in Acts 18:10, "I am with you."

Practice God's presence, stopping in the midst of your busy day to say to yourself, "The Lord is here." And pray that you will see Him who is invisible—and see Him everywhere.   —DR

God's unseen presence comforts me,
I know He's always near;
And when life's storms besiege my soul,
He says, "My child, I'm here." —D. DeHaan

Seek the Lord while He may be found, call
upon Him while He is near. —Isaiah 55:6

Faithfulness in Everything

READ: Colossians 3:12–17

Whatever you do in word or deed, do all in the name of the Lord Jesus. —COLOSSIANS 3:17

In August 2007, a major bridge in Minneapolis collapsed into the Mississippi River, killing thirteen people. In the weeks that followed, it was difficult for me not to think about that tragedy whenever crossing a bridge over a body of water.

Some time later, I was watching an episode of *Dirty Jobs* on the Discovery Channel. Host Mike Rowe was talking to an industrial painter whose work he was trying to duplicate. "There's really no glory in what you do," he said.

"No," the painter agreed, "but it's a job that needs to be done."

You see, that man paints the inside of the Mackinac Bridge towers in Northern Michigan. His unnoticed job is done to ensure that the steel of the magnificent suspended structure won't rust from the inside out, compromising the integrity of the bridge. Most of the 12,000 people who cross the Straits of Mackinac each day aren't even aware that they are depending on workers like this painter to faithfully do their jobs well.

God also sees our faithfulness in the things we do. Though we may think our deeds—big and small—sometimes go un-noticed, they are being observed by the one who matters most. Whatever our task today, let's "do all in the name of the Lord Jesus" (Colossians 3:17). —CHK

Whatever task you find to do,
Regardless if it's big or small,
Perform it well, with all your might,
Because there's One who sees it all. —Sper

Daily work takes on eternal value when it is done for God.

I'm Innocent!

READ: James 1:19–25

Be doers of the Word. —JAMES 1:22

All of the students at a school in Florida—2,550 in total—were in trouble. A message system notified every parent that their child (or children) had detention that weekend for bad behavior. Many kids pleaded their innocence, yet some parents meted out punishment anyway. One mother, Amy, admitted that she yelled at her son and made sure he showed up for his detention on Saturday.

To the relief of 2,534 kids, and to the embarrassment of some parents, they discovered that the automated message was sent in error to the entire student body when only sixteen kids actually deserved detention. Amy felt so bad about not listening to and believing her son that she took him out for breakfast that Saturday morning.

We all have stories to tell about circumstances that have shown us our need to listen before we speak. We're naturally tempted to come to quick judgments and react angrily. The book of James gives us these three practical exhortations to deal with life's stressful situations: "Be swift to hear, slow to speak, slow to wrath" (James 1:19).

In life's stressful times, let's be "doers of the Word" (v. 22) and take the time to listen and show restraint with our words and anger. —AC

A judgment made without the facts
Is sure to be unfair;
So always listen to both sides—
You'll find the answer there. —Branon

Listen to understand; then speak with love.

Have You Left a Tip?

READ: 2 Corinthians 8:1–9

Though He was rich, yet for your sakes
He became poor. —2 CORINTHIANS 8:9

The practice of tipping is commonly accepted in many countries. But I wonder: Has this courtesy influenced our attitude toward giving money to the church?

Many Christians regard their financial giving as little more than a goodwill gesture to God for the service He has rendered us. They think that as long as they have given their tithe to God, the rest is theirs to handle as they please. But the Christian life is about so much more than money!

The Bible tells us that our Creator owns "the cattle on a thousand hills" (Psalm 50:10). "The world is Mine," God says, "and all its fullness" (v. 12). Everything comes from Him, and everything we have belongs to Him. God has not only given us every material thing we have, He has also given us His Son, the Lord Jesus Christ, who provides our very salvation.

Paul used the Macedonian Christians as an illustration of what our giving should look like in the light of God's incredible generosity toward us. The Macedonians, who were in "deep poverty," gave with "liberality" (2 Corinthians 8:2). But "they first gave themselves to the Lord" (v. 5).

God the Creator of the universe does not need anything from us. He doesn't want a tip. He wants us!   —CPH

Whatever, Lord, we lend to Thee,
Repaid a thousand-fold will be;
Then gladly will we give to Thee,
Who givest all—who givest all. —C. Wordsworth

No matter how much you give, you can't outgive God.

Resolve

READ: Romans 14:1–13

Resolve this, not to put a stumbling block or a cause to fall in our brother's way. —ROMANS 14:13

I once decorated a notebook with definitions of the words *idea, thought, opinion, preference, belief,* and *conviction* to remind myself that they do not mean the same thing. For example, the temptation to elevate an opinion to the level of a conviction can be strong, but doing so is wrong, as we learn from Romans 14.

In the first century, religious traditions based on the law were so important to religious leaders that they failed to recognize the one who personified the law, Jesus. They were so focused on minor matters that they neglected the important ones (Matthew 23:23).

Scripture says that we need to subjugate even our beliefs and convictions to the law of love, for love fulfills the law and leads to peace and mutual edification (Romans 13:8, 10; Galatians 5:14; James 2:8).

When opinions and preferences become more important to us than what God says is valuable to Him, we have made idols out of our own beliefs. Idolatry is a serious offense because it violates the first and most important command: "You shall have no other gods before Me" (Exodus 20:3).

Let's resolve not to elevate our own opinions above God's, lest they become a stumbling block and keep others from knowing the love of Jesus.
—JAL

—— A PRAYER ——

Lord, help me not to elevate my opinions and make others follow. You are the convicter of hearts. May others learn of your love through me. The greatest force on earth is not the compulsion of law but the compassion of love.

Unclean? Be Cleansed!

READ: Mark 1:40–45

Jesus, moved with compassion, stretched out His hand and touched him, and said to him, "I am willing; be cleansed." —MARK 1:41

As I read Mark 1:40–45, I imagine the following scene:

They saw him coming toward them from across the way. He was waving his arms to warn them away. They recognized him by the piece of cloth covering his nose and mouth, his torn garments, and the skin peeling away from his body. He was a leper—unclean!

The crowd around Jesus scattered as the leper charged into their midst. Everyone was afraid of being touched by him because they themselves would then become unclean. Lepers were barred from the religious life of the community, isolated from society, and compelled to mourn their own death by tearing their clothes.

But this leper threw himself at Jesus' feet, appealing to Him out of desperation and faith to restore him to wholeness: "If You are willing, You can make me clean" (v. 40). Moved with compassion, Jesus touched the man and said, "I am willing; be cleansed" (v. 41). Jesus healed the man of his leprosy and told him to show himself to the temple priest.

Jesus has the power to cleanse, forgive, and restore those who are hopelessly and helplessly caught up in their sin and can see no way out. Trust Him to say to you, "I am willing; be cleansed." —MW

> *The Savior is waiting to save you*
> *And wash every sin-stain away;*
> *By faith you can know full forgiveness*
> *And be a new creature today! —Bosch*

Jesus specializes in restoration.

Which Way Am I Growing?

READ: Galatians 6:7–10

Whatever a man sows, that he will also reap. —GALATIANS 6:7

Some folks grow old gracefully, while others become grouchy and ill-tempered. It's important to know which way we're growing, because we're all growing older.

People don't get irritable and short-tempered merely because they're getting older. Aging doesn't have to make us hypercritical and cranky. No, it's more likely that we've become what we've been becoming all along.

Paul wrote: "He who sows to his flesh will . . . reap corruption, but he who sows to the Spirit will . . . reap everlasting life" (Galatians 6:8). Those who pander to self-interest and think only of themselves are sowing seeds that will produce a harvest of misery in themselves and in others. On the other hand, those who love God and care for others are sowing seeds that, in time, will yield a harvest of joy.

C. S. Lewis put it this way: "Every time you make a choice you are turning the central part of you, the part of you that chooses, into something a little different from what it was before." We can choose to submit our will to God each day, asking Him to give us strength to live for Him and for others. As He works in us, we will grow in grace and in kindness.

So the question we need to ask ourselves is: Which way am I growing? —DR

> *Surer than autumn's harvests*
> *Are harvests of thought and deed;*
> *Like those that our hands have planted,*
> *The yield will be like the seed.* —Harris

The seeds we sow today determine the kind of fruit we'll reap tomorrow.

The Measure of Mercy

READ: Philippians 2:5–11

You were not redeemed with corruptible things, . . . but with the precious blood of Christ. —1 PETER 1:18–19

What is the distance from God's throne of splendor down to the abyss of Calvary's cross? What is the measure of the Savior's love for us? In Paul's letter to the Philippians, he described Jesus' descent from the heights of glory to the depths of shame and agony and back again (2:5–11).

Christ is the eternal Creator and Lord of all existence, exalted infinitely above earth's foulness and decay. He is the source of life, with myriads of angels to sing His praises and do His bidding. Yet, motivated by love for our lost human race, "He humbled Himself and became obedient to the point of death, even the death of the cross" (v. 8). He came to our puny planet, was born in a cavelike barn with its smells and filth, and was placed as a helpless baby in a feeding trough.

When He grew to manhood, He endured homelessness (Matthew 8:20). Thirsty, He asked an adulteress for water (John 4:7–9). Weary, He fell asleep in a boat on a storm-tossed sea (Mark 4:37–38). Sinless, He was adored by the multitudes one day (Matthew 21:9), and just a few days later condemned as a criminal and died on a Roman cross in excruciating pain.

That's the distance from God's throne down to Calvary! That's the measure of His mercy and grace!

—VG

> *O the love that drew salvation's plan!*
> *O the grace that brought it down to man!*
> *O the mighty gulf that God did span*
> *At Calvary!* —Newell

God broke into human history to offer us the eternal gift of salvation.

His Part; Our Part

READ: Joshua 1:1–9

Arise, go over this Jordan. . . . I will not
leave you nor forsake you. —JOSHUA 1:2, 5

Whenever the Lord assigns us a difficult task, He gives us what we need to carry it out. John Wesley wrote, "Among the many difficulties of our early ministry, my brother Charles often said, 'If the Lord would give me wings, I'd fly.' I used to answer, 'If God bids me fly, I will trust Him for the wings.'"

Today's Scripture tells us that Joshua was thrust into a position of great responsibility. No doubt the enormity of the challenge before him made him tremble with fear. How could he ever follow such a great leader as Moses? In his own strength it would be impossible to lead the people into the Promised Land. But along with the marching orders, the Lord gave him an assuring promise: "I will not leave you nor forsake you" (Joshua 1:5). Then He said, "Have I not commanded you? Be strong and of good courage; do not be afraid, nor be dismayed, for the Lord your God is with you wherever you go" (v. 9). Such reassurances were the backing Joshua needed.

If God has given you some special work to do that frightens you, it's your responsibility to jump at it. It's up to the Lord to see you through. As you faithfully do your part, He will do His part. —RD

> *I'll go where You want me to go, dear Lord,*
> *O'er mountain or plain or sea;*
> *I'll say what You want me to say, dear Lord,*
> *I'll be what You want me to be.* —Brown

The Journey Home

READ: Hebrews 11:1–10

*[Abraham] waited for the city . . . whose
builder and maker is God.* —HEBREWS 11:10

Bill Bright, the founder of Campus Crusade for Christ, was diagnosed years ago with the terminal disease pulmonary fibrosis. Eventually he required prolonged bed rest. Bright used this time of quiet reflection to write a book called *The Journey Home.*

In his book, Bright quotes Charles Haddon Spurgeon, who said: "May we live here like strangers and make the world not a house, but an inn, in which we sup and lodge, expecting to be on our journey tomorrow."

Struck by Spurgeon's perspective concerning his own terminal prognosis, Bright commented: "Knowing that heaven is our real home makes it easier to pass through the tough times here on earth. I have taken comfort often in the knowledge that the perils of a journey on earth will be nothing compared to the glories of heaven."

Abraham, the friend of God, illustrates this same otherworldly orientation: "By faith he dwelt in the land of promise as in a foreign country . . . for he waited for the city which has foundations, whose builder and maker is God" (Hebrews 11:9–10). His sojourn was that of a traveling foreigner, who by faith sought an eternal city constructed by God.

Whether death is near or somewhere in the unknown future, let's exhibit a faith that focuses on our eternal home.   —DF

> *Home from the earthly journey,*
> *Safe for eternity;*
> *All that the Savior promised—*
> *That is what heaven will be.* —Anonymous

We may walk a desert pathway, but the
end of the journey is the garden of God.

Humility and Greatness

READ: Matthew 20:20–28

*Whoever desires to become great among you,
let him be your servant.* —MATTHEW 20:26

As a seven-year-old, Richard Bernstein admired Jackie Robinson's athletic ability and courage as the first African-American man to play Major League baseball in the modern era. A few years later, while working at a small-town golf course, Bernstein was astonished to find himself carrying the bag of his hero, Jackie Robinson. When rain postponed the game, Robinson held an umbrella over the two of them and shared his chocolate bar with the young caddy. Writing in the *International Herald Tribune,* Bernstein cited that humble act of kindness as a mark of greatness he has never forgotten.

True greatness is shown by humility, not pride. This was powerfully demonstrated and taught by Jesus Christ, who told His ambitious disciples: "Whoever desires to become great among you, let him be your servant. And whoever desires to be first among you, let him be your slave—just as the Son of Man did not come to be served, but to serve, and to give His life a ransom for many" (Matthew 20:26–28).

When God himself walked on earth as a man, He washed feet, welcomed children, and willingly gave His life to deliver us from the self-centered tyranny of sin. His example gives credence to His command.

—DM

*True greatness does not lie with those
Who strive for worldly fame,
It lies instead with those who choose
To serve in Jesus' name.* —D. DeHaan

We can do great things for the Lord if we
are willing to do little things for others.

Servant-Friendship

READ: 1 Thessalonians 2:1–8

We were gentle among you, just as a nursing mother cherishes her own children. —1 THESSALONIANS 2:7

Don Tack wanted to know what life was like for homeless people. So he concealed his identity and went to live on the streets of his city. He found out that food and shelter were offered by many organizations. At one shelter he could spend the night if he listened to a sermon beforehand. He appreciated the guest speaker's message and wanted to talk with him afterward. But as Don reached out to shake the man's hand and asked if he could talk with him, the speaker walked right past him as if he didn't exist.

Don learned that what was missing most in ministry to the homeless in his area were people who were willing to build relationships. So he began an organization called Servants Center to offer help through friendship.

What Don encountered at the shelter was the opposite of what the people who heard the apostle Paul experienced. When he shared the gospel, he gave himself too. He testified in his letter to the Thessalonians, "We were well pleased to impart to you not only the gospel of God, but also our own lives, because you had become dear to us" (1 Thessalonians 2:8). He said, "We were gentle among you," like a mother (v. 7).

In our service for the Lord, do we share not just our words or money but our time and friendship?　　　　　　　　　　　　　　　—AC

I want to do service for Christ while I live,
And comfort and cheer to poor lonely hearts give;
For this is the program approved by the Word,
To visit the needy and speak of the Lord. —Bosch

One measure of our likeness to Christ
is our sensitivity to the suffering of others.

Who Crucified Jesus?

READ: Luke 23:33–38

When they had come to the place called Calvary, there they crucified Him. —LUKE 23:33

When looking at Rembrandt's painting of *The Three Crosses,* your attention is drawn first to the cross on which Jesus died. Then as you look at the crowd gathered around the foot of that cross, you are impressed by the various facial expressions and actions of the people involved in the awful crime of crucifying the Son of God. Finally, your eyes drift to the edge of the painting to catch sight of another figure, almost hidden in the shadows. Some art critics say this is a representation of Rembrandt himself, for he recognized that by his sins he helped nail Jesus to the cross.

Someone has said, "It is a simple thing to say that Christ died for the sins of the world. It is quite another thing to say that Christ died for my sins. . . . It is a shocking thought that we can be as indifferent as Pilate, as scheming as Caiaphas, as callous as the soldiers, as ruthless as the mob, or as cowardly as the disciples. It wasn't just what *they* did—it was *I* who nailed Him to the tree. I crucified the Christ of God. I joined the mockery."

Place yourself in the shadows with Rembrandt. You too are standing there. But then recall what Jesus said as He hung on that cross, "Father, forgive them." Thank God, that includes you and me. —HB

Behold the Savior of mankind
Nailed to the shameful tree!
How vast the love that Him inclined
To bleed and die for thee! —Wesley

The cross of Christ reveals the love of God at its best and the sin of the world at its worst.

God Will Move the Stone

READ: Mark 16:1–14

When they looked up, they saw that the stone had been rolled away. —MARK 16:4

The women who sought to anoint the dead body of Jesus are to be commended for their tender love and regard for the Savior. Yet, as they came near the place of burial, the practical difficulty of moving the heavy stone that sealed His tomb brought them unnecessary anxiety. Their fears were groundless; it had already been moved.

So too, we are often needlessly concerned over prospective difficulties that God graciously removes or helps us overcome. Let us exercise greater faith in facing possible obstructions on the pathway of duty. We may be sure of the Lord's assistance in such matters when we press on in His name and for His glory.

Go forward today on the pathway of service, undaunted by possible future obstacles. Let your heart be cheered by the certainty that whatever difficulty you may face, God will move the stone. —HB

In today's bright sunlight basking,
Leave tomorrow's cares alone—
Spoil not present joys by asking:
"Who shall roll away the stone?"
Oft, before we've faced the trial
We have come with joy to own,
Angels have from heaven descended
And have rolled away the stone. —Anonymous

If God doesn't remove an obstacle, He'll help you find a way around it.

Much More!

READ: Romans 5:12–21

Where sin abounded, grace abounded much more. —ROMANS 5:20

A statement I heard at an Easter service stays with me: "More has been gained in the resurrection of Jesus than was lost in the fall." More gained than lost? Can it be true?

Each day we experience the damage caused by sin entering our world. Greed, injustice, and cruelty all trace their origins back to Adam and Eve's decision to follow their own path rather than God's (Genesis 3). The legacy of their disobedience is passed down to every generation. Without God's intervention, we would be in a hopeless situation. But Jesus overpowered sin through His cross and conquered death through His resurrection.

The victory of Christ is celebrated in Romans 5, often called the "much more" chapter of the New Testament, where Paul contrasts the devastation caused by sin with the restoring power of God's grace. In every case, grace overpowers the consequences of sin. In a grand conclusion, Paul says: "Where sin abounded, grace abounded much more, so that as sin reigned in death, even so grace might reign through righteousness to eternal life through Jesus Christ our Lord" (5:20–21).

No matter how much we have personally lost because of sin, we have gained far more through the resurrection victory of Christ.   —DM

> *Sin and despair, like the sea-waves cold,*
> *Threaten the soul with infinite loss;*
> *Grace that is greater—yes, grace untold—*
> *Points to the refuge, the mighty cross.* —Johnston

Our sin is great. God's grace is greater.

The Honor of Your Friendship

READ: John 15:9–17

I have called you friends. —JOHN 15:15

During the marriage ceremony of a British couple, the best man remained motionless. Even after vows were exchanged, he didn't move.

The still figure was a race car driver who was trying to be in two places at one time. Because of contractual commitments, Andy Priaulx, three-time world touring-car champion, had to break his promise to participate in his friend's wedding. So he sent a life-size cardboard cut-out of himself, as well as a prerecorded speech. The bride said she was moved by his effort to honor their marriage.

Priaulx's gesture was certainly creative, and we shouldn't second-guess his actions. But Jesus gave us another standard by which to gauge friendship.

Jesus asked His disciples to show their friendship to Him by loving one another as He had loved them. Then, He raised the bar. In anticipation of His death on the cross, He said, "Greater love has no one than this, than to lay down one's life for his friends" (John 15:13).

This depth of friendship isn't merely about doing the right thing. It's about sacrifice, and it springs out of a relationship with the one who truly did lay down His life for us.

Are we showing others that we have been loved by Jesus as He is loved by His Father? (v. 9).

—MD

―――――― **FOR FURTHER STUDY** ――――――
*In 1 Corinthians 13 we find a description of what real
love looks like. Take some time to study this passage.*

Love is more than a sentiment; love is putting
another's needs ahead of your own.

Nothing Left but God

READ: 2 Chronicles 20:3–17

Do not be afraid nor dismayed because of this great multitude, for the battle is not yours, but God's. —2 CHRONICLES 20:15

A wise Bible teacher once said, "Sooner or later God will bring self-sufficient people to the place where they have no resource but Him—no strength, no answers, nothing but Him. Without God's help, they're sunk."

He then told of a despairing man who confessed to his pastor, "My life is really in bad shape."

"How bad?" the pastor inquired.

Burying his head in his hands, the man moaned, "I'll tell you how bad—all I've got left is God."

The pastor's face lit up. "I'm happy to assure you that a person with nothing left but God has more than enough for great victory!"

In today's Bible reading, the people of Judah were also in trouble. They admitted their lack of power and wisdom to conquer their foes. All they had left was God! But King Jehoshaphat and the people saw this as reason for hope, not despair. "Our eyes are upon You," they declared to God (2 Chronicles 20:12). And their hope was not disappointed as He fulfilled His promise: "The battle is not yours, but God's" (v. 15).

Are you in a position where all self-sufficiency is gone? As you turn your eyes on the Lord and put your hope in Him, you have God's reassuring promise that you need nothing more. —JY

Turn your eyes upon Jesus,
Look full in His wonderful face;
And the things of earth will grow strangely dim
In the light of His glory and grace. —Lemmel

When all you have is God, you have all you need.

Loss and Gain

READ: Luke 24:13–35

Then their eyes were opened and they knew Him; and He vanished from their sight. —LUKE 24:31

A Texas high school football team began the 2002 season with a 57-game winning streak and hopes for an unprecedented fifth consecutive state championship. In spite of losing their longtime coach and competing against larger schools, the Celina Bobcats remained undefeated through the regular season. But then they lost a quarterfinal playoff game by one point. It felt like the end of the world—even though they had won 68 straight games and five state championships in seven years.

When our dreams are shattered and our hearts are broken, we may feel that all has been lost and nothing has been gained. It takes the touch of God to open our eyes to the greater glory of His plan.

When the crucified and risen Christ joined two disciples on the road to Emmaus, they were grieving over His death. "We were hoping that it was He who was going to redeem Israel," they told Jesus, whom they didn't recognize (Luke 24:21). But Jesus said, "Ought not the Christ to have suffered these things and to enter into His glory?" (v. 26). Later they realized they had been talking with Jesus. He was alive!

In our time of loss, the risen Lord comes to us with comfort and peace, revealing His glory and the eternal gain that is ours because of His cross.   —DM

When circumstances overwhelm
And seem too much to bear,
Depend upon the Lord for strength
And trust His tender care. —Sper

Present pains can lead to permanent gains.

The Other Goat

READ: Leviticus 16:5–22

He Himself is the propitiation for our sins, and not for ours only but also for the whole world. —I JOHN 2:2

The Scapegoat, a novel by Daphne du Maurier, is about two men who are amazed at the striking similarity in their appearance. They spend an evening together, but one runs off, stealing the other's identity and leaving him to step into a life filled with problems. The second man becomes a *scapegoat.*

The origin of that word comes from a ceremony performed on the Day of Atonement in the Old Testament (known today in the Jewish calendar of feasts and holidays as Yom Kippur). The high priest would sacrifice one goat and symbolically place the sins of the people on the head of a second goat—the scapegoat—before it was sent into the wilderness, carrying away the blame of the sin (Leviticus 16:7–10).

But when Jesus came, *He* became our scapegoat. He offered himself up "once for all" as a sacrifice to pay for the sins of "the whole world" (1 John 2:2; Hebrews 7:27). That first goat had been sacrificed as a sin offering for God's people and symbolized Jesus' sacrifice on the cross. The second goat was a representation of the completely innocent Jesus accepting and removing our sin and guilt.

None of us is without sin, but the Father laid on Jesus "the iniquity of us all" (Isaiah 53:6). God sees followers of His Son as blameless—because Jesus took all the blame we deserve. —CHK

> *Jesus our Savior left heaven above,*
> *Coming to earth as a Servant with love;*
> *Laying aside all His glory, He came,*
> *Giving His life, taking all of our blame.* —Hess

Jesus takes our sin and gives us His salvation.

It's Bubbling in My Soul

READ: John 7:33–39

If anyone thirsts, let him come to Me and drink. . . . Out of his heart will flow rivers of living water. —JOHN 7:37–38

Decades ago, I visited a ministry center in West Africa and saw a little girl climb onto a truck that had a public address system. Smiling, she began to sing over the microphone:

It's bubbling, it's bubbling, it's bubbling in my soul;
I'm singing and laughing since Jesus made me whole.
Since Jesus came within, and cleansed my heart from sin,
It's bubbling, bubbling, bubbling, bubbling, bubbling in my soul!

I heard her sing that song only once. But the joy in her voice was so evident and powerful that I remember the lyrics and tune to this day.

The parallel in the song between water and spiritual refreshment is a biblical one. During the Feast of Tabernacles, a Levite priest would pour out water as a symbol of God providing water for Israel in the wilderness. During that feast, "Jesus stood and cried out, saying, 'If anyone thirsts, let him come to Me and drink. He who believes in Me, as the Scripture has said, out of his heart will flow rivers of living water'" (John 7:37–38). Jesus was talking about the Holy Spirit promised to those who would believe in Him (v. 39). This thirst-quenching water is a picture of the spiritual satisfaction that only He can provide.

Perhaps you've lost that joy you first experienced at salvation. Confess all known sin right now (1 John 1:9). Be filled with God's Holy Spirit (Ephesians 5:18), and let Him provide you with a "bubbling in your soul."

—DF

Christ departed so that the Holy Spirit could be imparted.

God Remembers

READ: Genesis 8:1–17

God remembered Noah, and every living thing, and all the animals that were with him in the ark. —GENESIS 8:1

A Chinese festival called *Qing Ming* is a time to express grief for lost relatives. Customs include grooming gravesites and taking walks with loved ones in the countryside. Legend has it that it began when a youth's rude and foolish behavior resulted in the death of his mother. So he decided that henceforth he would visit her grave every year to remember what she had done for him. Sadly, it was only after her death that he remembered her.

How differently God deals with us! In Genesis, we read how the flood destroyed the world. Only those who were with Noah in the ark remained alive. But God remembered them and sent a wind to dry the waters so that they could leave the ark (8:1).

God also remembered Hannah when she prayed for a son (1 Samuel 1:19). He gave her a child, Samuel.

Jesus remembered the dying thief who said, "Lord, remember me when You come into Your kingdom." Jesus replied, "Today You will be with Me in Paradise" (Luke 23:42–43).

God remembers us wherever we are. Our concerns are His concerns. Our pain is His pain. Commit your challenges and difficulties to Him. He is the all-seeing God who remembers us as a mother remembers her children, and He waits to meet our needs. —CPH

> *There is an Arm that never tires*
> *When human strength gives way;*
> *There is a Love that never fails*
> *When earthly loves decay.* —Wallace

To know that God sees us brings both conviction and comfort.

Check Your Attitude

READ: John 3:22–31

He must increase, but I must decrease. —JOHN 3:30

A music professor with a well-trained voice usually sang the major male solo parts in the choir of a large church. A young man named Bob who had no training sometimes took a few shorter solos. As the choir director prepared for the Christmas cantata, she felt that Bob's voice and style made him a natural for the lead role. However, she didn't know how she could give it to him without offending the older man.

Her anxiety was unnecessary. The professor had the same thoughts as she did, and he told her that Bob should take the part. He continued to sing faithfully in the chorus and was a source of much encouragement to Bob.

People who can set aside selfish ambition and genuinely seek the good of others have an attitude that pleases God. Do you remember how John the Baptist reacted when the crowds left him and began following Jesus? He said, "He must increase, but I must decrease" (John 3:30).

What did John the Baptist and the music professor have in common? They were able to set aside "selfish ambition." They were happy to see others elevated above themselves when it was for the common good. Can the same be said about us? —HVL

> *This is the highest learning,*
> *The hardest and the best—*
> *From self to keep still turning*
> *And honor all the rest.* —MacDonald

When we forget about ourselves, we do things others will remember.

Gatekeepers

READ: 1 Corinthians 3:1–17

The temple of God is holy, which temple you are. —1 CORINTHIANS 3:17

In journalism, the term *gatekeeper* refers to reporters, editors, and publishers who consider various news items and determine which stories are newsworthy. Some longtime news professionals warn that the Internet allows information to get through without being checked at the gate.

In Old Testament times, gatekeepers guarded the temple to prevent those who were unclean from entering (2 Chronicles 23:19). In AD 70, the temple was destroyed by the Roman armies. But the destruction began years earlier when the Levites assigned to guard it failed to do so after coming under the corrupt influence of the Syrian king Antiochus IV.

Paul called our bodies God's "temple" (1 Corinthians 3:16–17), and many forces are at work to assault God's new dwelling. Evil may gain a foothold through unfortified areas of our spiritual life—places where envy, strife, or divisions may undermine us (3:3). Each of us must be on guard against the enemy of our souls and never give place to the devil (Ephesians 4:27).

The criteria for what may enter is found in Philippians 4:8—whatever is true, noble, just, pure, lovely, of good report, virtuous, and praiseworthy. The resulting peace will guard the gate of our hearts and minds. —JAL

Help me to guard my troubled soul
By constant, active self-control.
Clean up my thought, my speech, my play;
Lord, keep me pure from day to day. —Thomas

If you're not on guard against evil, you'll be influenced by evil.

The Bus Driver

READ: 1 John 4:7–12

Be imitators of God . . . and walk in love. —EPHESIANS 5:1–2

In the middle of carting seventy pieces of luggage, an electronic piano, and other equipment through airports and on and off a tour bus, it's easy to wonder, "Why are we doing this?"

Taking twenty-eight teenagers on an eleven-day ministry trip to a land across the ocean is not easy. But at the end of the trip our bus driver, who had carted us all over England and Scotland, grabbed the bus microphone and in tears thanked the kids for how wonderful they had been. Then after we got home, he e-mailed us to say how much he appreciated the thank you cards the kids had written to him—many of which contained the gospel.

Although the students ministered to hundreds through song during the trip, perhaps it was the bus driver who most benefited from their Christlikeness. In Ephesians we are told to be imitators of God and to walk in love (5:1–2). Others see God in us when we show love to one another (1 John 4:12). The bus driver saw Jesus in the students and told them that they might just convert him to faith in Christ. Maybe it was for this man that we took that trip.

Why do you do what you do? Whose life are you affecting? Sometimes it's not our target audience that we impact most. Sometimes it's the bus drivers of the world.   —DB

> *Lord, may I be a shining light*
> *For all the world to see*
> *Your goodness and Your love displayed*
> *As You reach out through me.* —Sper

Witnessing is not just something a Christian says, but what he is.

What's Next?

READ: Philippians 3:7–16

I press toward the goal for the prize of the upward call of God in Christ Jesus. —PHILIPPIANS 3:14

In the television series *The West Wing*, fictional president Josiah Bartlet regularly ended staff meetings with two words: "What's next?" It was his way of signaling that he was finished with the issue at hand and ready to move on to other concerns. The pressures and responsibilities of life in the White House demanded that he not focus on what was in the rearview mirror; he needed to keep his eyes ahead, moving forward to what was next.

In a sense, the apostle Paul had a similar perspective on life. He knew that he had not "arrived" spiritually, and that he had a long way to go in becoming like Christ. What could he do? He could either fixate on the past, with its failures, disappointments, struggles, and disputes, or he could learn from those things and move on to "what's next."

In Philippians 3, Paul tells us how he chose to live his life: "Forgetting those things which are behind and reaching forward to those things which are ahead, I press toward the goal for the prize of the upward call of God in Christ Jesus" (vv. 13–14). It's a perspective that speaks of moving on—of embracing what's next. It is where we too must focus as we seek to be shaped into the image of the Savior while we look forward to eternity with Him. —BC

> *Onward and upward your course plan today,*
> *Seeking new heights as you walk Jesus' way;*
> *Heed not past failures, but strive for the prize,*
> *Aiming for goals fit for His holy eyes.* —Brandt

Keep your eyes fixed on the prize.

The Best Eraser

READ: Luke 16:19–31

I have blotted out, like a thick cloud, your transgressions. —ISAIAH 44:22

What is memory? What is this faculty that enables us to recall past feelings, sights, sounds, and experiences? By what process are events recorded, stored, and preserved in our brain to be brought back again and again? Much is still mystery.

We do know that memories can be blessings—full of comfort, assurance, and joy. Old age can be happy and satisfying if we have stored up memories of purity, faith, fellowship, and love. If a saint looks back on a life of Christian service and remembers the faithfulness of Him who promised, "I will never leave you nor forsake you" (Hebrews 13:5), his or her sunset years can be the sweetest of all.

But memory can also be a curse and a tormentor. Many people as they approach the end of life would give all they possess to erase from their minds the past sins that haunt them. What can a person do who is plagued by such remembrances? Just one thing. He can take them to the one who is able to forgive them and blot them out forever. He's the one who said, "Their sins and their lawless deeds I will remember no more" (Hebrews 10:17).

You may not be able to forget your past. But the Lord offers to blot out, "like a thick cloud, your transgressions" (Isaiah 44:22). —MRD

> *The deep remorse that's in the soul*
> *No human eye may trace;*
> *But Jesus sees the broken heart,*
> *And can its woes erase.* —Bosch

The best eraser is honest confession to God.

Go Home and Tell

READ: Luke 8:26–39

Return to your own house, and tell what great things God has done for you. —LUKE 8:39

Two young men had been friends from childhood. One was a Christian, the other was not. The second man was about to embark on a long ocean voyage, and the believer felt the urge to speak to his friend about Christ before he left. "I'll do it on the way to the dock," he promised himself. But when they reached the dock, he still hadn't done so.

He went on board to say good-bye and thought, "When we bring the baggage to his room, I'll speak to him." But the porter took the trunks and suitcases, so they did not visit the stateroom.

Finally the Christian said to himself, "I'll be sure to witness to him in some quiet place before the ship departs." Suddenly, however, there came the announcement that all visitors must leave the ship immediately.

Two months later word came that the Christian's friend had died overseas.

In Luke's gospel we read of a man possessed by many demons who had been wonderfully restored by Jesus. In gratitude to the Lord he wanted to stay with Him to worship Him (8:38). But Jesus said, "Return to your own house, and tell what great things God has done for you" (v. 39).

Will you apply Jesus' words to your life and tell someone of His grace and salvation—beginning at home? Don't put it off. Tell someone now about Jesus!

—MD

To the work! To the work! Let the hungry be fed;
To the fountain of life let the weary be led;
In the cross and its banner our glory shall be,
While we herald the tidings, "Salvation is free!" —Crosby

Any place can be the right place to witness.

Thunderstorm Thoughts

READ: Matthew 8:23–27

The God of peace will be with you. —PHILIPPIANS 4:9

Recently I've been hearing a clever radio commercial that has a woman shouting to her friend in conversation. She's trying to talk above the sounds of the thunderstorm in her own head. Ever since a storm damaged part of her home, that's all she hears because her insurance company isn't taking care of her claims.

I've heard thunderstorms in my head, and maybe you have too. It happens when a tragedy occurs—to us, to someone close to us, or to someone we hear about in the news. Our minds become a tempest of "what if" questions. We focus on all the possible bad outcomes. Our fear, worry, and trust in God fluctuate as we wait, we pray, we grieve, and we wonder what the Lord will do.

It's natural for us to be fearful in a storm (literal or figurative). The disciples had Jesus right there in the boat with them, yet they were afraid (Matthew 8:23–27). He used the calming of the storm as a lesson to show them who He was—a powerful God who also cares for them.

We wish that Jesus would always calm the storms of our life as He calmed the storm for the disciples that day. But we can find moments of peace when we're anchored to the truth that He's in the boat with us and He cares.

—AC

Fierce drives the storm, but wind and waves
Within His hand are held,
And trusting His omnipotence
My fears are sweetly quelled. —Brown

To realize the worth of the anchor, we need to feel the stress of the storm.

Too Old?

READ: Genesis 17:15–22

My covenant is with you, and you shall be a father of many nations. —GENESIS 17:4

When God promised Abraham and his wife Sarah that they would have a son, Abraham laughed in unbelief and replied, "Shall a child be born to a man who is one hundred years old? And shall Sarah, who is ninety years old, bear a child?" (Genesis 17:17).

Later, Sarah laughed for the same reason: "After I have grown old, shall I have pleasure, my lord being old also?" (18:12).

We too grow old and wonder if the Lord can fulfill His promises to us. We no longer have prominence or status. Our minds are not as nimble as they once were. We're hampered by physical problems that limit our mobility and keep us close to home. Every day we seem to lose more of the things we have spent a lifetime acquiring. Robert Frost underscores something that we sometimes ask ourselves: "The question . . . is what to make of a diminished thing."

Not much—if we are left to ourselves. But God is able to do more with us than we can imagine. He asks us, as He asked Sarah, "Is anything too hard for the Lord?" (18:14). Of course not!

We're never too old to be useful if we make ourselves available to God for His purposes.   —DR

Growing old but not retiring,
For the battle still is on;
Going on without relenting
Till the final victory's won. —*Anonymous*

As God adds years to your life, ask Him to add life to your years.

Agreeing with God

READ: Matthew 15:1–9

These people draw near to Me with their mouth, and honor Me with their lips, but their heart is far from Me. —MATTHEW 15:8

The caller to the radio program mentioned religion, so the radio talk show host began to rant about hypocrites. "I can't stand religious hypocrites," he said. "They talk about religion, but they're no better than I am. That's why I don't like all this religious stuff."

This man didn't realize it, but he was agreeing with God. God has made it clear that He can't stand hypocrisy either. It's ironic, though, that something God opposes is used by some people as an excuse not to seek Him.

Jesus said this about hypocrisy: "These people draw near to Me with their mouth, and honor Me with their lips, but their heart is far from Me. And in vain they worship Me, teaching as doctrines the commandments of men" (Matthew 15:8–9).

Notice what Jesus said to perhaps the biggest hypocrites of His day, the Pharisees. He called them hypocrites—not once, not twice, but seven times (see Matthew 23). They were religious people who were putting on a big show, but God knew their hearts. He knew they were far from Him.

Non-Christians who point out hypocrisy in us when they see it are right in doing so. They are agreeing with God, who also despises it. Our task is to make sure our lives honor the one who deserves our total dedication. —DB

Hypocrisy is a common sin
That grieves the Lord above;
He longs for those who'll worship Him
In faith and truth and love. —Bosch

The devil is content to let us profess
Christianity as long as we do not practice it.

The Father's Faithfulness

READ: Psalm 107:1–16

*Through the Lord's mercies we are not consumed,
because His compassions fail not. . . . Great is
Your faithfulness.* —LAMENTATIONS 3:22–23

Hudson Taylor, the humble servant of God to China, demonstrated extraordinary trust in God's faithfulness. In his journal he wrote: "Our heavenly Father . . . knows very well that His children wake up with a good appetite every morning. . . . He sustained three million Israelites in the wilderness for forty years. We do not expect He will send three million missionaries to China; but if He did, He would have ample means to sustain them all. . . . Depend on it, God's work done in God's way will never lack God's supply."

We may be faint and weary, but our heavenly Father is all-powerful. Our feelings may fluctuate, but He is unchangeable. Even creation itself is a record of His steadfastness. That's why we can sing these words from a hymn by Thomas Chisholm:

Summer and winter, and springtime and harvest,
Sun, moon, and stars in their courses above
Join with all nature in manifold witness
To Thy great faithfulness, mercy, and love.

What an encouragement to live for Him! Our strength for the present and hope for the future are not based on the stability of our own perseverance, but on the fidelity of God. No matter what our need, we can count on the Father's faithfulness. —PVG

*Great is Thy faithfulness! Great is Thy faithfulness!
Morning by morning new mercies I see;
All I have needed Thy hand hath provided—
Great is Thy faithfulness, Lord, unto me!* —Chisholm

He who abandons himself to God will never be abandoned by God.

Against the Wall

READ: Romans 8:31–39

Who shall separate us from the love of Christ? —ROMANS 8:35

On April 25, 1915, soldiers of the Australian and New Zealand Army Corps landed on the Gallipoli peninsula expecting a quick victory. But fierce resistance by the Turkish defenders resulted in an eight-month stalemate during which thousands on both sides were wounded or killed.

Many of the ANZAC troops who were evacuated to Egypt visited the YMCA camp outside Cairo where chaplain Oswald Chambers offered hospitality and hope to these men so broken and disillusioned by war. With great insight and compassion, Chambers told them: "No man is the same after an agony; he is either better or worse, and the agony of a man's experience is nearly always the first thing that opens his mind to understand the need of redemption worked out by Jesus Christ. At the back of the wall of the world stands God with His arms outstretched, and every man driven there is driven into the arms of God. The cross of Jesus is the supreme evidence of the love of God."

Paul asked: "Who shall separate us from the love of Christ?" (Romans 8:35). His confident answer was that nothing can remove us from God's love in Christ (vv. 38–39).

When we're up against the wall, God is there with open arms.

—DM

> *God knows each winding way I take*
> *And every sorrow, pain, and ache;*
> *His children He will not forsake—*
> *He knows and loves His own.* —Bosch

God's love still stands when all else has fallen.

Lip Service

READ: Mark 7:5–15

This people honors Me with their lips, but their heart is far from Me. —MARK 7:6

Smile," said Jay as we drove to church. "You look so unhappy." I wasn't; I was just thinking, and I can't do two things at once. But to make him happy, I smiled.

"Not like that," he said. "I mean a real smile."

His comment got me thinking even more intently. Is it reasonable to expect a real smile from someone who's being issued a command? A real smile comes from inside; it's an expression of the heart, not of the face.

We settle for phony smiles in photographs. We're happy when everyone cooperates at the photographer's studio and we get at least one picture with everyone smiling. After all, we're creating an icon of happiness, so it doesn't have to be genuine.

But phoniness before God is unacceptable. Whether we're happy or sad or mad, honesty is essential. God doesn't want false expressions of worship any more than He wants false statements about people or circumstances (Mark 7:6).

Changing our facial expression is easier than changing our attitude, but true worship requires that all of our heart, soul, mind, and strength agree that God is worthy of praise. Even when our circumstances are sad, we can be grateful for God's mercy and compassion, which are worth more than the "lip service" of a phony smile. —JAL

What a God we have to worship!
What a Son we have to praise!
What a future lies before us—
Everlasting, love-filled days! —Maynard

A song in the heart puts a smile on the face.

First Things First

READ: Matthew 6:25–34

Seek first the kingdom of God and His righteousness. —MATTHEW 6:33

A seminar leader wanted to make an important point, so he took a wide-mouth jar and filled it with rocks. "Is the jar full?" he asked.

"Yes," came a reply.

"Oh, really?" he said. Then he poured smaller pebbles into the jar to fill the spaces between the rocks. "Is it full now?"

"Yes," said someone else.

"Oh, really?" He then filled the remaining spaces between the rocks and stones with sand. "Is it full now?" he asked.

"Probably not," said another, to the amusement of the audience. And the person was right. The seminar leader then took a pitcher of water and poured it into the jar.

"What's the lesson we learn from this?" he asked.

An eager participant spoke up, "No matter how full the jar is, there's always room for more."

"Not quite," said the leader. "The lesson is: to get everything in the jar, you must always put the big things in first."

Jesus proclaimed a similar principle in the Sermon on the Mount. He knew that we waste our time worrying about the little things that seem so urgent but crowd out the big things of eternal value. "Your heavenly Father knows that you need all these things," Jesus reminded His hearers. "But seek first the kingdom of God and His righteousness, and all these things shall be added to you" (Matthew 6:32–33).

What are you putting first in your life?　　　　　—DD

MAKE IT PRACTICAL

- *Always pray before planning.*
- *Always love people more than things.*
- *Do all things to please God.*

Those who lay up treasures in heaven are the richest people on earth.

Slapton Sands

READ: 1 Peter 5:1–11

Be sober, be vigilant; because your adversary the devil walks about like a roaring lion, seeking whom he may devour. —1 PETER 5:8

On the southern shores of England is Slapton Sands. It is a beautiful beach area that carries a tragic memory from its past.

On April 28, 1944, during World War II, Allied soldiers were engaged in Operation Tiger, a training exercise in amphibious beach landings in preparation for the D-Day invasion of Normandy. Suddenly, enemy gunboats appeared and killed over 700 American servicemen in a surprise attack. Today, a monument stands on Slapton Sands to commemorate the sacrifice of those young men who died while training for battle.

This tragedy is a metaphor that warns the believer in Christ. We too are involved in combat with an enemy who is powerful and deceptive. That is why the apostle Peter warned: "Be sober, be vigilant; because your adversary the devil walks about like a roaring lion, seeking whom he may devour" (1 Peter 5:8).

Like the soldiers on Slapton Sands, we face an enemy who desires our undoing. In the service of our King, we must be on the alert. The call to be effective in battle (2 Timothy 2:3–4) challenges us to be ready for the surprise attacks of our spiritual enemy, so that we can endure to serve another day. —BC

The devil's tactic is surprise
To stop you in your tracks,
So keep on guard and trust God's Word;
Resist his strong attacks. —Branon

Satan's ploys are no match for the Savior's power.

Drifting Away

READ: Job 1:13–22

Shall we indeed accept good from God, and
shall we not accept adversity? —Job 2:10

Imagine relaxing on a rubber raft along the shore, eyes closed, soaking up the sun and listening to the gentle crash of waves. You don't have a care in the world—until you open your eyes! Suddenly the shore is alarmingly distant.

We tend to drift like that spiritually. It's subtle yet shocking when we suddenly realize how far we've drifted from God. The point of departure begins when Satan steals our affection for our loving Creator by putting a deceitful twist on our experiences and causing us to suspect God instead of trust Him.

Consider Job and his wife. Both had plenty of reasons to be mad at God. Their children were dead, their fortune lost, and Job's health destroyed. His wife told him, "Curse God and die!" But Job replied, "Shall we indeed accept good from God, and . . . not accept adversity?" (Job 2:9–10).

There are many attitudes that can set us adrift: believing that we need more than God to be happy; placing meaningful relationships above loyalty to God; thinking God should live up to our expectations; resisting His reproofs; turning a deaf ear when His Word is uncomfortable.

If you're beginning to drift, remember: stay close to the Lord—the sole source of satisfaction.   —JS

> *Lord, help me to stay close to You*
> *And trust You more each day,*
> *So when the storms of life appear*
> *I will not drift away.* —Sper

To avoid drifting away from God, stay anchored to the Rock.

I Will Never Leave You

READ: Deuteronomy 31:1–8

I am with you always, even to the end of the age. —MATTHEW 28:20

One of my earliest memories of hearing good music was when a male quartet rehearsed at our home. I was about ten years old, and I was especially attentive to my dad, who sang first tenor. One of the quartet's favorites was titled "I Am with You." Even at that tender age, I not only appreciated the music but I "got the message."

Those words of Jesus to His disciples just before He ascended—"I am with you always"—became precious to me as the quartet sang, "In the sunlight, in the shadow, I am with you where you go."

One of the first references to God's unfailing presence was spoken by Moses in Deuteronomy 31:6–8, when he instructed his successor about leading God's people into the "land of promise." And Joshua himself heard the same word from the Lord: "As I was with Moses, so I will be with you. I will not leave you nor forsake you" (Joshua 1:5).

That promise is repeated in the New Testament, where the writer of Hebrews gave this assurance: "He Himself has said, 'I will never leave you nor forsake you'" (13:5).

Wherever you may be today, you are not alone. If you've placed your trust in Jesus for your eternal salvation, you can be certain that He will never leave you. —CHK

Jesus whispers "I am with you"
In the hour of deepest need;
When the way is dark and lonesome,
"I am with you, I will lead." —Morris

First make sure you are with Him; then you can be sure He'll be with you.

The Cheat Test

READ: Psalm 119:129–136

Direct my steps by Your Word, and let no iniquity have dominion over me. —PSALM 119:133

Dan Ariely, an economics professor at the Massachusetts Institute of Technology, conducted some tests on human behavior. In one experiment, the participants took an examination in which they would receive money for each correct answer. The participants didn't know, however, that Ariely was not testing their knowledge but whether they would cheat. He set up the test so that the groups thought it would be easy to get away with cheating.

Prior to taking the exam, one group was asked to write down as many of the Ten Commandments as they could remember. To Ariely's astonishment, none from this group cheated! But all the other groups did have those who cheated. Recalling a moral benchmark made the difference.

Centuries ago, the psalmist understood the need for a moral benchmark and asked for divine aid in following it. He prayed to the Lord, "Direct my steps by Your Word, and let no iniquity have dominion over me. . . . Teach me Your statutes" (Psalm 119:133–135).

Ariely's "cheat test" experiment illustrates our need for moral guidance. The Lord has given us His Word as a lamp for our feet and a light for our path (v.105) to direct us in our moral choices. —DF

> *How precious is the Book divine*
> *By inspiration given!*
> *Bright as a lamp its doctrines shine,*
> *To guide our souls to heaven.* —Fawcett

Like a compass, the Bible always points us in the right direction.

The Work of Our Hands

READ: Psalm 112

The righteous will be in everlasting remembrance. —PSALM 112:6

One reason we're left here on earth and not taken to heaven immediately after trusting in Christ for salvation is that God has work for us to do. "Man is immortal," Augustine said, "until his work is done."

The time of our death is not determined by anyone or anything here on earth. That decision is made in the councils of heaven. When we have done all that God has in mind for us to do, then and only then will He take us home—and not one second before. As Paul put it, "David, after he had served his own generation by the will of God, fell asleep" (Acts 13:36).

In the meantime, until God takes us home, there's plenty to do. "I must work the works of Him who sent Me while it is day," Jesus said. "Night is coming when no one can work" (John 9:4). Night is coming when we will once for all close our eyes on this world, or our Lord will return to take us to be with Him. Each day brings that time a little closer.

As long as we have the light of day, we must work—not to conquer, acquire, accumulate, and retire, but to make visible the invisible Christ by touching people with His love. We can then be confident that our "labor is not in vain in the Lord" (1 Corinthians 15:58).   —DR

> *If you rely upon God's strength*
> *And live a life that's true,*
> *Then what you do in Jesus' name*
> *Will be His work through you.* —D. DeHaan

In God's eyes, true greatness is serving others.

Eliana Level

READ: Luke 22:7–20

Do this in remembrance of Me. —LUKE 22:19

My wife babysits for our young granddaughter Eliana during the school year while her mom teaches. We do many things to make her feel at home. For example, we put pictures of her and her parents on our refrigerator at "Eliana level." That way she can see them or carry them around with her during the day. We want her to think of her mom and dad often throughout the day.

Why do this? Is there a chance she would forget them? Of course not. But it is comforting for her to have an ongoing remembrance of them.

Now think about this. Before Jesus was crucified, He created a remembrance of himself. He told His disciples—and us by extension—to "do this [eat the bread and drink from the cup] in remembrance of Me" (Luke 22:19). Is this because we might forget Jesus? Of course not! How could we forget the one who died for our sins? Yet He started this way of remembrance—the Lord's Supper—as a comforting reminder of His great sacrifice, His presence, His power, and His promises.

Just as Eliana's photos remind her of her parents' love, so the celebration of Communion provides a valuable reminder of the one who will come again to take us home.

Partake. And remember.

—DB

> *But drops of grief can ne'er repay*
> *The debt of love I owe;*
> *Here, Lord, I give myself away—*
> *'Tis all that I can do.* —Watts

Those who take their sin seriously remember Christ's cross gratefully.

Connectors

READ: 1 Thessalonians 1:2–10

From you the word of the Lord has sounded forth, not only in Macedonia and Achaia, but also in every place. —1 THESSALONIANS 1:8

Marketing professionals have known for years that a product recommendation from a friend is among the most effective means of advertising. That's why many large companies recruit consumers who receive free samples of their products along with the encouragement to recommend them to family and friends. One major US corporation regularly sends coupons and products to 725,000 selected people called "connectors," who spread the word to others.

The gospel of Jesus Christ is more than a product. It is God's great plan for bringing people into a living, vital relationship with Him. But the gospel is conveyed most effectively by example and by word of mouth. Paul commended the Christians at Thessalonica for their exemplary living and their effective witness: "From you the word of the Lord has sounded forth. . . . Your faith toward God has gone out, so that we do not need to say anything" (1 Thessalonians 1:8). Because their lives had been radically changed (v. 9), they found it impossible to keep silent about their faith.

A university professor who trains advertising professionals says, "It's human nature to talk about things that excite us." God's grace is all the incentive we need to recommend our Savior to a friend.   —DM

> *I'll tell the world how Jesus saved me*
> *And how He gave me a life brand new;*
> *And I know that if you trust Him*
> *That all He gave me He'll give to you.* —Fox

If you want others to know what Christ will do for
them, tell them what He has done for you.

Still Small Voice

READ: 1 Kings 19:11–18

Be still, and know that I am God; I will be exalted among the nations, I will be exalted in the earth! —PSALM 46:10

When God spoke to Elijah on Mount Horeb, He could have done so in the wind, earthquake, or fire. But He didn't. He spoke with a "still small voice" (1 Kings 19:12). God asked, "What are you doing here, Elijah?" (v. 13), as the prophet hid from Jezebel who had threatened to kill him.

Elijah's reply revealed what God already knew—the depth of his fear and discouragement. He said, in effect, "Lord, I have been most zealous when others have forsaken You. What do I get for being the only one standing up for You?" (see v. 14).

Was Elijah really the only one serving God? No. God had "seven thousand in Israel . . . whose knees have not bowed to Baal" (v. 18).

In the depths of our fear or despair, we too may think we're the only one serving God. That may happen right after the height of a success, as it did for Elijah. Psalm 46:10 reminds us to "be still, and know" that He is God. The sooner we focus on Him and His power, the quicker we will see relief from our fear and self-pity.

Both the clashing cymbals of our failures and the loud trumpeting of our successes can drown out God's still small voice. It's time for us to quiet our hearts to listen for Him as we meditate on His Word. —AL

Keep listening for the "still small voice"
If you are weary on life's road;
The Lord will make your heart rejoice
If you will let Him take your load. —Hess

To tune in to God's voice we must tune out this world's noise.

At Just the Right Time

READ: Galatians 4:1–7

When the fullness of the time had come,
God sent forth His Son. —GALATIANS 4:4

Why is being on time so challenging for some of us? Even when we start early, something inevitably gets in our way to make us late.

But here's the good news: God is always on time! Speaking of the arrival of Jesus, Paul said, "When the fullness of the time had come, God sent forth His Son" (Galatians 4:4). The long-awaited, promised Savior came at just the right time.

Jesus' arrival during the Roman Empire's *Pax Romana* (the peace of Rome) was perfect timing. The known world was united by one language of commerce. A network of global trade routes provided open access to the whole world. All of this guaranteed that the gospel could move rapidly in one tongue. No visas. No impenetrable borders. Only unhindered access to help spread the news of the Savior whose crucifixion fulfilled the prophecy of the Lamb who would be slain for our sins (Isaiah 53). All in God's perfect timing!

All of this should remind us that the Lord knows what time is best for us as well. If you're waiting for answered prayer or the fulfillment of one of His promises, don't give up. If you think He has forgotten you, think again. When the fullness of time is right for you, He'll show up—and you'll be amazed by His brilliant timing!   —JS

> *Not ours to know the reason why*
> *Unanswered is our prayer,*
> *But ours to wait for God's own time*
> *To lift the cross we bear.* —Anonymous

God's timing is always perfect.

"Good Buddy"

READ: John 15:9–17

You are My friends if you do whatever I command you. —JOHN 15:14

The congregation listened intently as the pastor began to pray: "Dear heavenly Father . . ." Suddenly he was interrupted by a voice saying, "Hey there, good buddy!"

Everyone began to laugh when they realized the voice was coming from the organ. It was picking up the conversation of a truck driver on his CB radio! Not much was accomplished in the service that day, because the congregation continued to chuckle about the voice that made them think God was responding to their pastor and calling him His "good buddy."

Moses knew what it was like to be a friend of God—a relationship that went beyond buddies. The Lord often talked with Moses "face to face, as a man speaks to his friend" (Exodus 33:11). The patriarch Abraham was also called God's friend (2 Chronicles 20:7).

But can you and I be a friend of God? In our Bible reading for today, Jesus, the supreme example of loving friendship, called His disciples friends (John 15:13, 15). He put it simply: "You are My friends if you do whatever I command you" (v. 14).

And what does He command? That we love Him with all our heart and love others as ourselves (Mark 12:30–31). That's how we can be God's friend. —AC

Friendship with Jesus,
Fellowship divine,
Oh, what blessed, sweet communion,
Jesus is a friend of mine. —Ludgate

The dearest friend on earth is but a mere
shadow compared to Jesus. —Chambers

In Every Bad Experience

READ: 2 Kings 5:1–15

Now I know that there is no God in all the earth, except in Israel. —2 KINGS 5:15

When I rear-ended a truck with my nearly new car, positive thoughts did not immediately come to mind. I was thinking primarily of the cost, the inconvenience, and the injury to my ego. But I did find some hope in this thought, which I often share with other writers: "In every bad experience, there's a good illustration."

Finding the good can be a challenge, but Scripture confirms that God uses bad circumstances for good purposes.

In 2 Kings 5, we find two people who had bad things happen to them. First is a young girl from Israel who was taken captive by the Syrian army. Second is Naaman, the commander of the army, who had leprosy. Even though the girl had good reason to desire bad things for her captors, she offered help instead. Israel's prophet Elisha, she said, could heal Naaman. Eager to be cured, Naaman went to Israel. However, he was reluctant to follow Elisha's humiliating directions. When he finally did, he was healed, which caused him to proclaim that Israel's God is the only God (v. 15).

God used two bad things—a kidnapping and a deadly disease—to change Israel's enemy into a friend. Even when we don't know why something bad has happened, we know that God has the power to use it for good.   —JAL

> *His purposes will ripen fast,*
> *Unfolding every hour;*
> *The bud may have a bitter taste*
> *But sweet will be the flower.* —Cowper

God is the master of turning burdens into blessings.

Childlike Faith

READS: Matthew 8:5–10

The things which are impossible with men are possible with God. —LUKE 18:27

On the way home from a family camping trip, six-year-old Tanya and her dad were the only ones still awake in the car. As Tanya looked at the full moon through the car window, she asked, "Daddy, do you think I can touch the moon if I stand on my tiptoes?"

"No, I don't think so," he smiled.

"Can you reach it?"

"No, I don't think I can either."

She was quiet for a moment, then said confidently, "Daddy, maybe if you hold me up on your shoulders?"

Faith? Yes—the childlike faith that daddies can do anything. True faith, though, has the written promise of God for its foundation. In Hebrews 11:1 we read, "Faith is the substance of things hoped for, the evidence of things not seen." Jesus talked a lot about faith, and throughout the Gospels we read of His response to those who had great faith.

When a paralyzed man's friends brought him to Jesus, He "saw their faith," forgave the man of his sins, and healed him (Matthew 9:2–6). When the centurion asked Jesus to "speak a word, and my servant will be healed," Jesus "marveled" and said, "I have not found such great faith" (8:8, 10).

When we have faith in God, we will find that all things are possible (Luke 18:27). —CHK

> God, give me the faith of a little child
> Who trusts so implicitly,
> Who simply and gladly believes Thy Word,
> And never would question Thee. —Showerman

A childlike faith unlocks the door to the kingdom of heaven.

Godly Sorrow

READ: 2 Corinthians 7:5–10

I rejoice, not that you were made sorry, but that your sorrow led to repentance. For you were made sorry in a godly manner. —2 CORINTHIANS 7:9

Thieves stole nearly $5,000 in sound and office equipment from a church in West Virginia, only to break in the following night to return the items they had taken. Apparently, the guilt of stealing from a church weighed so heavily on their conscience that they felt the need to correct their criminal behavior of breaking the commandment: "You shall not steal" (Exodus 20:15). Their actions make me think about the differences between worldly sorrow and godly sorrow.

Paul praised the Corinthians for understanding this difference. His first letter to them was biting, as he addressed issues of sin. His words caused sorrow among them, and because of this Paul rejoiced. Why? Their sorrow did not stop at just feeling sad about getting caught or suffering the unpleasant consequences of their sins. Their sorrow was godly sorrow, a genuine remorse for their sins. This led them to repentance—a change in their thinking that led to a renouncing of their sin and turning to God. Their repentance ultimately led to deliverance from their sinful habits.

Repentance is prompted by the Holy Spirit; it's a gift from God. Pray for repentance today (2 Timothy 2:24–26). —MW

O Wind of God, come bend us, break us,
Till humbly we confess our need;
Then in Thy tenderness remake us,
Revive, restore—for this we plead. —Head

Repentance means hating sin enough to turn from it.

The World Is Watching

READ: John 13:31–35

By this all will know that you are My disciples,
if you have love for one another. —JOHN 13:35

My friends were serving in a ministry that was directed mainly to Christians when an opportunity came for them to change jobs and touch the lives of thousands of nonbelievers. They decided to make what they believed to be an exciting change.

Many people, even some who didn't personally know them, were shocked and accused them of seeking fame and fortune in the world. But believing that Jesus came "to seek and to save that which was lost" (Luke 19:10), they decided to pursue what they considered an even greater opportunity to serve the "lost" in their community.

They said later, "Some Christians were so cruel to us, and wrote hateful e-mails. Our new non-Christian friends were kinder to us than our fellow Christians. We didn't understand that, and were hurt deeply." They told me that their desire was to follow God's directive to be "salt" and "light" in the world (Matthew 5:13–14).

When someone we know is making a decision or change, it can be helpful to ask about his or her motives. But we can't fully know another's heart. We don't want to "bite and devour" our fellow Christians (Galatians 5:15), but instead to love them in a way that others will know we are Jesus' followers (John 13:35). The world is watching.   —AC

We join our hearts and hands together,
Faithful to the Lord's command:
We hold each other to God's standards—
All that truth and love demand. —D. DeHaan

Only God sees the heart.

Getting Better

READS: Philippians 1:19–26

I am hard-pressed between the two, having a desire to depart and be with Christ, which is far better. —PHILIPPIANS 1:23

A popular song from the 1960s was titled "Getting Better." In it, the singer considers his young life and happily declares that he sees things "getting better all the time." It is a song of optimism. Unfortunately, it is also a song without any real basis for that hope.

By contrast, the Bible warns us that we live in a world that in many ways is actually getting worse (2 Timothy 3:13). Daily we're faced with increasing evidence to support that contention. So how do we respond to the realities of life in such a badly marred world? With empty optimism? With hopeless discouragement? The apostle Paul shows us how.

While imprisoned in Rome, Paul wrote to the church at Philippi to offer them genuine hope in a broken world. He encouraged his readers by telling them that though life in this world is often hard and painful, for the Christian things will get better. He wrote, "I am hard-pressed between the two, having a desire to depart and be with Christ, which is far better" (Philippians 1:23). It is a reminder to us that we can face the difficulties of living for Christ now because one day we will be with Him in an eternal home of splendor and fullness.

Life can be hard, but one day when we see Christ it will truly get better! —BC

> *To see His face, this is my goal,*
> *The deepest longing of my soul;*
> *Through storm and stress my path I'll trace*
> *Till, satisfied, I see His face!* —Chisholm

To be with Jesus forever is the sum of all happiness.

Magnets and Mothers

READ: Proverbs 31:26–31

Honor your father and your mother, as the Lord your God has commanded you. —DEUTERONOMY 5:16

A teacher gave her class of second-graders a lesson about the magnet and what it does. The next day, in a written test, she included this question: "My name has six letters. The first one is *m*. I pick up things. What am I?" When the test papers were turned in, the teacher was astonished to find that almost 50 percent of the students answered the question with the word *mother*.

Yes, mothers do pick up things. But they are much more than "magnets," gathering up clothes and picking up toys around the house. As willing as many mothers are to do such chores, they have a higher calling than that.

A good mother loves her family and provides an atmosphere where each member can find acceptance, security, and understanding. She is there when the children need a listening ear, a comforting word, a warm hug, or a loving touch on a fevered brow. And for the Christian mother, her greatest joy is in teaching her children to trust and to love Jesus as their Savior.

That kind of mother deserves to be honored—not just on one special day a year but every day. And that recognition should involve more than words; it ought to be shown in respect, thoughtfulness, and loving deeds.

—RD

Of all the earthly things God gives,
There's one above all others:
It is the precious, priceless gift
Of loving Christian mothers. —*Anonymous*

Godly mothers not only bring you up, they bring you to God.

Making the Cut

READ: Matthew 4:18–22

[Jesus] said to them, "Follow Me, and I will make you fishers of men." —MATTHEW 4:19

Every year, high school seniors apply to their favorite universities and then watch the mailbox for the letter announcing their acceptance.

It was different for Jewish boys in New Testament times. Jewish boys would often attend rabbinical schools until age thirteen. Then only the best and brightest would be chosen to "follow" the local rabbi. This small, select group of disciples would go where the rabbi went and eat what he ate—modeling their lives after the rabbi. Those who didn't make the cut would learn a trade like carpentry, sheep-herding, or fishing.

Guys like Simon, Andrew, James, and John hadn't made the cut. So instead of following the local rabbi, they were down by the docks, knee-deep in the family business. It's interesting that Jesus sought out these men that the local rabbi had rejected. Instead of targeting the best and brightest, Jesus offered His invitation, "Follow Me," to ordinary run-of-the-mill fishermen. What an honor! They would become followers of the ultimate Rabbi.

Jesus extends the same honor to you and me—not because we are the best or brightest, but because He needs ordinary people like us to model His life and to lovingly rescue people on His behalf. So follow Him and let Him make something of your life! —JS

As followers of Jesus
Who love Him from the heart,
We may be ordinary,
But we've been set apart. —Sper

Even the ordinary and the outcast can make the cut to follow Jesus.

The Secret Is

READ: 1 Corinthians 2:6–16

We speak the wisdom of God in a mystery, the hidden wisdom which God ordained before the ages. —1 CORINTHIANS 2:7

If you believe Rhonda Byrne, author of the bestselling book *The Secret,* "The shortcut to anything you want in your life is to *be* and *feel* happy now!" According to Byrne, this has to do with something called the law of attraction. If you think only about things that make you happy, she says, happy things will be attracted to you.

Sounds easy enough.

However, the Bible says that "the secret" to life is something very different. It has to do with "the law of the Spirit of life" that sets us free from "the law of sin and death" (Romans 8:2), not with the "law of attraction."

According to the apostle Paul, the most important thing to know is "Jesus Christ and Him crucified" (1 Corinthians 2:2). To those who are concerned with happiness now, this is indeed foolishness (v. 14). They do not recognize the power of God in what appears to them as weakness.

The Lord created us with a desire to know what is secret. And in His wisdom, He kept certain things hidden in mystery for a time (v. 7). But now, through His Holy Spirit, He has made them known. And the secret He reveals has nothing to do with having happy thoughts in order to obtain happy things; it has to do with having the mind of Jesus Christ (v. 16).   —JAL

There is a law that made us free—
In Romans 8 this truth is heard;
The secret is to walk with God
And daily lean upon His Word. —Hess

To know lasting happiness, we must get to know Jesus.

The Gift of Self-Indulgence

READ: Ezekiel 16:48–57

She and her daughter had pride, fullness of food, and abundance of idleness; neither did she strengthen the hand of the poor and needy. —EZEKIEL 16:49

An upscale London department store launched a new gift card with the slogan, "The Gift of Self-Indulgence." Throughout the store, signs, slogans, and even nametags called attention to the cards. According to one employee, sales of the gift cards during the first weeks of the promotion had been very strong, far exceeding company expectations. Generosity may prompt a person to give a luxurious gift to someone special, but too often we find it easier to purchase what we want for ourselves.

The prophet Ezekiel sheds light on an ancient city whose people suffered God's judgment, in part, because they embraced a self-indulgent lifestyle. "This was the iniquity of your sister Sodom: She and her daughter had pride, fullness of food, and abundance of idleness; neither did she strengthen the hand of the poor and needy. And they were haughty and committed abomination before Me; therefore I took them away as I saw fit" (Ezekiel 16:49–50). Historically, the Lord dealt harshly with His people when they became arrogant, overfed, and unconcerned (v. 49).

The antidote to the poison of self-indulgence is the desire to please God and serve others, not ourselves (Philippians 2:4).

Self-indulgence is a gift we don't need. —DM

Some are discouraged and weary in heart,
Help somebody today!
Someone the journey to heaven should start,
Help somebody today! —Breck

The more we serve Christ, the less we serve self.

Wake-Up Music

READUH: Deuteronomy 31:16–22

Let the word of Christ dwell in you richly in all wisdom; teaching and admonishing one another in psalms and hymns and spiritual songs. —COLOSSIANS 3:16

In a suburb of Nairobi, Kenya, a group of international refugees has been singing songs that they hope will wake up their homeland. According to the BBC, the group Waayah Cusub has been enjoying extensive airplay on radio stations and television channels by using bold lyrics to address social issues. One of the musicians says, "We are not happy with what is happening back home; in fact we have recorded a thought-provoking song that we hope will bring our leaders back to their senses."

Long before Waayah Cusub began using songs to call for an end to social pain and violence, God taught Moses to use music in a bold and provocative way. Knowing that His people's sinful inclinations would distract them when they began to enjoy the prosperity of the Promised Land, God told Moses to teach them the song we call "The Song of Moses," which begins, "Listen, O heavens, and I will speak" (Deuteronomy 31:21; 32). It is a shocking song of warning, designed to get the attention of those who would forget God and fill their lives with trouble.

Could our wise and loving God be repeating that strategy with us? Is there a psalm, a hymn, or a spiritual song that is calling us back to His faithfulness and amazing grace? What song might He be using to get under the radar of our natural defenses and renew our hearts today?

—MD

Come, Thou fount of every blessing,
Tune my heart to sing Thy grace;
Streams of mercy, never ceasing,
Call for songs of loudest praise. —*Robinson*

Where words fail, music speaks. —Hans Christian Andersen

The Heavenly Alternative

READ: 2 Corinthians 5:1–11

We are confident, yes, well pleased rather to be absent from the body and to be present with the Lord. —2 CORINTHIANS 5:8

Recently, I wished a young friend "happy birthday" and asked him how it felt to be a year older. His playful response? "Well, I guess it's better than the alternative!"

We laughed together, but I later thought, Is it really? Don't misunderstand me. I'm happy to live as long as the Lord allows me to live and to watch my kids and grandkids grow and experience life. I'm not excited about the inevitability of death. But as a believer, the alternative to getting older is heaven—and that's not bad!

In 2 Corinthians 5, Paul talks about the reality of living with the aches and pains of our physical bodies, our "tents" of flesh. But we should not live in despair about aging. In fact, the apostle calls us to just the opposite. He wrote, "We are confident, yes, well pleased rather to be absent from the body and to be present with the Lord" (v. 8). Confident! Pleased! Why? Because our alternative to earthly life is that we will be present with the Lord—forever! The heavenly perspective of what awaits us can give us confidence for living now.

If you know Christ, His promise can give you what the hymnwriter called, "Strength for today and bright hope for tomorrow." What a great alternative! —BC

He's gone "to prepare a place for you,"
That where He is "there you may be."
Our death is not the end of life—
We'll be with Christ eternally! —Hess

Death is gain because it means heaven, holiness, and Him!

War in Heaven

READ: Revelation 12:7–12

*War broke out in heaven . . . . [And Satan]
was cast to the earth.* —REVELATION 12:7–9

Philip Pullman is a gifted writer of fantasy books. His Dark Materials trilogy includes *The Golden Compass, The Subtle Knife,* and *The Amber Spyglass* and is very popular among young readers. But below the surface of these sympathetic characters and compelling subplots is a sinister purpose, for the story culminates in a great war against God.

In these books, Pullman views the fall of Satan as a righteous cause for personal independence from God's "tyrannical" control. He implies that Satan's attempt to usurp the throne of God was the right thing to do!

In the book of Revelation we read of the endtimes: "War broke out in heaven. . . . [And Satan] was cast to the earth" (12:7–9). That future war is being preceded by an earthly conflict on the battlefield of our minds.

We must recognize Satan for what he is—a liar (John 8:44). His strategy is to take God's words out of context and twist them into falsehood (Genesis 3:1–7). Our best defense against him is to hold firmly to the truth of God's Word (Ephesians 6:10–18).

Our loving heavenly Father is "not willing that any should perish" (2 Peter 3:9). But neither will He force our obedience. He leaves the choice to us.   —DF

When Satan strikes, strike back with the Word of God.

Restoring Spiritual Sight

READ: John 9:1–11

The entrance of Your words gives light; it gives
understanding to the simple. —PSALM 119:130

Sanduk Ruit is a Nepalese doctor who has used his scalpel, microscope, and simplified cataract surgery technique to give sight to almost 70,000 people over the past twenty-three years. The poorest patients who visit his nonprofit eye center in Katmandu pay with just their gratitude.

Our Lord Jesus Christ healed many of physical blindness during His time on earth. But of greater concern to Him were the spiritually blind. Many of the religious authorities who investigated the healing of the blind man refused to believe that Jesus was not a sinner (John 9:13–34). This caused Jesus to say, "For judgment I have come into this world, that those who do not see may see, and that those who see may be made blind" (v. 39).

The apostle Paul wrote of this spiritual blindness when he said, "If our gospel is veiled, it is veiled to those who are perishing, whose minds the god of this age has blinded, who do not believe, lest the light of the gospel of the glory of Christ, who is the image of God, should shine on them" (2 Corinthians 4:3–4).

The psalmist said, "The entrance of Your words gives light" (Psalm 119:130). God's Word is what will open our eyes and cure spiritual blindness. —CPH

> *Come to the Light, 'tis shining for thee!*
> *Sweetly the Light has dawned upon me;*
> *Once I was blind, but now I can see—*
> *The Light of the world is Jesus.* —Bliss

A world in darkness needs the light of Jesus.

Is He Enough?

READ: Acts 3:1–10

Silver and gold I do not have, but
what I do have I give you. —ACTS 3:6

Is Jesus enough? That's a question many Christians need to ask themselves. They have abundant material possessions, but is that what they depend on? Do they depend on Jesus—or on their stuff?

While having wealth is not condemned in Scripture as long as priorities are in order and the needs of others are addressed, those of us with relative wealth must remind ourselves that Jesus—not riches—sustains us.

The apostle Peter helps us with this in the story of the lame man begging at the temple gate in Jerusalem. This man asked Peter for money, but Peter replied, "Silver and gold I do not have, but what I do have I give you: In the name of Jesus Christ of Nazareth, rise up and walk" (Acts 3:6).

The man lying at the gate thought the answer to his problems that day was money, but Peter showed him that the answer was Jesus. And He still is.

I read about a group of Chinese Christians who have much to teach us as they seek to spread the gospel in their homeland and beyond. These believers say, "We can't afford any big programs or fancy gospel presentations. All we have to give people is Jesus."

Jesus is enough for our brothers and sisters in China. He is enough for the poor. Is He enough for you? —DB

> *You may have much gold and grandeur,*
> *Yet by God be reckoned poor;*
> *He alone has riches truly*
> *Who has Christ, though nothing more.* —Anonymous

Our greatest riches are the riches we have in Christ.

I'm Right; You Must Be Wrong

READ: Luke 6:37–42

Judge not, and you shall not be judged. Condemn not,
and you shall not be condemned. —LUKE 6:37

My friend Ria admires the great blue heron's amazing six-foot spread of wings and marvels at his majestic appearance. She welcomes the sight of him gliding in for a landing on a small island in the middle of the pond near her home.

Now, I can appreciate that the heron is a marvelous and unique creature. But I don't ever want to spot him in my backyard! That's because I know he won't be there just to admire the garden. No, this not-so-fine-feathered version of *persona non grata* (someone not welcome) will be checking out our pond for a take-out fish dinner!

So, am I right? Or is Ria? Why can't we agree? Different personalities, history, or knowledge can color people's views. It doesn't mean that one person is right and the other wrong. Yet sometimes we can be unkind, rigid, and judgmental if there is not agreement. I'm not talking about sin, but just a difference in opinion or perspective. We need to take care in judging others' thinking, motives, and actions because we too desire that kind of benefit of the doubt (Luke 6:37).

Can we learn from someone who sees things with a different perspective? Do we need to practice a little patience and love? I'm so grateful that God is abundantly patient and loving with me. —CHK

You've been so patient with us, Lord,
Though we are slow to hear;
Give us the grace to show such love
To those we hold so dear. —K. DeHaan

A little love can make a big difference.

Make Way

READ: Isaiah 40:3–5

Prepare the way of the Lord; make straight in the desert a highway for our God. —ISAIAH 40:3

Dwight D. Eisenhower was known for his courageous leadership during World War II. His battle-tested skill equipped the troops to reclaim Europe. Soon after returning to the US as a hero, he was elected president.

While in Europe, Eisenhower had experienced the danger and difficulty of navigating the twisting roads. So, for the sake of US national security, he commissioned a network of roads that became the nation's interstate highway system. Mountains were tunneled through and valleys were traversed by mammoth bridges.

In ancient times, conquering kings gained access to newly acquired territories through highways built for their troops. Isaiah had this in mind when he declared, "Make straight in the desert a highway for our God" (Isaiah 40:3). And John the Baptist called people to repentance to "prepare the way" into their hearts for the arrival of King Jesus.

What preparation needs to be done to allow Jesus unhindered access to your own heart? Are there rough places of bitterness that need the bulldozer of forgiveness? Are there valleys of complaining that need to be filled with contentment? We can't afford to neglect this spiritual engineering. Let's prepare the way for the King! —JS

Repentance clears the way for our relationship with the King.

The Witness of Friends

READ: 1 John 1:1–7

We have seen, and bear witness, and declare to you that eternal life which was with the Father and was manifested to us. —1 JOHN 1:2

Pulitzer Prize-winning author David Halberstam died in a traffic accident five months before the publication of his landmark book about the US war in Korea. In the days following the author's death, fellow writers and colleagues volunteered to conduct a national book tour on his behalf. During every engagement, they paid tribute to Halberstam by reading from his new book and offering personal recollections of their friend.

When it comes to conveying the essence and importance of a person, there's no substitute for a friend. After the resurrection and ascension of Jesus Christ, His followers began to tell others about the unique person they had known. "We have seen, and bear witness, and declare to you that eternal life which was with the Father and was manifested to us" (1 John 1:2). Their purpose was that others might come to know God the Father and Christ His Son (v. 3).

At times we may feel that witnessing to others about our faith in Christ is a frightening task or a burdensome duty. But talking about our Savior and friend Jesus, whose presence and influence have transformed our lives, helps us see witnessing in a new light.

The gospel of Christ has always been most powerfully presented by the witness of His friends. —DM

> *Lord, help us see, through transformed eyes,*
> *This world of people in despair;*
> *We want to reach out with Your love*
> *To tell them just how much You care.* —Sper

The more you love Jesus, the more you'll talk about Him.

Witnesses

READ: Acts 1:1–11

You shall receive power when the Holy Spirit has come upon you; and you shall be witnesses to Me . . . to the end of the earth. —ACTS 1:8

In a criminal court case, witnesses provide vital information about a possible crime. Being a witness means telling the court the truth about what you know.

Just as the criminal justice system relies heavily on witnesses, Jesus uses bold, faithful, and credible witnesses to spread His Word and build His church.

Before Jesus ascended to His Father, He gave His disciples a final command—to launch a worldwide witnessing campaign. The Holy Spirit would come upon them and give them supernatural power to be His witnesses throughout the world (Acts 1:8).

Jesus called these early apostles to go into a world where people did not know about Him and to give a truthful account of what they had seen, heard, and experienced (Acts 4:19–20). Since they had witnessed His perfect life, teachings, suffering, death, burial, and resurrection, they were to go out and give a truthful testimony about Him (Luke 24:48; Acts 1–5). As the apostle Paul later wrote, "How shall they believe in Him of whom they have not heard?" (Romans 10:14).

In taking the gospel to the ends of the earth, we are called to testify to the truth about Jesus and how He has changed our lives. What are you doing to tell others?   —MW

> *Lord and Savior, Christ divine,*
> *Reign within this heart of mine;*
> *May my witness ever be*
> *Always, only, Lord, for Thee.* —Brandt

God has left us in the world to witness to the world.

Calling Evil Good

READ: Isaiah 5:18–23

Woe to those who call evil good, and good evil! —ISAIAH 5:20

The Wizard of Oz has remained popular for years. People of all ages have learned moral lessons from Dorothy, the Scarecrow, the Tin Man, and the Cowardly Lion as they travel down the yellow brick road. Of course, in the plot line the great enemy to be overcome is the Wicked Witch of the West. Evil is clearly depicted and overcome by good.

A new Broadway musical, however, turns the moral sense of the original story on its head. In this rewriting of the story, the wicked witch is presented as a sympathetic character. Born with green skin, she feels like an outsider. Major characters, plot lines, roles, and other details are altered so that the wicked witch is seen as just a misunderstood person. The audience might come away with the idea that evil is good and good is evil.

During the ministry of the prophet Isaiah, a reversal of moral values took place in Israel. Some actually lifted up the evils of murder, idolatry, and adultery as good. In response, Isaiah gave a stern warning: "Woe to those who call evil good, and good evil!" (Isaiah 5:20).

In our relativistic world, popular culture constantly challenges biblical values. But studying, memorizing, and meditating on God's Word can strengthen our ability to discern between good and evil.   —DF

> *In our day-to-day existence,*
> *Evil sometimes wears a mask;*
> *Trust the Lord for true discernment—*
> *He gives wisdom when we ask.* —Hess

If we know the truth, we can discern what's false.

None So Blind

READ: Psalm 82

Inasmuch as you did it to one of the least of these My brethren, you did it to Me. —MATTHEW 25:40

Singer Ray Stevens is generally given credit for writing the phrase "There is none so blind as he who will not see," a line from the song "Everything Is Beautiful." But preacher Matthew Henry used the phrase 250 years ago when commenting on the lyrics of another songwriter, Asaph.

Asaph's lyrics were not as upbeat as those of Stevens. His song was a rebuke to the Israelites for failing to fulfill their God-given purpose. God had chosen them to show the world how to live right and judge justly, but they were failing miserably. Instead of defending the weak and fatherless, they were defending the unjust and showing partiality to the wicked (Psalm 82:2–3).

In his commentary on Psalm 82, Henry wrote: "A gift in secret blinds their eyes. They know not because they will not understand. None so blind as those that will not see. They have baffled their own consciences, and so they walk on in darkness."

Jesus confirmed God's interest in the weak and helpless. He explained that whatever is done for the "least of these" is done for Him (see Matthew 25:34–40). And He chided His disciples for keeping children away from Him (Luke 18:16).

Those who have eyes that see what God sees find ways to help the helpless.   —JAL

> *Love through me, Love of God,*
> *There is no love in me;*
> *O Fire of love, light Thou the love*
> *That burns perpetually.* —*Carmichael*

A test of true Christian love: Do you help those who can't help you in return?

The Arlington Ladies

READ: Matthew 26:6–13

What this woman has done will also be told as a memorial to her. —MATTHEW 26:13

In 1948, the US Air Force Chief of Staff noticed that no one attended the funeral of an airman at Arlington National Cemetery, and that deeply disturbed him. He talked with his wife about his concern that each soldier be honored at burial, and she began a group called the Arlington Ladies.

Someone from the Arlington Ladies group honors each deceased soldier by attending his or her funeral. The ladies also write personal notes of sympathy and speak words of gratitude to family members when they are present. If possible, a representative keeps in contact with the family for months afterward.

Margaret Mensch, an Arlington Lady, says, "The important thing is to be there for the families. . . . It's an honor to . . . pay tribute to the everyday heroes that make up the armed forces."

Jesus showed the importance of paying tribute. After a woman poured a costly, fragrant oil on His head, He said that she would be honored for years to come (Matthew 26:13). The disciples were indignant and thought her act was wasteful, but Jesus called it "a good work" for which she would be remembered (v. 10).

We know heroes who have given their lives in service to God and their country. Let's honor them today. —AC

> *Lord, help us to appreciate*
> *The work that others do,*
> *The service given from their hearts,*
> *Their sacrifice for You.* —Sper

We honor God when we honor one another.

Armed for the Fray

READ: Ephesians 6:10–18

Put on the whole armor of God, that you may be able to stand against the wiles of the devil. —EPHESIANS 6:11

Paul the apostle, a spiritual warrior, testified as he came to the end of his embattled life: "I have fought the good fight, I have finished the race, I have kept the faith" (2 Timothy 4:7).

Years earlier, that valiant soldier of Jesus Christ had pleaded with his fellow Christians to put on the armor of God, which would enable them to stand firm in their conflict with the powers of darkness. He knew the vital importance of donning that armor every day. In his service for Christ, Paul had been whipped, beaten, stoned, and imprisoned, and was often hungry, thirsty, cold, and weary (2 Corinthians 11:22–28).

Strapping on the belt of truth, the breastplate of righteousness, the shoes of peace, the shield of faith, the helmet of salvation, and the sword of the Spirit (God's Word) enabled Paul to "quench all the fiery darts of the wicked one" (Ephesians 6:14–17). With God's armor we too are fully covered and prepared for battle.

The prince of darkness with his hosts of demonic helpers is an incredibly crafty foe. That's why we need to guard against his deceitful devices and put on the whole armor of God every day. When we do, like Paul when he was nearing the end of his days, we can be confident that we have "kept the faith."   —VG

Sound the battle cry! See—the foe is nigh!
Raise the standard high for the Lord;
Gird your armor on, stand firm, everyone;
Rest your cause upon His holy Word. —Sherwin

God's armor is tailormade for you, but you must put it on.

Wow!

READ: Romans 11:33–36

Who is like You, O Lord, among the gods? Who is like You, glorious in holiness, fearful in praises, doing wonders? —EXODUS 15:11

One blustery day in June, our family, holidaying in the Canadian Rockies, went to a tourist site that was billed as a "must see." The cold wind made me reluctant to go on until I saw a group of people returning from the scenic spot.

"Is it worth it?" I asked.

"Definitely!" was their response.

That gave us the incentive to go on. When we finally reached the spot, its beauty rendered us virtually speechless. "Wow!" was all we could manage.

Paul reached that point as he wrote about the work of God in saving Jew and Gentile. Three things about God "wowed" him.

First, God is all-wise. His perfect plan of salvation shows that He has far better solutions to the problems of life than we are capable of devising (Romans 11:33).

Second, God is all-knowing. His knowledge is infinite. He needs no counselor and nothing surprises Him (v. 34).

Third, God is all-sufficient. No one can give to God what He has not first given to them. Nor can anyone ever repay Him for His goodness (v. 35).

We can say with Moses, "Who is like You, majestic in holiness, awesome in glorious deeds, doing wonders?" (Exodus 15:11 ESV). What a marvelous God we serve!   —CPH

By God's grace I stand on tiptoe,
Viewing all His wonders grand,
Praising Him who freely gave me
Simple faith to understand! —Bosch

In God's character and in His creation, we see His majesty.

For Sale: One Soul

READ: Matthew 16:24–28

What will a man give in exchange for his soul? —MATTHEW 16:26

One would think that selling one's soul, as the character Faust did when he offered his to the devil in Goethe's *Dr. Faustus,* is only a figment of literary fiction. Unlikely as it seems, however, *Wired* magazine reported that a 29-year-old university instructor succeeded in selling his immortal soul for $1,325. He said, "In America, you can metaphorically and literally sell your soul and be rewarded for it." One wonders how the purchaser intended to collect.

We can't literally sell our soul, but we can lose our soul to gain something else. Which means that we need to ponder Jesus' question, "What will a man give in exchange for his soul?" (Matthew 16:26). Our answers today would differ only in specifics from the responses of Jesus' day: the world, the flesh, and the devil. The lusts that captivate us and the thirst for unbridled pleasure, success, revenge, or material things have certainly taken on far more importance to many people than any considerations of eternity.

Nothing on earth compares to the gifts of God's love and forgiveness. If the pleasures of this world are preventing you from trusting in Jesus Christ, please think again. It's not worth the cost of your eternal soul. —DE

Rejoice, O soul, the debt is paid,
For all our sins on Christ were laid;
We've been redeemed, we're justified—
And all because the Savior died. —D. DeHaan

Jesus is the only fountain who can satisfy the thirsty soul.

He Would Not Go In

READ: Luke 15:25–32

He was angry and would not go in. —LUKE 15:28

Some theologians divide transgressions into "sins of the flesh" and "sins of the spirit." This means that some sins originate in our physical passions; others come from our "heart" or disposition. In the story of the prodigal son, the elder brother's attitude gives us an example of the latter.

We're inclined to single out the prodigal son as worse than his brother. But it's worth noting that when the story ends, the prodigal is restored, forgiven, and full of joy, while the elder brother stands outside and refuses to go in and join in the welcome-home festivities for his brother.

The stay-at-home son is more than background filler for the story. He makes us think about the state of our heart, for sour moods create untold misery. Discontent, jealousy, bitterness, resentment, defensiveness, touchiness, and ingratitude are the dispositions that ruin our marriages, wither our children, alienate our friends, and embitter every life—including our own.

It's easy to defend our bad moods and to slide into deception and hypocrisy. But we must guard our hearts against such destructive attitudes. When they arise, we need to confess them, let them go, and experience God's forgiveness.

Don't let your bad attitude cause you to lose out while others enter into joy.　　　　　　　　　　　　　　　　　　　　—DR

> *When anger lingers in our heart,*
> *It poisons all we think and do;*
> *When faith seeks ways to show God's love*
> *It keeps our spirit strong and true.* —D. DeHaan

Resentment comes from looking at others;
contentment comes from looking at God.

Pay It Forward

READ: John 13:3–15

I have given you an example, that you should do as I have done to you. —JOHN 13:15

Pay It Forward is a movie about a twelve-year-old's plan to make a difference in the world. Motivated by a teacher at his school, Trevor invites a homeless man to sleep in his garage. Unaware of this arrangement, his mother awakens one evening to find the man working on her truck. Holding him at gunpoint, she asks him to explain himself. He shows her that he has successfully repaired her truck and tells her about Trevor's kindness. He says, "I'm just paying it forward."

I think this is what Jesus had in mind in one of His last conversations with His disciples. He wanted to show them the full extent of His love. So before their last meal together, He took off His outer garment, wrapped a towel around His waist, and began to wash His disciples' feet. This was shocking because only slaves washed feet. It was an act of servanthood and a symbol that pointed to Jesus' sacrifice, passion, and humiliation on the cross. His request to His disciples was: "If I then, your Lord and Teacher, have washed your feet, you also ought to wash one another's feet" (John 13:14). They were to "pay it forward."

Imagine how different our world would look if we gave the kind of love to others that God has given us through Jesus.   —MW

> *Christ's example teaches us*
> *That we should follow Him each day,*
> *Meeting one another's needs,*
> *Though humble service be the way.* —Hess

To know love, open your heart to Jesus.
To show love, open your heart to others.

The Lord of Our Years

READ: Psalm 90

*Before the mountains were brought forth, or ever You
had formed the earth and the world, even from
everlasting to everlasting, You are God.* —PSALM 90:2

When the *Concise Oxford English Dictionary* announced in 2006 that the word *time* was the most-often used noun in the English language, it didn't seem surprising. We live in a world where people are obsessed with using days, saving minutes, and trying to find more hours in the day. Although each of us has all the time that there is, few of us think we have enough.

Perhaps that's why Psalm 90 is such a treasured passage. It shifts the focus from our time-bound lives to our eternal God. "Before the mountains were brought forth, or ever You had formed the earth and the world, even from everlasting to everlasting, You are God" (v. 2).

A stanza in Matthew Bridges' well-known hymn "Crown Him with Many Crowns" begins: "Crown Him the Lord of years, the Potentate of time." A potentate is a sovereign, a monarch, an anointed majesty—one who does not seek appointment or run for election.

God created time. He rules and transcends it. When we feel frustrated by the calendar or captured by the clock, a quiet reading of Psalm 90 reminds us that our days and years are in the hands of our eternal God.

As we humbly bow before Him, we see time from a new perspective.
—DM

Crown Him the Lord of years,
The Potentate of time,
Creator of the rolling spheres,
Ineffably sublime. —*Bridges*

We must have a right view of eternity to know the real value of time.

The Circle of Fear

READ: 1 John 2:1–11

If anyone sins, we have an Advocate with the
Father, Jesus Christ the righteous. —1 JOHN 2:1

When the popular band The Eagles prepares a new song for concert, they sit in a circle with acoustic guitars and unamplified voices and rehearse their intricate vocals. They call this exercise "The Circle of Fear" because there is no place to hide and no way to conceal any errors they might make in the harmonies. That sense of absolute exposure for their mistakes is what makes this drill so frightening to them.

Apart from Christ, we would suffer a far worse kind of exposure before the God of all justice. If we had no advocate and no escape, we would also have no hope. But in Christ, the believer has a defender who stands before the Father on our behalf. First John 2:1 says, "My little children, these things I write to you, so that you may not sin. And if anyone sins, we have an Advocate with the Father, Jesus Christ the righteous." With our failings exposed, He takes our defense. Christ our defender carries our relationship with God beyond a "circle of fear" to a fellowship of grace and truth.

Our challenge is to live lives of purity and integrity that honor our heavenly Father. But when we do fail, we do not need to fear abandonment or ridicule from our Father. We have an advocate who will carry us through. —BC

Frail children of dust, and feeble as frail,
In Thee do we trust, nor find Thee to fail.
Thy mercies how tender! How firm to the end!
Our Maker, Defender, Redeemer, and Friend. —Grant

The one who died as our substitute now lives as our advocate.

Adopted

READ: Colossians 3:1–12

*Put to death your members which are on
the earth: fornication, uncleanness, passion,
evil desire, and covetousness.* —COLOSSIANS 3:5

In ancient Rome, adoption was occasionally used by the emperors to pass on succession to competent heirs. Augustus Caesar was adopted by his great-uncle Julius Caesar. Other notable adoptees include the emperors Tiberius, Trajan, and Hadrian. All of them proved to be strong rulers because each lived like a child of his adoptive father.

Every Christian is an adopted child of the King of kings. We are greatly indebted to Him for His favor. But God, who has everything, does not need us to repay Him.

What does God desire? He wants us to live in a way that befits His children. Activities and values that are not in keeping with our position as God's children must be done away with (Colossians 3:5). Selfish and destructive ways are to be replaced by activities and values that showcase our gratitude and love for God and reflect our status as His children. Paul wrote, "Put on tender mercies, kindness, humility, meekness, long-suffering" (v. 12).

Can others around you tell that you are indeed a child of the King? Ask the Holy Spirit what you need to put off and put on in your life so that you can reflect more truly your status as God's adopted child.
—CPH

I once was an outcast stranger on earth,
A sinner by choice and an alien by birth;
But I've been adopted, my name's written down—
An heir to a mansion, a robe, and a crown. —*Buell*

We honor God's name when we call Him our Father and live like His children.

Day of Days

READ: 2 Timothy 2:1–4

*You therefore must endure hardship as a good
soldier of Jesus Christ.* —2 TIMOTHY 2:3

In the television miniseries *Band of Brothers,* the 101st Airborne is flown over their drop zone during D-Day, the major offensive to liberate Europe from Nazi control. As the main character, Lt. Richard Winters, parachutes from the plane, the crack of antiaircraft and machine-gun fire fills the air.

Winters later reflected on his first day in combat: "That night, I took time to thank God for seeing me through that day of days. . . . And if somehow I manage to get home again, I promise God and myself that I will find a quiet piece of land someplace and spend the rest of my life in peace." Winters knew he must endure until that day came.

The Bible tells us that believers are caught in a conflict initiated by Satan's rebellion against God. Because of this, we are challenged to "endure hardship as a good soldier of Jesus Christ" (2 Timothy 2:3). In Paul's day, the Roman legionnaires suffered in service for the emperor. As followers of Jesus, we may be called upon to do the same for the King of kings.

In heaven, we will no longer experience such difficulties but will enjoy lasting peace with the Savior. For now, we are to persevere by faith. —DF

Lord, the trials we face at times seem too much to bear. We're grateful, though, for the reminders in your Word that you will stay by our side and help us endure till you call us Home. Amen.

Victory is sure for those who endure.

Words and Numbers

READ: John 17:20–26

I and My Father are one. —JOHN 10:30

My husband is a "numbers" person; I am a "word" person. When my incompetence with numbers gets the best of me, I try to boost my ego by reminding Jay that word people are superior because Jesus called himself the Word, not the Number.

Instead of trying to defend himself, Jay just smiles and goes on about his business, which consists of much more important things than my silly arguments.

Since Jay will not defend himself, I feel compelled to do so. Although I am right about Jesus being the Word, I am wrong in saying that He didn't refer to himself as a number. One of the most moving passages of Scripture is Christ's prayer just before His arrest and crucifixion. Facing death, Jesus prayed not only for himself, but also for His disciples and for us. His most urgent request on our behalf involved a number: "[I pray] that they all may be one, as You, Father, are in Me, and I in You; that they also may be one in Us, that the world may believe that You sent Me" (John 17:21).

As people who live by the Word, we need to remember that "right words" sound hollow to the world unless we, being one in Christ, are glorifying God with one mind and one voice.   —JAL

God calls His children to unity.

A Life Remembered

READ: Psalm 139:1–16

That we may be able to comfort those who are in any trouble, with the comfort with which we ourselves are comforted by God. —2 CORINTHIANS 1:4

Daddy, help me." Those were the last words Dianne and Gary Cronin heard their daughter say as she struggled to breathe. Kristin, fourteen years old, died suddenly—just two days after saying she didn't feel well. A strep infection attacked her body on Thursday. By Saturday, she was pleading with her daddy to help her.

Before Kristin died, I was scheduled to speak at her family's church in Soldotna, Alaska. In God's timing, I stood before the congregation the day after her funeral.

Kristin was one of those vivacious teens who loved Jesus and lived for Him—and whose sudden death leaves us with a million questions.

Because I went through a similar loss of my own teenage daughter a few years ago, I was able to offer some advice to this stunned and grieving church. First, I said, we must recognize God's sovereignty. Psalm 139:16 reminds us that Kristin's life was the exact length God intended. Second, I asked the church never to forget her family. Whether it's two months or five years later, the family will never "get over" losing Kristin. They will never stop needing Christians who care and remember.

In times like this, don't forget that God is in control and that He wants us to be a comfort to others. —DB

When we sustain a heartbreaking loss,
When grief overwhelms our soul,
The Savior who gave himself on the cross
Reminds us that He's in control. —D. DeHaan

In every desert of despair God has an oasis of comfort.

Risk

READ: Proverbs 6:16–19

Humble yourselves under the mighty hand of God,
that He may exalt you in due time. —1 PETER 5:6

When our children were young, one of our favorite board games was Risk. World conquest was the objective. Each player mobilized his troops to take possession of countries and continents. It always amused me that the person who initially was leading the game seldom won. The reason is obvious. When other players sensed his mounting pride, they would join together against him.

Whether consciously or subconsciously, it is easy to dislike powerful people who have proud looks. Their very countenance seems to encourage others to throw obstacles in their paths or to be silent objectors.

In today's Bible reading, we are told that God hates seven things. Tellingly, the first is pride. When someone overvalues himself by undervaluing others, he inevitably reveals it with his proud look. Puffed up in self-conceit, he may also devise evil and sow discord. No wonder God hates proud looks.

Proud and powerful people may think they can disregard others' displeasure, but they cannot disregard God's opposition. Peter reminds us not to trust in ourselves but in the One who will exalt us "in due time" (1 Peter 5:6). As we submit to Him, we avoid the risk that pride brings to our character and we become thankful, humble servants of God.   —AL

Naught have I gotten but what I received;
Grace hath bestowed it since I have believed;
Boasting excluded, pride I abase;
I'm only a sinner saved by grace! —*Gray*

No one can glorify self and Christ at the same time.

Land of Eternal Spring

READ: Ecclesiastes 12:1–7

I have been young, and now am old; yet I have not seen the righteous forsaken. —PSALM 37:25

The former president of Columbia Bible College in South Carolina, J. Robertson McQuilkin, pointed out that God has a wise purpose in letting us grow old and weak.

"I think God has planned the strength and beauty of youth to be physical. But the strength and beauty of age is spiritual. We gradually lose the strength and beauty that is temporary so we'll be sure to concentrate on the strength and beauty which is forever. It makes us more eager to leave the temporary, deteriorating part of us and be truly home-sick for our eternal home. If we stayed young and strong and beautiful, we might never want to leave."

When we are young, happily occupied with all our relationships and activities, we may not long for our celestial home. But as time passes, we may find ourselves without family and friends, afflicted with dim vision and hearing difficulties, no longer able to relish food, or troubled by sleeplessness.

Here's the advice I give myself: Be grateful that, as the apostle Paul wrote in 1 Timothy 6:17, "God . . . gives us richly all things to enjoy" in life's summer and autumn. And rejoice too that with the onset of life's winter we can anticipate that we'll soon be living in the land of eternal spring.

—VG

There's a land that is fairer than day,
And by faith we can see it afar;
For the Father waits over the way,
To prepare us a dwelling-place there. —*Bennett*

The promise of heaven is our eternal hope.

Religious Nuts

READ: Matthew 10:16–22

Let your speech always be with grace, seasoned with salt, that you may know how you ought to answer each one. —COLOSSIANS 4:6

I have a friend who was invited to a dinner party where he was seated next to a belligerent unbeliever who delighted in taunting Christians. Throughout the evening, the man baited Matt mercilessly about the evils of Christendom throughout the ages. With each insult, my friend calmly replied, "That's an interesting point of view." And then he asked a question that revealed genuine interest in the man and deflected the discussion away from the issue that divided them.

As the two were walking out the door at the end of the evening, the man fired a final jab, at which point Matt put his arm around the other man's shoulders and chuckled. "My friend," he said, "all night long you've been trying to talk to me about religion. Are you a religious nut?"

The man's animosity dissolved in a burst of laughter and then in sobriety, for he was indeed a religious nut. All human beings are. We're insatiably and incurably religious—hounded by the relentless love of God, though we may try to keep Him away. In this case, Matt's kindness and deft humor awakened this man's heart so that he could be receptive to the gospel.

We are to be "wise as serpents" when dealing with non-Christians, speaking to them "with grace, seasoned with salt" (Matthew 10:16; Colossians 4:6).   —DR

You have called us, Lord, to witness—
Called to speak the truth in love;
O how much we need Your guidance
And Your wisdom from above. —D. DeHaan

As the "salt of the earth," Christians can
make others thirsty for the Water of Life.

A Fair Trade

READ: Psalm 119:161–168

*I rejoice at Your Word as one who
finds great treasure.* —PSALM 119:162

Scott and Mary Crickmore poured fifteen years of their lives into helping to translate the New Testament in the Maasina dialect. It was for
the Fulani tribe in the West African nation of Mali.

After the initial draft, Mary visited nearby villages and read it to
people. She sat in huts with a group of men or women listening to them
discuss what they understood. That helped her to make sure the words
they were using in the translation were accurate and clear.

Some people would think that the Crickmores' sacrifice was too
great—giving up their comfortable lifestyle, changing their diet to
mush and rice, and living in less-than-ideal circumstances for those
fifteen years. But the Crickmores say it was "a fair trade," because now
the Fulani people have the Word of God in a language they can read.

The psalmist delighted in God's Word. He stood in awe of it,
rejoiced over it, loved it, and obeyed it (Psalm 119:161–168). He found
great peace and hope in the Word.

The Fulani people are now able to discover the "great treasure"
(v. 162) of God's Word. Would you agree with the Crickmores that any
effort and sacrifice to get the Bible to others is "a fair trade"?   —AC

*The Bible brings great hope and peace,
Beyond all earthly measure;
So we must share it with all those
Who don't possess this treasure.* —Sper

One measure of our love for God is what we're
willing to do to share His Word with others.

Getting "In the Way"

READ: John 14:1–6

*Jesus said . . . , "I am the way, the truth, and the life. No one comes to the Father except through Me." —*JOHN 14:6

The ancient Romans were known for their roads, which crisscrossed their empire with wide, heavily traveled highways. It's what Jesus' audience would have pictured when He claimed, "I am the way" (John 14:6).

While this verse indicates that Jesus is the way to heaven, there's really more to His statement. Cutting through the underbrush of the dense jungle of our world, Jesus is our trail guide who makes a new way for us to live. While many follow the way of the world by loving their friends and hating their enemies, Jesus carves out a new way: "Love your enemies, bless those who curse you" (Matthew 5:44). It's easy to judge and criticize others; but Jesus the Way-maker says to take the plank out of our own eye first (7:3–4). And He cuts a path for us to live with generosity instead of greed (Luke 12:13–34).

When Jesus said "I am the way," He was calling us to leave the old ways that lead to destruction and to follow Him in His new way for us to live. In fact, the word *follow* (Mark 8:34) literally means, "to be found in the way" with Him.

You and I can make the choice to travel the familiar and ultimately destructive ways, or we can follow Him and be found in the way with the One who is the way! —JS

As people of the Lord we're called
To follow in His way;
And though the world won't understand,
They'll see Him on display. —Sper

We don't need to see the way if we're following the One who is the Way.

Meditate on These Things

READ: Psalm 119:89–105

I will meditate on the glorious splendor of Your majesty, and on Your wondrous works. —PSALM 145:5

Some Christians get a little skeptical when you start talking about meditation—not seeing the huge distinction between biblical meditation and some types of mystical meditation.

In mystical meditation, according to one explanation, "the rational mind is shifted into neutral . . . so that the psyche can take over." The focus is inward, and the aim is to "become one with God."

In contrast, biblical meditation focuses on the things of the Lord, and its purpose is to renew our minds (Romans 12:2) so that we think and act more like Christ. Its objective is to reflect on what God has said and done (Psalm 77:12; 119:15–16, 97) and on what He is like (48:9–14).

In Psalm 19:14, David wrote, "Let the words of my mouth and the meditation of my heart be acceptable in Your sight, O Lord." Other psalms reflect on God's love (48:9), His deeds (77:12), His law (119:97), and His testimonies (119:99).

Fill your mind with Scripture and focus on the Lord's commands and promises and goodness. And remember this: Whatever is true, noble, just, pure, lovely, and of good report, "if there is any virtue and if there is anything praiseworthy—meditate on these things" (Philippians 4:8).
—CHK

Of all God's creatures, only man
Can worship, meditate, and plan;
The gift of thought sets him apart
To love the Lord with all his heart. —D. DeHaan

To become more like Christ, meditate on who He is.

Common Cents

READ: Mark 12:41–44

[Jesus said,] "This poor widow has put in more than all those who have given to the treasury." —MARK 12:43

In 1987, Mike Hayes, a freshman at the University of Illinois, found a unique way to finance his education. He convinced a popular columnist at the *Chicago Tribune* to ask his readers to "send in a penny for Mike."

"Just one penny," Hayes said. "A penny doesn't mean anything to anyone. If everyone . . . looks around the room right now, there will be a penny under the couch cushion . . . or on the floor. That's all I'm asking. A penny from each of your readers."

In less than a month the fund was up to 2.3 million cents. Donations came in from all over the US, as well as from Mexico, Canada, and the Bahamas. Mike eventually ended up with $28,000!

The common cent just isn't worth much—unless it's added to a whole bunch of other pennies.

The woman we read about in Mark 12 gave the equivalent of a fraction of a penny, which was "all that she had" (v. 44). But Jesus honored that little bit. Her sacrifice was an example and an encouragement to the disciples—and to us. She gave all she had. Have we ever been so generous?

Jesus used an unnamed widow to teach us what giving is all about. It was less than a cent, yet it was a priceless gift of love to God.   —CHK

One grace each child of God can show
Is giving from a willing heart;
Yet if we wait till riches grow,
It well may be we'll never start. —D. DeHaan

God looks at the heart, not the hand; the giver, not the gift.

My Two Cents

READ: Acts 2:40–47

Do not withhold good from those to whom it is due, when it is in the power of your hand to do so. —PROVERBS 3:27

Recently, our family had to change Internet cable services. Our former provider promised to send us a postage-paid box to mail their equipment back to them. We waited. No box came. I phoned. The promised box still did not arrive, but we did get a bill for the equipment!

Wanting to get this resolved, I decided to return it at my own expense. I sent several faxes asking if they received it—but no reply. Then I got a refund check of $.02 for the returned equipment! An experience like that can be frustrating. A simple transaction was complicated by poor communication.

Sadly, some people in our churches may encounter an impersonal response to their needs. Whether seeking marital counseling, childcare, guidance for a troubled teen, or a loving community, they come away feeling uncared for.

The first-century church was not perfect, but it faithfully helped others. The church at Jerusalem "divided [their goods] among all, as anyone had need" (Acts 2:45).

Good communication is the starting point for learning others' needs. This enables us to provide personal and practical help to people when they need it. Resources, both material and spiritual, can then be directed to each person as the object of God's personal love.   —DF

All who serve within the church
Should show by word and deed
A sensitivity to those
Who have a special need. —D. DeHaan

God cares for you—care for others.

Ongoing Encouragement

READ: Colossians 3:14–25

Fathers, do not provoke your children, lest they become discouraged. —COLOSSIANS 3:21

Father's Day is celebrated in many countries worldwide. Although the origins, activities, and actual day of observance differ widely, they all share the common thread of honoring fathers for their role as parents.

This year for Father's Day, I've decided to do something different. Instead of waiting to receive a card or phone call from my children, I'm sending words of appreciation to them and to my wife. After all, without them, I wouldn't be a dad.

Paul instructed fathers to be a positive part of their children's development rather than a source of anger and discouragement. He wrote, "Fathers, do not provoke your children to wrath, but bring them up in the training and admonition of the Lord" (Ephesians 6:4). "Fathers, do not provoke your children, lest they become discouraged" (Colossians 3:21). Both of these verses are embedded in passages about loving and honoring each other in family relationships.

The role of a father changes as children grow, but it doesn't end. Praise and encouragement are welcomed whether a child is four or forty. Prayer is always powerful. And it's never too soon to mend a broken relationship with a son or daughter.

Fathers, now is a good time to tell your children how much you love and appreciate them. —DM

> *Our children need encouragement,*
> *Expressions of our love and care;*
> *Appreciation, when expressed,*
> *Accentuates the bond we share.* —Sper

The greatest gift a father can give to his children is himself.

Passionate Boldness

READ: Acts 4:5–13

When they saw the boldness of Peter and John, . . . they marveled.
And they realized that they had been with Jesus. —ACTS 4:13

A young man was preaching to the passersby in Hounslow, on the outskirts of London, England. Most ignored him, a few ridiculed, and several stopped to listen. But regardless of the reaction of the people, he was undeterred. With a strong voice and clear resolve, he poured out his heart—not with the words of an angry prophet, but with deep concern for the men and women on that street. His eyes, facial expressions, and tone of voice revealed an attitude of compassion, not condemnation. In it all, he boldly shared the love and grace of Jesus Christ.

In Acts 4, when the church was still new, Peter and John also boldly addressed the people of their generation. And what was the response of the leaders of their day? "Now when they saw the boldness of Peter and John, and perceived that they were uneducated and untrained men, they marveled. And they realized that they had been with Jesus" (v. 13). That boldness was not the fruit of ministerial training but of much time spent in the presence of the Master. As a result, Peter and John had become passionate about what concerned Christ—the eternal destiny of men and women.

That same passionate boldness was on the face of the young man in Hounslow. Do people see it in us? —BC

> *Will you be bold in your witness*
> *By giving lost sinners God's Word?*
> *Jesus will honor your service,*
> *And sinners will surely be stirred.* —Bosch

A Christian is an ambassador who speaks for the King of kings.

The Tempted Brothers

READ: Genesis 39:1–12

How then can I do this great wickedness,
and sin against God? —GENESIS 39:9

Two brothers—both far from home—faced similar temptations. One, working away from the family, fell to the schemes of a younger woman. His sin led to embarrassment and family turmoil. The other, separated from loved ones *because* of family turmoil, resisted the advances of an older woman. His faithfulness led to rescue and renewal for the family.

Who are these brothers? Judah, who fell to the desperate scheme of his neglected daughter-in-law Tamar (Genesis 38). And Joseph, who ran from the arms of Potiphar's wife (39). One chapter presents an ugly story of irresponsibility and deception; the other, a beautiful chapter of faithfulness.

The stories of Judah and Joseph, presented back-to-back in the midst of "the history of Jacob" (37:2), show us that temptation itself is not the problem. Everyone faces temptation; even Jesus did (Matthew 4:1–11). But *how* do we face temptation? Do we demonstrate that faith in God can shield us from giving in to sin?

Joseph gave us one way of escape: Recognize sin as an affront to God and run from it. Jesus gave another: Answer temptation with truth from God's Word.

Facing temptation? See it as an opportunity to make God and His Word real in your life. Then run!   —DB

We fall into temptation when we don't stand against it.

A Happy Reunion

READ: Revelation 21:1–5

Behold, the tabernacle of God is with men, and He will dwell with them, and they shall be His people. —REVELATION 21:3

In 2002, Elizabeth Smart was kidnapped from her home in Utah. She lived a vagabond life in the constant presence of the couple accused of abducting her. Nine months after she was abducted, Elizabeth was found and returned home. It was the happy reunion her family had been longing for.

In the book of Revelation, John describes a vision of a new heaven and a new earth and our future reunion with the Lord (21:1–5). The context is not just geographic; it is a context of life for God's people—a glorious reality of God and His people dwelling together for eternity.

John describes the benefits that come to God's people when He takes up His abode in their midst. Abolished forever are the debilitating consequences of sin. In John's vision, sorrow, death, pain, and separation are all part of the things that will be gone. The old order will give way to the new and perfect order—a reunion of eternal blessedness. "Behold, the tabernacle of God is with men, and He will dwell with them, and they shall be His people. . . . He who sat on the throne said, 'Behold, I make all things new'" (Revelation 21:3, 5).

One day, we'll rejoice over a happy reunion in heaven with our heavenly Father. What a day of rejoicing that will be!   —MW

> *Beyond the sunset, O glad reunion*
> *With our dear loved ones who've gone before;*
> *In that fair homeland we'll know no parting.*
> *Beyond the sunset forevermore.* —Brock

Separation is the law of earth; reunion is the law of heaven.

Our Legacy

READ: Psalm 127

Children are a heritage from the Lord. —PSALM 127:3

A friend of mine wrote recently, "If we died tomorrow, the company that we are working for could easily replace us in a matter of days. But the family left behind would feel the loss for the rest of their lives. Why then do we invest so much in our work and so little in our children's lives?"

Why do we sometimes exhaust ourselves rising up early and going late to rest, "eating the bread of anxious toil" (Psalm 127:1–2 ESV), busying ourselves to make our mark on this world, and overlooking the one investment that matters beyond everything else—our children?

Solomon declared, "Children are a heritage from the Lord"—an invaluable legacy He has bequeathed us. "Like arrows in the hand of a warrior, so are the children of one's youth" (v. 4) is his striking simile. Nothing is more worthy of our energy and time.

There is no need for "anxious toil," working night and day, the wise man Solomon proclaimed, for the Lord does take care of us (127:2). We can make time for our children and trust that the Lord will provide for all of our physical needs. Children, whether our own or those we disciple, are our lasting legacy—an investment we'll never regret.   —DR

> *Our children are a heritage,*
> *A blessing from the Lord;*
> *They bring a richness to our lives—*
> *In each, a treasure stored.* —Fasick

Time spent with your children is time wisely invested.

Open Invitation

READ: Ephesians 2:14–22

Let us therefore come boldly to the throne of grace, that we may obtain mercy and find grace to help in time of need. —HEBREWS 4:16

Versailles was made the capital of France by King Louis XIV in 1682 and remained the capital (except for a short time) until 1789 when it was moved back to Paris. The beautiful palace of Versailles included an opulent 241-foot-long Hall of Mirrors. When a visitor approached the king, he had to curtsy every five steps as he walked the entire distance to meet the king sitting on his dazzling silver throne.

Foreign emissaries to France submitted to that humiliating ritual to court the French monarch's favor toward their country. By contrast, our God, the King of kings, invites His people to come to His throne freely. We can come to Him anytime—no advance appointments and no bowing required.

How grateful we should be that our heavenly Father is so much more inviting. "Through [Christ] we . . . have access by one Spirit to the Father" (Ephesians 2:18). Because of this, the writer of Hebrews urges us to "come boldly to the throne of grace, that we may obtain mercy and find grace to help in time of need" (Hebrews 4:16).

Have you responded to God's open invitation? Come in awe and gratitude, for the God of this universe is willing to hear your petitions anytime.   —CPH

> *You need to talk with God today,*
> *Your heart's bowed down with care;*
> *Just speak the words you have to say—*
> *He'll always hear your prayer.* —Hess

Access to God's throne is always open.

A Powerful Message

READ: 1 Corinthians 1:18–25

*The gospel of Christ . . . is the power of God to
salvation for everyone who believes.* —ROMANS 1:16

Bible teacher Lehman Strauss was brought to Christ through the power of the Word when he was young. At his girlfriend's suggestion, he read Romans 3:23, 5:8, and 10:13. As he did, he was convicted of his sin. He wept and believed.

When his son Richard was seven years old, he asked his father how to be saved. Lehman used the same verses that his girlfriend (who was now his wife) had used years earlier. His son believed too, and eventually became a pastor.

God's Word has tremendous power! The first recorded time God spoke, He created light (Genesis 1:3). He spoke a promise to Abraham and enabled his ninety-year-old wife Sarah to bear a child (17:15–19; 21:1–2). God still speaks with power today, and all who hear and believe the gospel are saved (Romans 1:16).

Yes, the message of Christ and His saving work on the cross can change the direction of a person's life. It has the power to reach the heart of that person you love and have prayed for many times.

So don't give up in your witness. Be consistent in your daily walk. Keep praying and sharing the gospel with others. It's a powerful message!   —DE

Sweetly echo the gospel call—
Wonderful words of life;
Offer pardon and peace to all—
Wonderful words of life. —Bliss

Our words have power to influence; God's words have power to save.

Postponement Problems

READ: Romans 12:4–13

We have many members in one body, but all the members do not have the same function. —ROMANS 12:4

Many of us struggle with them—postponement problems. A professor at the University of Calgary in Alberta, Canada, studied the problem of procrastination for five years and reported that 95 percent of us put off doing one thing or another. One estimate showed that Americans lose approximately $400 million a year by putting off filing taxes! Because of fear of failure or other insecurities, we wait and wait before starting a project or making a decision.

Procrastination is a problem in the church too. Many of us postpone serving God. We know we should reach out to others, but we feel insecure or worried about what to do. Because we're unsure of our gifts or interests, we put off our involvement in the church. We worry. *What if I do a poor job? What if I find out I can't even do it?*

Romans 12 gives us some encouragement. Serving starts with presenting ourselves to God as "a living sacrifice" (v. 1). Pray and give yourself anew to the Lord and His work. Then look around at what others are doing in your church and ask if you can join in. Start small if you need to, and try a number of things.

Your church needs you. Ask God to help you overcome your postponement problems. —AC

Don't put off for tomorrow
What you can do today;
Postponement may bring sorrow;
Prompt action is the way. —Hess

For a healthier church, exercise your spiritual gifts.

Chimp Eden

READ: Numbers 14:1–10

*If the Lord delights in us, then He will bring us
into this land and give it to us.* —NUMBERS 14:8

Eugene Cussons rescues chimpanzees. Orphaned by those in the business of bush-meat trade and taken from the jungle as infants, many have lived their entire lives confined in a space smaller than a prison cell. When Cussons arrives to take them to the game reserve he calls "Chimp Eden," he often finds them hostile and untrusting.

"These chimps don't realize that I am one of the good guys," Cussons says. When he tries to put them into a smaller crate for the trip to their new home, they put up quite a fight. "They don't know that I'm going to take them back to Chimp Eden and give them a life so much better."

On a much grander scale, God's offer to liberate us from the slavery of sin is often met with resistance. When He rescued the children of Israel from Egypt, God took them through difficult places that caused them to doubt His good intentions. "Would it not be better for us to return to Egypt?" they cried (Numbers 14:3).

On our journey of faith, there are times when the "freedom" of sin that we left behind is more appealing than the restrictions of faith that lie ahead. We must trust the protective boundaries found in God's Word as the only way to get to the place of ultimate freedom.   —JAL

*Sin's lure may look like freedom
But in its grip we're bound;
It's when we're bound to Jesus
Real freedom will be found.* —D. DeHaan

Obedience to God is the key to freedom.

The Song of the Saints

READ: Revelation 15

Who shall not fear You, O Lord, and glorify Your name? For You alone are holy. . . . Your judgments have been manifested. —REVELATION 15:4

We've all heard the expression "I don't get mad; I just get even." Reading about the judgments described in Revelation, one might assume that God will get "even" with sinners for their phenomenal offenses throughout the history of mankind.

The truth is that God's final judgment is a necessary expression of His holy justice. He can't turn a blind eye to sin. In fact, if He doesn't finally carry out justice as described in Revelation, it would be a denial of His holy character. That's why in the midst of His judgments, the saints will sing His praise: "Who shall not fear You, O Lord, and glorify Your name? For You alone are holy. . . . Your judgments have been manifested" (15:4). Those who know God best do not judge Him for His judgments; rather, they worship and affirm His actions.

What should surprise us is not the massive scale of God's judgments, but that He's waiting so long! Desiring that none should perish but that all should come to repentance (2 Peter 3:9), God is now mercifully restraining His judgment and giving maximum space to His marvelous mercy and grace. Now is the time to repent and take advantage of His patient love. And when we do, we'll join the saints in praising Him for all eternity!   —JS

> *O love of God, how rich and pure!*
> *How measureless and strong!*
> *It shall forevermore endure—*
> *The saints' and angels' song.* —Lehman

When God's justice is finally and fully revealed, His praises will resound!

Advice for the Groom

READ: Proverbs 1:1–9

My son, hear the instruction of your father. —PROVERBS 1:8

The custom of a bachelor party before a wedding is often characterized by drunkenness and carousing. The party-hearty attitude seems driven by the belief that the groom will soon be married and have to settle down to a life of domestic boredom.

Not long ago, one of my nephews got married. The best man planned a get-together for Joel before the wedding, but with a refreshing difference. Those invited were asked to bring some thoughts to share that would help him in this new chapter of life.

When I arrived at the informal breakfast, I found a cheerful spirit of camaraderie. Fathers, uncles, brothers, and friends were animated in lively discussion. The father of the bride and the father of the groom were asked to share their advice on what they had learned in their own Christian marriage. Their thoughts were personal, realistic, and biblical.

The book of Proverbs mirrors this kind of mentoring in facing life's challenges and rewards. "My son, hear the instruction of your father . . . for [it] will be a graceful ornament on your head" (1:8–9).

How God-honoring it would be if more couples would begin their marriage with an attitude that heeds the wisdom of those who have walked the path before them.   —DF

> *Lord, give us ears to hear advice*
> *From loved ones wise and humble,*
> *So when life's challenges appear*
> *We will not have to stumble.* —Sper

He is truly wise who gains his wisdom from the experience of others.

Are You Ready?

READ: Acts 13:1–5

As they ministered to the Lord and fasted, the Holy Spirit said,
"Now separate to Me Barnabas and Saul for the work." —ACTS 13:2

Three months before a planned missions trip, a friend and I were talking about the upcoming event. He said to me, "If anyone can't go, I'd be willing to step in and join you." This was not going to be an easy eight days, for we would be painting, repairing, and fixing stuff in the July heat of Jamaica. Yet my friend seemed eager to go.

About six weeks before we were scheduled to leave, there was an opening. I e-mailed my friend—whom I hadn't seen in the interim—and asked if he was still interested. He immediately responded, "Sure! And I got a passport just in case you asked." He had made sure he was ready, just in case he got the call to go.

My friend's preparation reminds me of what happened back in the first century at Antioch. Paul and Barnabas were among a number of people getting themselves ready spiritually for whatever God might ask them to do, or wherever He might send them. They didn't prepare by getting a passport, but they "ministered to the Lord and fasted" (Acts 13:2). And when the Holy Spirit said, "Separate to Me Barnabas and Saul for the work" (v. 2), they were all set for the journey.

Are you preparing for what God might want you to do? When the Spirit says, "Go," will you be ready?   —DB

> *Available for God to use me,*
> *Available, if God should choose me;*
> *Should it be here or there, it doesn't matter where;*
> *My waiting heart prepare.* —Anthony

Be prepared; God will find work for you.

Macauley

READ: Isaiah 6:1–8

I heard the voice of the Lord, saying: "Whom shall I send, and who will go for Us?" Then I said, "Here am I! Send me." —ISAIAH 6:8

Macauley Rivera, one of my dearest friends in Bible college, had a passion for the Savior. His heart's desire was to graduate, marry his fiancée Sharon, return to the inner city of Washington, DC, and plant a church to reach his friends and family for Christ.

That dream ended, however, when Mac and Sharon were tragically killed in an accident, leaving the student body stunned at the loss. At Mac's memorial service, the challenge was issued: "Mac is gone. Who will serve in his place?" As evidence of the impact of Mac's example, more than two hundred students stood to take up the mantle of Christ's fallen servant.

The response of those students echoes the commitment of Isaiah. In a time of fear and insecurity, the prophet was summoned into the throne room of God, where he heard Him say, "Whom shall I send, and who will go for Us?" Isaiah responded, "Here am I! Send me" (Isaiah 6:8).

God still calls men and women to be His ambassadors today. He challenges us to serve Him—sometimes close to home, sometimes in distant lands. The question for us is, How will we respond to His call? May God give us the courage to say, "Here am I! Send me."   —BC

Take the task He gives you gladly;
Let His work your pleasure be;
Answer quickly when He calleth,
"Here am I, send me, send me." —March

Whom God calls, He qualifies; whom He qualifies, He sends.

Search and Rescue

READ: Luke 19:1–10

The Son of Man has come to seek and to save that which was lost. —LUKE 19:10

Almost every week we see news about a search-and-rescue mission. It may involve a child who wandered away from a family picnic and is lost, or a hiker stranded on a mountain, or people trapped in the rubble following an earthquake. In every case, the people at risk are unable to help themselves. And those who are found and saved usually have lasting gratitude for those who joined in the search and rescued them.

The account of Zacchaeus in Luke 19:1–10 is a story of search and rescue. At first glance it may seem like a series of chance events—Jesus was passing through Jericho and a rich tax collector climbed a tree to catch a glimpse of the miracle-working teacher and Jesus looked up and saw him. But this encounter with Jesus was not a coincidence. At the end of the narrative, Luke deliberately included Jesus' words to Zacchaeus, "Today salvation has come to this house . . . ; for the Son of Man has come to seek and to save that which was lost" (vv. 9–10).

Jesus began His search-and-rescue operation on earth by His life, death, and resurrection. He continues it today through the power of the Holy Spirit, and He graciously invites us to participate with Him by loving those who are lost. —DM

People can't believe in Jesus
If the gospel they don't hear,
So we must proclaim its message
To the world—both far and near. —Sper

Those rescued from sin are best able to rescue those in sin.

The Reveal

READ: Luke 2:25–35

*The glory of the Lord shall be revealed, and
all flesh shall see it together.* —ISAIAH 40:5

The room was a wreck. Mismatched furniture. Faded paint. Ugly light fixtures. Knickknacks crammed into crowded spaces. The home-owners tried to make some improvements, but the room kept getting worse.

Thus begins a home-improvement TV program. After interviewing the owners, the designer draws a plan to maximize the room's potential. Program producers create suspense by building up to a moment referred to as "the reveal." Viewers watch the progress and ooh and aah with the homeowners when they see the new room.

Over time, the world has become like a neglected room. People bring in things that don't belong. They arrange priorities in ways that hinder potential. Lives become dull, overcrowded, and ineffective. Self-improvement projects offer little help.

The Bible is God's plan that shows the best way to live. God builds suspense throughout the Old Testament. Then, at the appointed time, comes the great reveal—Jesus! Upon seeing Him, Simeon exclaimed, "My eyes have seen Your salvation . . . , a light to bring revelation to the Gentiles, and the glory of Your people Israel" (Luke 2:30–32).

We become part of God's great reveal when we follow His design and Christ's example. —JAL

*O send Thy Spirit, Lord, now unto me
That He may touch my eyes and make me see;
Show me the truth concealed within Thy Word,
And in Thy Book revealed I see Thee, Lord.* —Lathbury

All that I am I owe to Jesus Christ, revealed to me in His divine Book.

The Choice

READ: Genesis 2:16–17; 3:1–8

Of every tree of the garden you may freely eat; but of the tree of the knowledge of good and evil you shall not eat. —GENESIS 2:16–17

I watched as a young mother tried to get her two-year-old child to make a choice. "You can have fish or chicken," she told him. She limited his choice to just two because he was too young to understand beyond that. Choice often involves a wider variety of options, and it also must allow the person to reject the options.

Adam and Eve were in the best possible environment. God had given them freedom to eat of all the trees in Eden—with one exception. He drew the boundary lines around only one tree! They had a choice, and it should have been a no-brainer to choose wisely. But their choice was tragic.

Some blame God for what they see as His restrictions. They may even accuse Him of trying to control their lives. But God gives us a choice, just as He did Adam and Eve.

Yes, God draws boundary lines, but they are for our protection. David understood this. He wrote, "You, through Your commandments, make me wiser than my enemies. . . . I understand more than the ancients, because I keep Your precepts. I have restrained my feet from every evil way, that I may keep Your Word" (Psalm 119:98–101).

God cares so much about us that He gives us boundary lines so that we will choose what is right. —CPH

> Lord, help us to obey Your Word,
> To heed Your still, small voice;
> And may we not be swayed by men,
> But make Your will our choice. —D. DeHaan

God's commandments were given to fulfill us, not to frustrate us.

Job's Principle

READ: Philippians 4:10–13

*Shall we indeed accept good from God,
and shall we not accept adversity?* —JOB 2:10

When my wife accepted a position as Director of Special Education in a school district many miles from our home, it resulted in a very long commute each day. It was tolerable in the short term, but neither of us could see her doing this indefinitely. So we decided to relocate to another city halfway between our two jobs.

The real estate agent was not optimistic about our home selling quickly. Market trends showed many homes for sale with few buyers. After much prayer and strenuous cleaning, we finally put our home up for sale. To our surprise, our house sold in less than three weeks!

Sometimes I feel guilty about receiving material blessings. With so many needs around the world, why should I expect divine intervention in selling a home? Then I remember Job's reply to his wife: "Shall we indeed accept good from God, and shall we not accept adversity?" (Job 2:10).

This verse is most often applied to accepting disappointment. But the principle also applies to being grateful for blessings. The apostle Paul had learned how to rejoice in plenty and in want (Philippians 4:10–13). God has an interest in teaching us contentment through both gains and losses. Thanking God in all circumstances recognizes His sovereignty and nurtures a response of faith.　　　　—DF

*We thank You, Lord, for blessings
You give us on our way;
May we for these be grateful,
And praise You every day.* —Roworth

The Lord gave, and the Lord has taken away;
blessed be the name of the Lord. —Job

Dangerous Freedom

READ: Galatians 5:1–6, 16–21

Do not use liberty as an opportunity for the flesh,
but through love serve one another. —GALATIANS 5:13

Freedom is dangerous in the hands of those who don't know how to use it. That's why criminals are confined in prisons with barbed wire, steel bars, and concrete barriers. Or consider a campfire that is allowed to spread in a dry forest. It quickly becomes a blazing inferno. Unchecked freedom can create chaos.

Nowhere is this more evident than in the Christian life. Believers are free from the law's curse, its penalty, and its guilt-producing power. Fear, anxiety, and guilt are replaced by peace, forgiveness, and liberty. Who could be more free than one who is free in the depths of his soul? But here is where we often fail. We use freedom's luxury to live selfishly, or we claim ownership of what God has merely entrusted to us. We slip into patterns of self-indulgent living, especially in affluent societies.

The proper use of freedom is "faith working through love" to serve one another (Galatians 5:6, 13). When we rely on the Spirit and expend our energies on loving God and helping others, the destructive works of the flesh will be restrained by God (vv. 16–21). So let's always use our liberty to build up, not to tear down.

Like a raging fire, freedom without limits is dangerous. But when controlled, it is a blessing to all.　　　　　　　　　　　　—DD

> *Christ came to give us liberty*
> *By dying in our place;*
> *Now with new freedom we are bound*
> *To share His love and grace.* —D. DeHaan

Freedom doesn't give us the right to do
what we please, but to do what pleases God.

Hopeful Praise

READ: Psalm 103:1–14

Bless the Lord, O my soul, and forget not all His benefits. —PSALM 103:2

One of my friends was in tears on a beautiful summer day, unable to deal with life's difficulties. Another could not look beyond the life-altering sadnesses of her past. Still another struggled with the closing of the small church he had pastored faithfully. A fourth friend had lost his job at a local ministry.

What can our struggling friends—or any of us—do to find hope? Where do we turn when tomorrow offers no happy promises?

We can praise or "bless" the Lord, as David said in Psalm 103. In the middle of trouble, acknowledging God's role in our lives can redirect our thinking from the hurts of our hearts and force us to dwell instead on the greatness of our God.

David knew trouble. He faced the threat of enemies, the consequences of his own sin, and the challenges of sorrow. Yet he also recognized the healing power of praise. That's why in Psalm 103 he can list reasons to turn our attention to God, who gives us many benefits: He forgives us, heals us, redeems us, crowns us with love and compassion, satisfies our desires, and renews us. David reminds us that God provides justice and righteousness, and He is gracious and loving.

Take it from David: Praising God's greatness puts hope in our troubled hearts. —DB

Praise, my soul, the King of heaven,
To His feet thy tribute bring;
Ransomed, healed, restored, forgiven,
Evermore His praises sing! —Lyte

Praise can lighten your heaviest burden.

Bubbles on the Border

READ: 2 Corinthians 4:8–18

We do not look at the things which are seen, but at the things which are not seen. —2 CORINTHIANS 4:18

Stuck in a long line at the US-Canada border, Joel Schoon Tanis had to do something to lighten the mood. He reached for his bottles of bubble-making solution, bounded out of the car, and began blowing bubbles. He handed bottles to other drivers too, and he says that "soon there were bubbles everywhere. . . . It's amazing what bubbles do for people." The line didn't move any faster, but "suddenly everyone was happy," Joel says.

"What we see depends mainly on what we look for," said British statesman John Lubbock (1834–1913). A good attitude and the right focus help us to handle life joyfully, even though it doesn't change our circumstances.

Paul encouraged the Corinthians in their trials: "Do not look at the things which are seen, but at the things which are not seen. For the things which are seen are temporary, but the things which are not seen are eternal" (2 Corinthians 4:18).

So what's unseen and eternal that we can look at? The character of God is an excellent place to focus. He is good (Psalm 25:8), He is just (Isaiah 30:18), He is forgiving (1 John 1:9), and He is faithful (Deuteronomy 7:9).

Pondering God's character can give us joy in the midst of our struggles.

—AC

The eyes of faith when fixed on Christ
Give hope for what's ahead;
But focus on life's obstacles,
And faith gives way to dread. —D. DeHaan

When Christ is the center of your focus, all else will come into proper perspective.

Doing the Work of God

READ: John 6:25–33

Our sufficiency is from God. —2 CORINTHIANS 3:5

When I was a pastor I used to have a recurring nightmare. I would rise to preach on Sunday morning, look out at my congregation— and see no one in the pews!

It doesn't take a Daniel (Daniel 2:1, 19) or a dream therapist to interpret the vision. It grew out of my belief that everything depended on me. I mistakenly believed that if I did not preach with power and persuasion, the congregation would fade away and the church would fold. I thought I was responsible for the results of God's work.

In the Gospels, we read that some people asked Jesus, "What shall we do, that we may work the works of God?" (John 6:28). What audacity! Only God can do the works of God!

Jesus' answer instructs us all: "This is the work of God, that you believe in Him whom He sent" (v. 29). Whatever we have to do, then, whether teaching a Sunday school class, leading a small group, telling the gospel story to our neighbor, or preaching to thousands, it must be done by faith. There is no other way to "work the works of God."

Our responsibility is to serve God faithfully, wherever He has placed us. Then we're to leave the results to Him. As Jesus reminded His disciples in John 15:5, "Without Me you can do nothing."   —DR

> *The work of the Lord for us has been done—*
> *Jesus has paid the supreme sacrifice;*
> *Our service for God has only begun—*
> *And nothing we do can help pay the price.* —Hess

Christ's work on the cross equips us to do good works for Him.

Heaven's Greatest Delights

READ: Revelation 22:1–5

Eye has not seen, nor ear heard . . . the things which God
has prepared for those who love Him. —1 CORINTHIANS 2:9

What will be one of heaven's supreme joys?

Joni Eareckson Tada, disabled as a teenager in a diving accident, has been a quadriplegic for over forty years. One would imagine that her greatest longing would be the ability to walk, even run, free from the confinement of her wheelchair.

But Joni tells us that her greatest desire is to offer "a praise that is pure." She explains: "I won't be crippled by distractions, or disabled by insincerity. I won't be handicapped by a ho-hum half-heartedness. My heart will join with yours and bubble over with effervescent adoration. We will finally be able to fellowship fully with the Father and the Son. For me, this will be the best part of heaven."

How that speaks to my divided heart and grips my unfocused spirit! What a blessing to offer "a praise that is pure," with no wandering thoughts, no self-centered requests, no inability to soar above my earthbound language!

In heaven, "there shall be no more curse, but the throne of God and of the Lamb shall be in it, and His servants shall serve Him" (Revelation 22:3). May the prospect of heaven enable us to experience a foretaste of that God-glorifying worship even here and now.   —VG

> *To be with Him will crown it all!*
> *To see His face—before Him fall,*
> *To feast within His banquet hall;*
> *To be with Him will crown it all!* —Peterson

To see Jesus will be heaven's greatest joy.

Life, Love, Chocolate

READ: 1 John 3:16–23

Be imitators of God. . . . And walk in love, as Christ also has loved us and given Himself for us. —EPHESIANS 5:1–2

An entry I read on a favorite blog caught my eye. It was the morning of his ninth wedding anniversary. Not having a lot of money, the writer ran out to get his wife, Heidi, their favorite French pastry—*pain au chocolat.* After sprinting several miles, he arrived home, exhausted, to find her in the kitchen just pulling a chocolate-filled croissant out of the oven. It was *pain au chocolat.*

That husband, Jeff, compared his life with Heidi to the lives of the people in O. Henry's short story "Gift of the Magi." The story tells of a man who sold his lone possession of value—a pocket watch—to buy hair combs for his wife, who had sold her long, beautiful hair to buy a gold chain for his watch.

Having no money concerns would be great. But realizing the immeasurable value of the people we care about is more important. We sometimes need a reminder that acquiring "things" is not nearly as important as appreciating the people God has placed in our lives. When we practice putting others' interests before our own (Philippians 2:3–4), we learn what it means to love, serve, and sacrifice. In fact, that's how we pattern Christ in our relationships (Ephesians 5:1–2).

Life, love, and chocolate taste better when shared with others.

—CHK

I want to share with those I love
The highest joy I'm thinking of,
Not just what brightens all their days
But what will give God highest praise. —Hess

Love is never afraid of giving too much.

God's Masterpieces

READ: Ephesians 2:1–10

We are His workmanship, created in Christ Jesus for good works,
which God prepared beforehand that we should walk in them.
—EPHESIANS 2:10

The Grand Rapids Art Museum has over 5,000 works of art, including 3,500 prints, drawings, and photographs; 1,000 works of design; and 700 paintings and sculptures. As I read about the new museum and anticipated visiting, I couldn't help but think about God's "museum."

God is an artist, and His creation is unspeakably magnificent. But it is not His greatest work. God's greatest work is His redemption of us. When we were still dead in our sins, He made us alive in His Son, Jesus Christ (Ephesians 2:1, 5). Paul reminded the Ephesians that they were God's "workmanship," or *poiema* (v. 10), a Greek term that means "poem" or "work of art." God's art museum is the church, filled with millions of marvelous works—His people.

Being God's work of art, Paul said, should result in something from us. We are not supposed to sit silently in the museum of fellowship. Rather, we are to show God's love in practical ways through our good works. Jesus said these good works glorify our heavenly Father (Matthew 5:16).

God did not redeem us to be museum pieces. He redeemed us so that our good works would showcase the brilliant colors of His redemption and grace, and draw a world in darkness to the light of His love.
—MW

Sing, O sing of my Redeemer,
With His blood He purchased me;
On the cross He sealed my pardon,
Paid the debt and made me free. —Bliss

They witness best who witness with their lives.

Pioneer of the Pioneers

READ: 2 Corinthians 5:12–21

I have made it my aim to preach the gospel, not where Christ was named, lest I should build on another man's foundation.
—ROMANS 15:20

In the early nineteenth century, US President Thomas Jefferson completed the Louisiana Purchase, stretching the borders of the fledgling republic "from sea to shining sea." But there was a problem. No one really knew what was in that vast expanse of land. Maps were needed, with clear instructions for the pioneers who would travel to the Pacific.

Thus, they turned to explorers Lewis and Clark, who became, in effect, the pioneers of the pioneers—preparing the way for the most massive land migration in US history. Lewis and Clark cut a new trail that others would follow.

The apostle Paul's commitment to ministry was framed by a similar priority. In Romans 15:20, he wrote, "I have made it my aim to preach the gospel, not where Christ was named, lest I should build on another man's foundation." He wanted his efforts in ministry to cut a new trail—and others followed. Timothy, Titus, Mark, and Silas are just a few who followed the trail that Paul blazed.

Today that commitment is seen in Jesus' followers who take the message of the Savior to the uttermost parts of the world. As we pray today, let's ask for God's blessing on His Word as we, His "ambassadors," cut a new trail in our generation (2 Corinthians 5:20).   —BC

Be this our common enterprise:
That truth be preached and prayer arise,
That each may seek the other's good
And live and love as Jesus would! —Brewster

God gave you a message to share; don't keep it to yourself.

He Watches Me

READ: Matthew 10:16–31

Do not fear therefore; you are of more value than many sparrows. —MATTHEW 10:31

One Sunday morning at church we sang "His Eye Is on the Sparrow" as a congregational hymn. It was a rare opportunity to give voice to a song usually performed by a soloist.

During the first chorus, I noticed a friend weeping so hard that he couldn't sing. Knowing a bit of what he had been through recently, I recognized his tears as tears of joy at realizing that, no matter what our situation, God sees, knows, and cares for us.

Jesus said, "Are not two sparrows sold for a copper coin? And not one of them falls to the ground apart from your Father's will. But the very hairs of your head are all numbered. Do not fear therefore; you are of more value than many sparrows" (Matthew 10:29–31). The Lord spoke these words to His twelve disciples as He sent them out to teach, heal, and bear witness of Him to "the lost sheep of the house of Israel" (v. 6). He told them that even though they would face persecution for His sake, they should not be afraid, even of death (vv. 22–26).

When threatening circumstances press us to lose hope, we can find encouragement in the words of this song: "I sing because I'm happy, I sing because I'm free. For His eye is on the sparrow, and I know He watches me." We are under His watchful care. —DM

If God sees the sparrow's fall,
Paints the lilies short and tall,
Gives the skies their azure hue,
Will He not then care for you? —Anonymous

When you put your cares in God's hands,
He puts His peace in your heart.

First Church of the Lampstand

READ: Revelation 1:10–2:5

Repent and do the first works, or else I will come to you quickly and remove your lampstand. —REVELATION 2:5

I love it when churches have names like "King of Glory Lutheran Church" or "Alpha and Omega Missionary Baptist Church." If the church in Ephesus were still around, maybe we'd call them something nifty like "First Church of the Lampstand."

We often miss the significance of John's glorious vision in Revelation 1 of Jesus standing among the seven golden lampstands. These weren't just decorative candelabras; they were substantial sources of light. How significant, then, that the lampstands represent the seven churches who were called to bring the light of Jesus into a very dark world.

We live in a dark world that desperately needs the candlepower of Christ shining through us. Let's be careful, then, not to repeat the mistake of the Ephesians who "left [their] first love" (Revelations 2:4). Although praised for doing many things well, they had failed to keep Jesus in first place.

It's easy to let things crowd Jesus out until soon we're doing "church work" for all the wrong reasons. What then? We lose our impact. Jesus warned, "Repent and do the first works, or else I will . . . remove your lampstand from its place" (v. 5). We can't afford to let that happen. Keep Jesus in first place so that His light will continue to shine brightly in this dark world.   —JS

Lord, help us always put You first
In everything we say and do
So that Your light will shine through us
And show the world their need of You. —Sper

Works that are done out of love for
Jesus shine brightest in a dark world.

Love Is for Losers?

READ: 1 Corinthians 13

Now abide faith, hope, love, these three; but the greatest of these is love. —1 CORINTHIANS 13:13

You can learn a lot about a person by what his or her T-shirt says. Recently, one of these messages caught my attention as I walked through a local shopping mall. A young woman wore a bright red T-shirt that said, "Love Is for Losers." Maybe she thought it was clever or provocative, even funny. Or perhaps she had been hurt by a relationship and had pulled away from others rather than risk being hurt again. Either way, the T-shirt got me thinking.

Is love for losers? The fact is, when we love, we take risks. People could very well hurt us, disappoint us, or even leave us. Love can lead to loss.

The Bible, though, challenges us to higher ground in loving others. In 1 Corinthians 13, Paul describes what it means to live out God's kind of love. The person who exercises godly love doesn't do so for personal benefit or gain but rather "bears all things, believes all things, hopes all things, endures all things" (13:7). Why? Because godly love endures beyond life's hurts by pulling us relentlessly toward the never-diminishing care of the Father.

So, perhaps love is for losers—for it is in times of loss and disappointment that we need God the most. Even in our struggles, we know that "love never fails." —BC

Unfailing is God's matchless love,
So kind, so pure, so true;
And those who draw upon that love
Show love in what they do. —D. DeHaan

God's love never fails.

Rocks and Robots

READ: Psalm 8

*When I consider Your heavens, the work of Your fingers, the
moon and the stars, . . . what is man that you are mindful of him?"*
—PSALM 8:3–4

During a walk through the picturesque Garden of the Gods in Colorado Springs, our attention was diverted from the huge, majestic
sandstone rocks toward two people wearing homemade robot suits. The
park was thronged with summer tourists who immediately began taking pictures of the robots while their children gathered round to touch
and talk to them. Folks who had come to admire the silent beauty
of God's creation were now watching people in cardboard costumes
sprayed with silver paint.

It reminded me of my quiet time. How often I sit down to seek the
Lord through Bible reading and prayer, only to be drawn away by the
newspaper, an unpaid bill, or a list of things to be done. The psalmist
had better focus when he wrote:

> *"O Lord, our Lord,*
> *How excellent is Your name in all the earth,*
> *Who have set Your glory above the heavens! . . .*
> *When I consider Your heavens, . . .*
> *What is man that You are mindful of him,*
> *And the son of man that You visit him?" (Psalm 8:1, 3–4)*

While contemplating the Lord and meditating on His creation, the
psalmist's self-important attitude shifted to one of humble appreciation
for God's goodness. It can be true of us too—if we can keep the robots
and the rocks in proper perspective.   —DM

It's good to worship God in nature if it
leads us to worship the God of nature.

Behind the Building

READ: 1 Peter 4:8–11

Be steadfast, immovable, always abounding in the work of the Lord, knowing that your labor is not in vain in the Lord.
—1 CORINTHIANS 15:58

Where we were working was hot, dirty, and it smelled bad. We had traveled thousands of miles to do some work projects, and on this day we were painting the back of a classroom building at a school for the deaf. The only people who would ever see this part of the building would be the guy who cut the grass and any unfortunate person who would have to work on the septic pit.

Yet, as the young adults diligently painted away, one of the girls, Melissa, put it in perspective by saying, "Nobody will ever come back here to see this, but God will see it. So let's make it look nice." And so we did.

Sometimes we sit at our desk and think no one sees our work. Or we stand at a line assembling item after endless item. Perhaps we take care of crying babies in the church nursery. Or we live the best Christian life we can—without anyone noticing.

Often our work is "behind the building." But if that is what God has called us to do, we need to work with all our heart. As part of our calling to love others deeply (1 Peter 4:8), offer hospitality (v. 9), and use our gifts to serve others (v. 10), our task is to work with God's strength to bring praise and glory to God, not ourselves. The important thing is that God likes what He sees. —DB

Though others may not observe us
And see how we serve God today,
Our job as servants of Jesus
Is to please Him in every way. —Branon

No service for Christ goes unnoticed by Him.

When the Ground Shakes

READ: Psalm 18:1–6

In my distress, I called upon the Lord. —PSALM 18:6

Several days after a devastating earthquake in the San Francisco area, a young boy was seen rocking and swaying on the school playground. His principal asked him if he was okay, and the boy nodded yes and said, "I am moving like the earth, so if there's another earthquake I won't feel it." He wanted to prepare himself for another shaking of the ground.

Sometimes after a trauma we brace ourselves for what might be coming next. If we've had a phone call that brought bad news, every time the phone rings we feel panicky and wonder, *What has happened now?*

The "ground was shaking" for the psalmist David after King Saul tried to kill him (1 Samuel 19:10). He ran and hid. He thought death was next and told his friend Jonathan, "There is but a step between me and death" (20:3). He wrote, "The pangs of death surrounded me, and the floods of ungodliness made me afraid" (Psalm 18:4).

David cried to the Lord in his distress (v. 6) and found that He was a stabilizer, One he could trust would always be with him. He said, "The Lord is my rock and my fortress and my deliverer; my God, my strength, in whom I will trust; . . . my stronghold" (v. 2). The Lord will be that for us also when the ground shakes under us. —AC

> *The Lord's our Rock, in Him we hide,*
> *A shelter in the time of storm;*
> *Secure whatever ill betide,*
> *A shelter in the time of storm.* —Charlesworth

To survive the storms of life, be anchored to the Rock of Ages.

A Donkey in Lion's Clothing

READ: Matthew 7:15–23

Beware of false prophets . . . in sheep's clothing, but inwardly they are ravenous wolves. —MATTHEW 7:15

In the final book of C. S. Lewis's Chronicles of Narnia, *The Last Battle,* a devious ape named Shift finds an old lion's skin and persuades a simpleminded donkey to put it on. Shift then claims that the disguised donkey is Aslan (the Lion who is the rightful king of Narnia) and forms an alliance with Narnia's enemies. Together they set out to control and enslave the subjects of Narnia. Young King Tirian, however, can't believe that Aslan would actually be involved with such brutal practices. So, with the help of the real Aslan, he defeats Shift and his counterfeit lion.

The Bible tells us that the devil is in the business of imitating God. His goal is "to be like the Most High" (Isaiah 14:12–15). Through deception, Satan tries to replace Christ with a substitute. Jesus himself warned us of false prophets and false christs: "Take heed that no one deceives you. For many will come in My name, saying, 'I am the Christ,' and will deceive many" (Matthew 24:4–5).

How can we tell the real Christ from the counterfeit? The only authentic Christ is the one described in Scripture. Anyone or anything that portrays a different Jesus than the One presented in the Bible is promoting "a donkey in lion's clothing."   —DF

Beware of anyone who claims
To speak directly from the Lord
If what he says does not agree
With everything that's in God's Word. —Sper

God's Word gives wisdom to discern what is false.

Till He Became Strong

READ: 2 Chronicles 26:3–15

His fame spread far and wide, for he was marvelously helped till he became strong. —2 CHRONICLES 26:15

In George MacDonald's fairy tale *Lilith*, giants live among normal people. These giants must conduct their daily affairs very carefully. When they sleep, their snoring is disruptive. When they turn over, houses may be crushed under their weight.

In the Bible, Uzziah became a "giant" of a man after becoming king at age sixteen. The keys to his success are recorded in 2 Chronicles 26. His father Amaziah set a good example for him (v. 4). The prophet Zechariah instructed him (v. 5). He had an army of fighting men and capable generals who helped him (vv. 11–15). And God prospered him (v. 5).

Clearly, King Uzziah became a "giant" through the Lord's blessing. But after attaining success, he grew careless and stumbled badly. The clue to his demise is found in the phrase "he was marvelously helped till he became strong" (v. 15). Those last four words, "till he became strong," serve as a dire warning to us all. Uzziah's "heart was lifted up, to his destruction" (v. 16). He usurped the priestly duties and became leprous (vv. 16–21).

We have all been marvelously helped by our Lord God, by those He has given to set an example for us, and by those who serve alongside us. When we become strong, we must take heed, or we too will stumble.

—AL

When all goes well and I feel strong,
Oh, help me, Lord, to see
That I must place my confidence
In You and not in me. —Anonymous

I have never met a man who has given me
as much trouble as myself. —D. L. Moody

Small Step—Giant Leap

READ: Ephesians 4:17–24

Be renewed in the spirit of your mind. —EPHESIANS 4:23

In July 1969 I was at Fort Benning, Georgia, training to become a US Army officer. Infantry Officer Candidate School was intense and highly regimented with only rare moments of free time. Surprisingly, on the evening of July 20, we were ordered to our company Day Room, seated in front of a flickering television set, and told simply, "This is history."

Amazed, we watched Apollo 11 astronaut Neil Armstrong become the first human to set foot on the moon as he said, "That's one small step for man, one giant leap for mankind." Our usual curfew was suspended and we talked late into the night—not only about what we had witnessed but about life, God, and eternity. Our demanding routine had been interrupted, and our attention was shifted to what truly matters.

All of us need to shift our focus on a daily basis. Maintaining a regular time alone with God allows us to step away from our demanding jobs, break the routine, and concentrate on Him through the Bible and prayer. Our thoughts and actions will change as we follow Paul's urging to "be renewed in the spirit of your mind" (Ephesians 4:23).

What may seem like a small step can be a giant leap each day in our life of faith in Christ. —DM

A small step is a giant leap
In growth and faith each day
If this step is your time with God
To read His Word and pray. —Sper

Each small step of faith is a giant step of growth.

Becoming Useful

READ: John 5:19–23

The Son can do nothing of Himself. — JOHN 5:19

Jesus was fully God, yet He was fully man. As a man, His power, wisdom, and grace flowed not from His divine nature but from His utter dependence on God. "The Son can do nothing of Himself," He said (John 5:19).

How much did Jesus do apart from God? Nothing! Jesus always depended on His Father.

Luke reports that as news of Jesus' ministry spread, "Great multitudes came together to hear, and to be healed by Him of their infirmities. So He Himself often withdrew into the wilderness and prayed" (Luke 5:15–16). He knew He needed those quiet times to restore His soul.

What's done in secret is what matters. It's during those quiet times that we, like Jesus, are shaped and molded and made into people that God can put to His intended use.

"But," you say, "I'm in a place where I can't be useful." Perhaps you feel that circumstances limit you drastically. Illness, financial problems, a difficult boss or co-worker, or an uncooperative family member seem to conspire against you. Whatever your situation, use it to grow closer to the Savior.

Learn to have utter dependence on the Father, just as Jesus did. Leave it up to God to make you useful in whatever way He sees fit.

—DR

O that my life may useful be
As I serve Jesus faithfully;
And may the world see Christ in me—
This is my earnest plea. —Hess

The measure of your usefulness is the measure of your faithfulness.

Who Is Deaf?

READ: Isaiah 42:1–4, 23–25

The Lord's hand is not shortened, that it cannot save. . . . [But] your sins have hidden His face from you, so that He will not hear.
—ISAIAH 59:1–2

A man told his doctor that he thought his wife was going deaf. The doctor told him to conduct a simple test. When the man reached the front door of his home, he called out, "Darling, is dinner ready?" Hearing no response, he walked inside and repeated the question. Still no reply. On the third try, when he was just behind her, he finally heard her say, "For the third time, yes!"

Similarly, the ancient Israelites thought God was deaf when the problem was actually with them. Isaiah was a prophet sent to warn God's people about impending judgment, but his message fell on deaf ears. Instead of being God's covenant people, who were to bring light to those in darkness and release them from the dungeons of sin (42:7), they refused to hear Him. "They would not walk in His ways, nor were they obedient to His law" (v. 24).

The prophet explained why their prayers seemed to fall on deaf ears: "The Lord's hand is not shortened, that it cannot save; nor His ear heavy, that it cannot hear. But your iniquities have separated you from your God" (Isaiah 59:1–2). One reason for not receiving answers from God is that sin may be blocking our hearing.

Let's examine ourselves carefully. Our God isn't hard of hearing.
—CPH

Nothing between my soul and the Savior,
Naught of this world's delusive dream;
I have renounced all sinful pleasure,
Jesus is mine; there's nothing between. —Tindley

God speaks through His Word to those who listen with their heart.

Ready to Speak

READ: 1 Peter 3:13–22

Always be ready to give a defense to everyone who asks you a reason for the hope that is in you, with meekness and fear. —1 PETER 3:15

Lee Eclov and his wife were at a coffee shop in Estes Park, Colorado. At another table sat four men, one of whom was mocking Christianity and the resurrection of Jesus.

Lee could sense the Lord telling him to respond. But his fear kept him from doing so. Finally, he knew he had to make a stand. So he walked over to the men and began giving historical evidence for the resurrection.

How do we respond when we're in a similar situation? The apostle Peter encouraged his readers to make a commitment to stand up for Jesus, especially during extreme suffering. This commitment meant not remaining speechless when circumstances warranted them to defend their faith. He said, "Always be ready to give a defense to everyone who asks you a reason for the hope that is in you, with meekness and fear" (1 Peter 3:15). Their readiness to answer required them to know God's Word. They were to respond in godly meekness and fear, so that their persecutors would be ashamed of their own conduct.

Had Lee Eclov remained silent or responded rudely, the cause of Christ would have suffered. Lee later wrote, "God has a way of flushing us out of our quiet little places, and when He does we must be ready to speak for Him." —MW

> *When people wonder about our faith,*
> *What answer will we give?*
> *We'll tell of Jesus who bore our sins*
> *And shows us how to live.* —Fitzhugh

To be silent about the Savior and His
salvation is a dreadful sin of omission.

Walk the Walk

READ: 1 Timothy 4:6–16

*Be an example to the believers in word, in conduct,
in love, in spirit, in faith, in purity.* —1 TIMOTHY 4:12

The preacher was speaking tongue-in-cheek when he complained, "My wife is absolutely unreasonable. She actually expects me to live everything I preach!" It's so much easier to tell someone what is right than to practice it personally.

When my son and I play golf together, I can tell him exactly how to play the hole and hit the shots. But my own ability to hit those shots is sadly limited. I suppose this is what is meant when we refer to athletes who "talk the talk, but don't walk the walk." Anyone can talk a good game, but actually performing well is far more difficult.

This is particularly true in the challenge of following Jesus Christ. It is not enough for us to talk about faith—we must live out our faith. Perhaps that is why Paul, after giving instructions to his young protégé Timothy about how to preach, included this reminder: "Let no one despise your youth, but be an example to the believers in word, in conduct, in love, in spirit, in faith, in purity. . . . Meditate on these things; give yourself entirely to them" (1 Timothy 4:12, 15).

As Christ's followers, we do not have the luxury of just talking a good game. We must live lives of exemplary faith in Jesus Christ. We must walk the walk.   —BC

> *Do others know from how we act
> At home, at work, at play,
> That we have Jesus in our heart
> And live for Him each day?* —D. DeHaan

We please God when our walk matches our talk.

Change Your Mind

READ: Acts 26:12–23

Repent, turn to God, and do works befitting repentance.
—ACTS 26:20

One of my favorite *Peanuts* comic strips features Charlie Brown saying to Snoopy, "I hear you're writing a book on theology. I hope you have a good title."

Snoopy responds, "I have the perfect title: *Has It Ever Occurred to You that You Might Be Wrong?*"

Snoopy's title reminds us that our understanding of God and what He requires of us is sometimes twisted. Because our wrong beliefs lead to wrong behavior, we need to "repent, turn to God, and do works befitting repentance" (Acts 26:20).

The Greek word translated "repent" is *metanoeo,* which means "change your mind." As Paul indicated, repentance does not mean just nodding in polite agreement with God and continuing the same way we were going. When we turn our thoughts toward God—when we truly agree with Him about what is right—our behavior will follow. Like a car, we go in the direction we are pointed. So, when we truly turn our minds and hearts toward God, our actions change accordingly.

Instead of going happily along, assuming that our choices are right, we need to regularly stop and ask ourselves Snoopy's question. As Paul taught, it is only when we are willing to admit being wrong that we can be certain of being right with God.   —JAL

> *We must acknowledge when we're wrong,*
> *Confessing it as sin,*
> *If we would know God's power to heal*
> *And cleanse us from within.* —Fasick

Either we conform our desires to the truth or we
conform the truth to our desires. —Os Guinness

Role Models

READ: Philippians 2:12–18

Do all things without complaining and disputing, that you may become blameless and harmless, children of God without fault.
—PHILIPPIANS 2:14–15

During a summer of international sports scandals involving gambling and substance abuse, two athletes were applauded for their character as much as their professional accomplishments. A record crowd of 75,000 cheered Cal Ripken Jr. and Tony Gwynn during their 2007 induction into the National Baseball Hall of Fame.

"Whether we like it or not," Ripken said, "as big leaguers, we are role models. The only question is, will it be positive or will it be negative?"

Gwynn echoed the sentiment: "There's more than just playing the game of baseball. . . . You're responsible, you've got to make good decisions and show people how things are supposed to be done."

Every day, people are watching us. As followers of Christ, we are guided by Paul's challenge to "become blameless and harmless, children of God without fault in the midst of a crooked and perverse generation, among whom you shine as lights in the world" (Philippians 2:15).

Compromise causes others to become disillusioned, while character fosters hope. As the life of our Savior flows out from us, we can encourage others and point them to Him.

What kind of role model will you be for someone watching today?
—DM

The best role models model Christ.

God's Heart Revealed

READ: Revelation 3:14–22

As many as I love, I rebuke and chasten.
Therefore be zealous and repent. —REVELATION 3:19

It's easy to think of God as a divine flyswatter, just waiting for you to land so that—whap—He can nail you for your sins. But that's not what we see in Revelation 2–3 in His letters to the seven churches. The pattern of the letters demonstrates God's loving heart for wayward people.

Jesus began many of these letters by affirming the good things His people had done. This shows us that when we do what is good and right, the Lord is pleased.

But Jesus is also concerned about the faults in our lives. His commendation in these letters was often followed by clear words of reproof. And while it's not comfortable to hear Him say, "Nevertheless I have this against you" (2:4; also see vv. 14, 20), He reveals what needs to be changed in our lives to keep us from self-deceit.

This moves us to the real heart of the matter—repentance. When the Lord told these churches to repent, He was revealing His love for wayward saints. His goal was not to condemn but to restore them to intimate fellowship with Him.

And don't miss the fact that each letter ends with a specific promise for the "overcomers." Clearly God desires to reward those who live lives that are pleasing to Him. —JS

What's He saying to you today?
To live a life that pleases Christ,
It's crucial to obey His voice;
When He reveals our sin to us,
Repentance is the wisest choice. —Sper

Repentance restores and renews our intimacy with the Lord.

The Value of Friends

READ: 1 Samuel 20:12–17

Jonathan . . . loved [David] as he loved his own soul.
—1 SAMUEL 20:17

John Chrysostom (347–407) was one of the great preachers in the early church. He was given the name Chrysostom, which means "golden-mouthed," because of his eloquent sermons.

Here is one of his insights on the value of friends: "Such is friendship, that through it we love places and seasons; for as . . . flowers drop their sweet leaves on the ground around them, so friends impart favor even to the places where they dwell. With friends even poverty is pleasant. . . . It would be better for us that the sun were exhausted than that we should be without friends."

The story of Jonathan and David illustrates the value of friendship. Though David was hunted by the demented King Saul, he drew encouragement from his friendship with Saul's son. "Jonathan . . . loved [David] as he loved his own soul" (1 Samuel 20:17). Their relationship was characterized by trust, understanding, and encouragement. How difficult it would have been for David to endure this unjust persecution without the nourishment of friendship based in the Lord (v. 42).

The ancient voice of Chrysostom and the witness of David and Jonathan are reminders of the need to nurture the friendships God has given us.   —DF

> *Since I have no gold to give,*
> *And love alone must make amends,*
> *My daily prayer is while I live—*
> *"God, make me worthy of my friends." —Sherman*

A friend is the first person who comes
in when the whole world has gone out.

Homecoming

READ: Psalm 73:21–28

You will guide me with Your counsel, and
afterward receive me to glory. —PSALM 73:24

One of my favorite pastimes as a boy was walking the creek behind our home. Those walks were high adventure for me: rocks to skip, birds to watch, dams to build, animal tracks to follow. And if I made it to the mouth of the creek, my dog and I would sit and share lunch while we watched the biplanes land across the lake. We'd linger as long as we could, but only so long, for my father wanted me home before sunset. The shadows grew long and the hollows got dark fast in the woods. I'd be wishing along the way that I was already home.

Our house sat on a hill behind some trees, but the light was always on until all the family was in. Often my father would be sitting on the back porch, reading the paper, waiting for me.

"How did it go?" he would ask.

"Pretty good," I'd say. "But it sure is good to be home."

Those memories of walking that creek make me think of another journey—the one I'm making now. It isn't always easy, but I know at the end of it there's a caring Father and my eternal home. I can hardly wait to get there.

I'm expected there. The light is on and my heavenly Father is waiting for me. I suppose He'll ask, just like my father used to, "How did it go?"

"Pretty good," I'll say. "But it sure is good to be Home."　　—DR

He will be waiting for me—
Jesus so kind and true;
On His beautiful throne He will welcome me home—
After the day is through. —Vandall

For the Christian, heaven is spelled H-O-M-E.

Getting Involved

READ: Luke 10:30–37

The Lord is gracious and full of compassion. —PSALM 111:4

Isn't anybody going to help that poor guy?" Fred exclaimed as he and my husband, Tom, realized what had been causing traffic to creep down the busy five-lane road. A man lay sprawled between the lanes, bicycle on top of him, as vehicles simply drove around him. Fred turned on the warning flashers and blocked traffic with his car. Then both guys jumped out to help the shaken man.

Fred and Tom got involved, as did the Samaritan man in Jesus' story in Luke 10. Like him, they overcame any reluctance they might have had to reach out to a man in distress. The Samaritan also had to overcome racial and cultural prejudice. The people we would have expected to help showed indifference to the injured man's plight.

It's easy to find reasons not to get involved. Busyness, indifference, and fear often top the list. Yet as we seek to follow our Lord faithfully, we will become more aware of opportunities to show the kind of compassion He showed (Matthew 14:14; 15:32; Mark 6:34).

In the parable of the good Samaritan, Jesus commended the man who had acted out of compassion even though it was inconvenient, difficult, and costly to do so. Then, to us He says, "Go and do likewise" (Luke 10:37). —CHK

When we share another's burden,
We display God's love and care,
Offering relief and comfort
When life seems too much to bear. —Sper

True compassion puts love into action.

The Only Place to Start

READ: Galatians 1:6–12

If anyone preaches any other gospel to you than what you have received, let him be accursed. —GALATIANS 1:9

When a publishing company asked me to write an endorsement for a new book, I said I'd be glad to. It appeared to be a helpful book directed to young people, challenging them to live for God in a changing world.

But as I read the book, something troubled me. Although it had lots of Scripture and great spiritual advice, it didn't explain that the starting point for any relationship with God is salvation through Jesus Christ. The writer seemed to imply that the essence of living spiritually in modern society is based totally on action—good deeds—and not on saving faith in Christ. I didn't write the endorsement.

The culture of the church is changing rapidly. Often left behind in the rush to find exciting new ideas is the essential nature of the gospel. The apostle Paul was astonished that people so readily embraced a "different gospel" (Galatians 1:6). What he preached was not from man, but a direct revelation from Jesus himself (vv. 11–12).

We must never let go of that true gospel: Christ died for our sins, was buried, and rose again for our justification, declaring us righteous before God (Romans 4:25; 1 Corinthians 15:3–4). This alone offers the "power of God to salvation for everyone who believes" (Romans 1:16). If we want to live for God, this is the only place to start.   —DB

No one can say he doesn't need
Forgiveness for his sin,
For all must come to Christ by faith
To have new life within. —Branon

Faith is the hand that must take God's gift of salvation.

Biography of God

READ: Romans 1:16–20

Since the creation of the world His invisible attributes are clearly seen . . . even His eternal power and Godhead. —ROMANS 1:20

Let's say you were really famous. People would want to know all kinds of things about you. Then let's say you called me up and asked, "How'd you like to write my biography?" Let's say I agreed. I would be all over you like a moth on a streetlight, buzzing around trying to find out all I could about you. I'd ask you a thousand questions. I would ask for your list of contacts and call everyone on it to find out more about you. Then I would ask you to hand over anything related to your life. Papers. Pictures. The works.

I would look for three components, which are the secret to getting to know someone: What you say about yourself, what others say about you, and what you've done. Now think of what this means as you seek to know God: What does He say about himself, what do others say about Him, and what has He done?

To know God in a vibrant, new way, ask all three. Read the Bible to find out what God says about himself (Exodus 34:6–7; Leviticus 19:2; Jeremiah 32:27). Then find out what the writers say about Him and His remarkable attributes (Psalm 19:1–4; Romans 1:16–20; 1 John 4:8–10). Finally, take a look at the amazing things God has done (Genesis 1:1; Exodus 14:10–31; John 3:16).

Get to know God. Be His biographer. It will teach you more about Him than you ever thought possible. —DB

> *Immortal, invisible, God only wise,*
> *In light inaccessible hid from our eyes,*
> *Most blessed, most glorious, the Ancient of Days,*
> *Almighty, victorious—Thy great name we praise.* —Smith

The God who created the universe is the God you can know.

Best Friends

READ: 1 Samuel 20:30–42

The righteous should choose his friends carefully. —PROVERBS 12:26

When I signed up for a popular Internet social network, I was shocked to be greeted with the words, "You have no friends." Although I knew it was untrue, I still felt sad for a moment. The idea that anyone, even an impersonal website, would call me friendless was upsetting. Friends are essential for our emotional, physical, and spiritual well-being.

Friends listen to our heartaches without blaming us for having problems. They defend us when we're under attack. They are happy when we succeed and sad when we fail. They give us wise counsel to keep us from making foolish choices. They even risk making us angry for the sake of making us right. My friends have done all of this and more for me.

Perhaps the best-known friendship in the Bible is that of Jonathan and David. Jonathan was heir to the throne of his father, Saul. But he knew that the Lord had chosen David for that role, so he risked his own life to save his friend (1 Samuel 20).

As the Bible shows us, we need to choose friends carefully (Proverbs 12:26). The very best friends are those who are friends with God and who strengthen our relationship with Him (1 Samuel 23:16).   —JAL

> *I do not ask for many friends,*
> *But give me, Lord, the few*
> *Whose loyalty and faithfulness*
> *Are first of all to You.* —Meadows

True friends are like diamonds—precious and rare.

Being Glad

READ: Psalm 30

This is the day the Lord has made; we will rejoice and be glad in it. —PSALM 118:24

One of my favorite childhood books was *Pollyanna*, the story of the optimistic young girl who always found something to be glad about—even when bad things happened.

I was reminded recently of that literary friend when my real-life friend fell and broke her arm while riding her bicycle. Marianne told me how thankful she was that she was able to ride all the way back home and how grateful she was that she wouldn't need to have surgery. It was her left arm (she's right-handed), she said, so she would still be able to work. And wasn't it great, she marveled, that she has good bones, so her arm should heal fine! And wasn't it wonderful that it hadn't been any worse!

Whew! Marianne is an example of someone who has learned to rejoice in spite of trouble. She has a confidence that God will care for her—no matter what.

Suffering eventually touches us all. And in times of difficulty, thankfulness is usually not our first response. But I think God looks at us with pleasure when we find reasons to be thankful (1 Thessalonians 5:16–18). As we realistically look for the good despite our bad circumstances, we can be grateful that God is holding us close. It is when we trust in His goodness that we find gladness. —CHK

Under His wings, what a refuge in sorrow!
How the heart yearningly turns to His rest!
Often when earth has no balm for my healing,
There I find comfort, and there I am blessed. —Cushing

Thankfulness finds something good in every circumstance.

Our Moral Compass

READ: 2 Chronicles 7:1–14

If My people . . . turn from their wicked ways, then I will . . . forgive their sin and heal their land. —2 CHRONICLES 7:14

When Abraham Lincoln was introduced to author Harriet Beecher Stowe, he reportedly said that she was "the little woman who wrote the book that started this great war."

Although President Lincoln's comment wasn't entirely serious, Stowe's novel *Uncle Tom's Cabin* was instrumental in abolishing slavery in the US. Its graphic depiction of racism and the injustice of slavery helped lead to the start of civil war. Later, the thirteenth amendment to the US Constitution would abolish all slavery. Thus, Stowe's novel helped to change a nation's moral compass.

Centuries earlier, King Solomon was told about what would change the moral compass of God's people Israel. It was to start with humility and confession. The Lord told Solomon: "If My people who are called by My name will humble themselves, and pray and seek My face, and turn from their wicked ways, then I will hear from heaven, and will forgive their sin and heal their land" (2 Chronicles 7:14).

As a Christian community, we should first take an inventory of our own personal lives. As we humbly seek God in prayer and repentance of sin, changes begin in our lives. God may then use us to change a nation's moral compass. —DF

> *Revive us again,*
> *Fill each heart with Thy love;*
> *May each soul be rekindled*
> *With fire from above.* —Mackay

Nothing is politically right which is morally wrong. —O'Connell

Matters of the Heart

READ: Matthew 13:10–15

The hearts of this people have grown dull. Their ears are hard of hearing, and their eyes they have closed. —MATTHEW 13:15

At the beginning of a spiritual retreat, our speaker Matt Heard asked, "How's your heart?" It stunned me, because I tend to focus on believing with my mind and working with my hands. In the activity of thinking and serving, my heart is pushed to the side. As we were led through the Bible's repeated emphasis on this crucial center of our lives, however, I began to grasp his premise that belief and service are, more than anything else, matters of the heart.

When Jesus told a story to illustrate how people receive and respond to His teaching (Matthew 13:1–9), His disciples asked, "Why do You speak to them in parables?" (v. 10). In reply, Jesus quoted the prophet Isaiah: "For the hearts of this people have grown dull. Their ears are hard of hearing, and their eyes they have closed, lest they should see with their eyes and hear with their ears, lest they should understand with their hearts and turn, so that I should heal them" (v. 15; see Isaiah 6:10).

How dangerously easy it is to neglect our hearts. If we become callous, we find no joy in living or serving, and life seems hollow. But when our hearts are tender toward God, understanding and gratefulness flow through us to others.

So, how's your heart?

—DM

Our service for the Lord becomes
A duty that is hollow
If we neglect our heart for God
And Him we do not follow. —Sper

We can become so busy doing
good that we lose our heart for God.

Breath Mint, Anyone?

READ: Galatians 6:1–5

Bear one another's burdens, and so fulfill the law of Christ.
—GALATIANS 6:2

A new website helps you tell a co-worker what you're afraid to say in person. Comments like: "A breath mint would be beneficial today," or "Your cell phone ringer is very loud today," or "Your perfume/cologne is very strong on a regular basis." You confront issues anonymously by having the website send an e-mail message for you.

It's understandable that we're cautious in talking to others about something that bothers us. But when it comes to confronting fellow believers about their sin, that's serious. We might wish we could do it anonymously, yet we have to do it face to face.

Galatians 6:1–5 offers some guidelines for confronting a fellow Christian who is living a sinful lifestyle. The first requirement is that we're close to the Lord ourselves, and that we don't exalt ourselves as superior to the one who is sinning. Then we are to look at the situation as restoring the person, not bringing condemnation. We're to have "a spirit of gentleness," all the while keeping in mind that we too may be tempted. Jesus also gave instructions that can help us with issues of sin against us personally (Matthew 7:1–5; 18:15–20).

With God's enablement we can courageously and sensitively confront and restore others. —AC

Lord, give us courage to confront
Believers who have strayed,
And then with gentleness restore
By coming to their aid. —Sper

To help people get back on the right path,
walk with them and show them the way.

Subtle Wisdom

READ: Mark 8:34–38

If anyone serves Me, let him follow Me; and where I am, there My servant will be also. —JOHN 12:26

When I was in college, my co-worker Bud, a fork-truck driver, often enriched my life with his pithy wisdom. We were eating lunch one day, sitting on the back of his fork truck, when I announced that I was transferring to another school.

"Why?" he asked.

"All my friends are transferring," I answered.

Bud chewed his sandwich for a moment and then replied quietly and with subtle irony, "I guess that's one way to pick a school."

His words struck me with rare force. *Of course,* I thought. *But is this the only way to choose a school? Will I follow my friends for the rest of my days, or will I follow Jesus? Will I seek His face and His will and go where He wants me to go?*

Twenty-five times in the New Testament, Jesus said to His disciples, "Follow Me." In Mark 8:34, He said, "Whoever desires to come after Me, let him deny himself, and take up his cross, and follow Me." No matter what others do or what direction their lives may take, we must do what He asks us to do.

The words of an old song come to mind: "My Lord knows the way through the wilderness; all I have to do is follow!"   —DR

> *As I walk along life's pathway,*
> *Though the way I cannot see,*
> *I shall follow in Christ's footsteps,*
> *For He has a plan for me.* —Thiesen

To find your way through life, follow Jesus.

Granville Sharp

READ: James 1:19–27

*Be doers of the Word, and not hearers
only, deceiving yourselves.* —JAMES 1:22

When I was a Bible college student, a name occasionally mentioned in Greek class was that of Granville Sharp. He was a renowned Greek scholar (1735–1813) whose studies resulted in principles of biblical interpretation that continue to guide our understanding of the original language of the New Testament.

To study the Scriptures and learn the powerful truths they contain is a noble exercise; but no matter how deeply we study, it is not enough. James challenged us to understand this when he wrote: "But be doers of the Word, and not hearers only, deceiving yourselves. For if anyone is a hearer of the Word and not a doer, he is like a man observing his natural face in a mirror; for he observes himself, goes away, and immediately forgets what kind of man he was" (James 1:22–24).

Granville Sharp understood this and put his faith into practice. In addition to being a biblical scholar, he fought to eradicate slavery in England. Sharp said, "A toleration of slavery is, in effect, a toleration of inhumanity." His biblical understanding of the worth of a human soul and the justice of a holy God compelled him to act on his beliefs.

We can benefit from Sharp's passion for the Word—and for living out the truth that Word contains. —BC

It is God's will that we should read
His Word from day to day,
Not just for knowledge, but much more—
To love Him and obey. —Hess

We don't really know the Bible unless we obey the Bible.

Yeah, But...

READ: 2 Timothy 4:1–8

They will turn their ears away from the truth.
—2 TIMOTHY 4:4

Grading university papers is full of surprises. Sometimes, one of my students will successfully handle a subject and display good writing style, and I feel as if my instruction was worthwhile.

Other surprises aren't so pleasant. Like the paper in which a student wrote, "The Bible says, 'Thou shalt not _____.'" He filled in the blank with the activity he was writing about—even though Scripture does not contain such a verse. I thought his biggest problem was not knowing Scripture, until he concluded, "Although the Bible says this is wrong, I don't see why, so I think it's okay."

It's dangerous—and the worst kind of arrogance—to think we know more about an issue than God does. But Scripture predicted this kind of thinking. Paul said in 2 Timothy 4: "They will not endure sound doctrine, but according to their own desires . . . they will heap up for themselves teachers; and they will turn their ears away from the truth" (vv. 3–4). This points to people who set aside the inspired Word of God (3:16) in order to accept teaching they think is "okay."

When the Bible clearly spells out a principle, we honor God by obeying Him. For believers, there's no room for "Yeah, but . . ." responses to Scripture. —DB

God who formed worlds by the power of His Word
Speaks through the Scriptures His truth to be heard;
And if we read with the will to obey,
He by His Spirit will show us His way. —D. DeHaan

The Bible: Read it, believe it, obey it!

The Heart of the Gospel

READ: 2 Corinthians 4:1–6

We all, with unveiled face, beholding as in a mirror the glory of the Lord, are being transformed. —2 CORINTHIANS 3:18

When E. Stanley Jones, well-known missionary to India, had the opportunity to meet with Mahatma Gandhi, he asked a searching question of India's revered leader: "How can Christianity make a stronger impact on your country?"

Gandhi thoughtfully replied that three things would be required. First, Christians must begin to live more like Jesus. Second, the Christian faith should be presented without any adulteration. Third, Christians should emphasize love, which is at the heart of the gospel.

These insightful suggestions are the key to effective evangelism around the world. As messengers of God's love, we are to be human mirrors who reflect without distortion a growing likeness to our Lord; we are not to walk in "craftiness" (2 Corinthians 4:2). If our lives reflect an image that is spiritually blurred, the truth of saving grace may not be clearly communicated (vv. 3–5). We are also to share the biblical essentials of our faith clearly. We must not handle the Word of God "deceitfully" (v. 2). And our lives are to be marked by love for God and others (1 John 5:1–2).

Let's be sure that we reflect a clear image of Jesus' likeness, the truth of God, and love. —VG

Called to be salt and light in this world,
Called to preserve and to shine,
Called to reflect the glory of God—
Oh, what a calling is mine! —Fitzhugh

The primary reason for living in this
world is to reflect the likeness of Christ.

GAD or God?

READ: 1 Peter 5:6–11

Casting all your care upon Him, for He cares for you.
—1 PETER 5:7

Are you a chronic worrier? Do you worry about bills, the future, health, debt, marriage issues? Has worry so consumed you that you have become "a fret machine"? If this describes you, perhaps you have generalized anxiety disorder, or GAD—a condition marked by a perpetual state of worry about most aspects of life. According to David Barlow, professor of psychology at Boston University, "the key psychological feature of GAD is a state of chronic, uncontrollable worry." A little anxiety is normal, but constant worry is not.

Overwhelmed by suffering and persecution, the first-century Christians were driven out of Jerusalem and scattered throughout Asia (1 Peter 1:1–7). Many of these Jesus-followers were experiencing feelings of distress because of possible danger or misfortune. Peter encouraged these believers not to be filled with anxiety but to cast all their worries upon God (5:7). He wanted them to realize that it made very little sense for them to carry their worries when they could cast them on God who cared deeply about what happened to them.

Are you a chronic worrier? Let God be responsible for your anxieties. Stop worrying and start trusting Him completely.   —MW

> *When every worry, every care*
> *To God in faith is brought,*
> *We have no place whereon to found*
> *One single anxious thought.* —Anonymous

Worry is a burden God never intended us to bear.

He Is Enough

READ: Matthew 14:22–33

*Jesus spoke to them, saying, "Be of good cheer! It is I; do not be afraid." —*MATTHEW 14:27

Sometimes we are overwhelmed by life. The crushing waves of disappointment, endless debt, debilitating illness, or trouble with people can cause hopelessness, depression, or despair. It happened to Jesus' disciples. And it has happened to me.

Three statements by the Lord beginning with the words "It is . . ." offer us comfort, reassurance, and hope that Jesus is enough.

The first is in Matthew 4 and is repeated three times: "It is written" (vv. 4, 7, 10). In responding to the three temptations of Satan, Jesus gave us proof enough that the Word of God is true and overcomes the most powerful forms of temptation and pressure.

The second statement, "It is I" (Matthew 14:27), was spoken when Jesus told His terrified disciples that He himself was presence enough to stop the howling storm and calm the raging seas.

Jesus spoke the third "It is" from the cross: "It is finished!" (John 19:30). He assured us that His death was provision enough to pay the debt for our sins and set us free.

Whatever our circumstances, Jesus is present with His love, compassion, and grace. He is proof, presence, and provision enough to carry us safely through.　　　　　　　　　　　　　　　　　　　　　　　—DE

When trials overwhelm our souls
And tempt us to despair,
We need to reach out to the Lord
And trust His tender care. —Sper

God's love does not keep us from
trials; it helps us get through them.

The Love of Rules

READ: Romans 13:1–10

Love is the fulfillment of the law. —ROMANS 13:10

When I teach writing, I explain that it's generally better to use short words or phrases first in a series, as in "arts and letters" and "life, liberty, and the pursuit of happiness." Early in my career, I explained to authors that it just sounds better this way. But then I discovered a "rule" about this use of words, and I found it more effective than my earlier explanation. I learned that authors are more likely to accept editorial changes when I can point them to a rule than when I just say, "Trust me."

This is typical of human nature. We have a love/hate relationship with rules. We don't like rules, but we're unsure how to determine right from wrong without them.

God had a relationship with Adam and Eve that was based on loving trust. The only rule necessary was one that protected them from knowledge that would end in death. But when disobedience broke the trusting relationship, God added more rules to protect the wayward couple and their offspring.

In Christ, God proclaimed once more that the good life He wants for us is not about rules but a relationship. As Paul wrote, all the commandments can be summarized in one word: love. Because we are "in Christ," we can enjoy peace with God and others—not because there's a rule, but because there is love.   —JAL

> *Though freed from the law with its stern commands—*
> *No longer ruled by its harsh demands—*
> *I'm bound by Christ's love and am only free*
> *To live and to act responsibly.* —D. DeHaan

The greatest force on earth is not the
compulsion of law but the compassion of love.

The Deadliest Disease

READ: Joshua 7:1, 19–26

[Jesus] was wounded for our transgressions, . . .
and by His stripes we are healed. —ISAIAH 53:5

Severe Acute Respiratory Syndrome (SARS) was identified in 2003 in Vietnam. By the time it was brought under control, SARS had spread globally and killed nearly eight hundred people. One reason for the high mortality rate was that the virus was not recognized initially. But once recognized and understood, SARS was contained.

An even more dangerous disease is on the loose in our world—sin. It too is difficult to bring under control because many people do not recognize its deadliness. And many dispute the Bible's diagnosis of sin.

In Joshua 7, we read the tragic story of Achan. Against God's command, he had taken some of the spoils from Jericho and hid them in his tent (v. 21). He and his entire family paid with their lives (v. 25).

Thankfully, God does not deal with us in that way. If He did, none of us would remain alive. Yet we must never underestimate sin's deadliness. It sent Christ to the cross for us.

Like SARS, the first step to deal with sin is to recognize it for what it is. Receive with gratitude the gift of eternal life. Then "put to death . . . what is earthly in you"—the selfish things that displease God (Colossians 3:5 ESV). That's the way to deal with our deadliest disease.

—CPH

The Remedy for Sin: Have you received Christ's gift of salvation?
He died for your sins and rose from the dead. He offers forgiveness
to all who believe in Him (Romans 10:9).

Sin is a heart disease that can be cured only by the Great Physician.

Running Every Day

READ: 1 Corinthians 9:24–27

Run in such a way that you may obtain [the prize].
—1 CORINTHIANS 9:24

The Pikes Peak Ascent is a challenging mountain foot race, covering 13.32 miles while gaining 7,815 feet in altitude. My good friend Don Wallace ran it twenty times. In his final race, he crossed the finish line one week before his sixty-seventh birthday!

Instead of training just before a race, Don ran six miles a day, year round, with rare exceptions, wherever he happened to be. He's done that for most of his adult life and continues to this day.

In 1 Corinthians 9, Paul uses running as a picture of his own discipline as a Christian in the race of life. He ran with purpose and discipline to win an eternal crown, and he encouraged others to do the same: "Run in such a way that you may obtain [the prize]" (v. 24). Then he says, "And everyone who competes for the prize is temperate in all things" (v. 25). The word *temperate* carries the meaning of self-control practiced by athletes who train to win the prize. As a consistent habit of life, regular discipline is of far greater value to any athlete than last-minute preparation.

Are we approaching "the race that is set before us" (Hebrews 12:1) with a hit-or-miss spiritual regimen, or with purpose and discipline born from a desire to please God?

The key to going the distance is the discipline of running every day.
—DM

> *Run the straight race through God's good grace,*
> *Lift up thine eyes and seek His face;*
> *Life with its way before us lies,*
> *Christ is the path and Christ the prize.* —*Monsell*

Running the Christian race takes dedication and discipline.

Royalty Recognized

READ: Philippians 2:5–11

At the name of Jesus every knee should bow, . . . [and] every tongue should confess that Jesus Christ is Lord. —PHILIPPIANS 2:10-11

As a kid, I loved watching the film *Little Lord Fauntleroy*. The story focuses on Cedric, a boy growing up in a poor home with his mother in Brooklyn. He discovers the stunning news that he is actually the direct descendant of the Earl of Dorincourt and the heir of a vast fortune. One day he's a nobody playing "kick the can" on the streets of New York, and then suddenly he's traveling through an English town to the cries of "Your lordship!" from adoring villagers.

If you had seen Jesus playing in the streets of Nazareth as a boy, you wouldn't have taken any special notice of Him (except that He probably wasn't playing "kick the can"). If you had seen Him in the carpentry shop, you wouldn't have had a clue about His deity. And if you had seen Him hanging on the cross, that horrific scene wouldn't have enticed your heart to adore Him if you didn't know what was behind it.

But in His resurrection, Jesus revealed His true identity. He is the conquering King—ultimate royalty! Since "God also has highly exalted Him and given Him the name which is above every name" (Philippians 2:9), how much more should we adoringly worship Him who, in such surrendered humility, died so that He could become our victorious King!   —JS

> *Behold Him there! The risen Lamb!*
> *My perfect, spotless righteousness;*
> *The great, unchangeable I AM,*
> *The King of glory and of grace.*   —*Bancroft*

Recognize and respond to the royalty of God—worship Him!

Sing a New Song

READ: Psalm 98

Shout joyfully to the Lord, all the earth; break forth in song, rejoice, and sing praises. —PSALM 98:4

At age ninety-four, Pastor Willis was admitted into a care facility. From his wheelchair, he shared with joy how God had given him a new mission field to share the gospel. When he was bedridden a few years later, he spoke with enthusiasm of being in the best possible position to look up to God. When he died at age one hundred, Pastor Willis left behind a legacy of one who sang a new song of praise at every turn of his earthly life.

Psalm 98 exhorts us to sing a new song for God who "has done marvelous things; His right hand and His holy arm have gained Him the victory" (v. 1). We ought to praise Him—even in times of difficulty—for God remembers "His mercy and His faithfulness" (v. 3). Though this psalm is about God freeing the Israelites from slavery, it is prophetically also about our salvation through Jesus Christ our Lord. And as we remember what God has done for us, we can trust Him to help us with today's difficulties as well as tomorrow's uncertainties.

The psalmist wrote: "Let the sea roar, and all its fullness, the world and those who dwell in it; . . . let the hills be joyful together before the Lord" (vv. 7–9). Let us join God's creation in singing praise to our Savior!

—AL

I don't know about tomorrow,
Nor what coming days will bring;
But I know my Lord is with me,
And His praise my heart will sing. —Fitzhugh

A heart in tune with God sings melodies of praise.

Beware the Rupert

READ: 2 Corinthians 11:3–4, 12–15

Satan himself transforms himself into an angel of light.
—2 CORINTHIANS 11:14

In the June 6, 1944, D-Day invasion of Europe, an armada of Allied ships assaulted the beaches of Normandy, France. Simultaneously, thousands of airplanes dropped paratroopers into the action. Along with the paratroopers, the Allies also dropped hundreds of rubber dummies behind the enemy lines. Called "Ruperts," these dummies were intended to simulate an attack to confuse the enemy. As the Ruperts landed, some German outposts were tricked into fighting the "paradummies," creating a vital crack in the walls of Fortress Europe.

We accept that kind of deception as part of a legitimate military operation designed to thwart oppressive forces. What we should not accept is the deception Satan throws our way. Paul explained that the devil "transforms himself into an angel of light" (2 Corinthians 11:14), and his servants appear to be people who are promoting righteousness (v. 15).

We must be alert! Our spiritual enemy would love to have followers of Christ distracted by false teaching and faulty doctrine. But as we keep our eyes on Jesus and the clear teachings of Scripture, our Lord can keep us aimed in the right direction.

Don't be tricked by Satan's Ruperts. —BC

God's truth uncovers Satan's lies.

It's All About the Heart

READ: Matthew 15:7–20

Those things which proceed out of the mouth
come from the heart. —MATTHEW 15:18

Every time Susan opens her mouth it sounds like the blare of an ambulance siren. This TV commercial uses humor to indicate that a dental problem could reveal a more serious physical ailment. So she'd better see her dentist soon!

The commercial made me think about what comes out of my mouth when I open it. Jesus said that our words come from our heart (Matthew 15:18). He offended the Pharisees when He said, "Not what goes into the mouth defiles a man; but what comes out of the mouth, this defiles a man" (vv. 11–12). They thought they were right with God because they followed strict rules, including ritual cleansing of their hands before eating, and eating only "clean" foods. Jesus upset their pride.

Jesus upsets our pride too. We may think we're godly people because we go to church regularly or pray, but then we gossip or talk about people behind their backs. James 3:9–10 says, "With [our tongue] we bless our God and Father, and with it we curse men. . . . Out of the same mouth proceed blessing and cursing. . . . These things ought not to be so."

If a siren blares from our mouth when we open it, we need to examine our heart and ask the Lord to forgive us and to help us be a blessing to others. —AC

Let the words of my mouth
and the meditation of my heart
Be acceptable in Your sight,
O Lord, my strength and my Redeemer. —Psalm 19:14

I Know I Can

READ: Ephesians 3:14–21

[God] is able to do exceedingly abundantly above all that we ask or think, according to the power that works in us. —EPHESIANS 3:20

Remember the story of *The Little Engine That Could?* That determined little train climbed the steep hill by chanting positively, "I think I can. I think I can." And then, as it gained more resolve, it declared, "I know I can. I know I can."

It is true that followers of Christ should think and live in a positive way. But do you ever find yourself depending too much on your own abilities rather than on the power of the indwelling Holy Spirit?

Jesus explained our need for complete dependence on Him when He said, "He who abides in Me, and I in him, bears much fruit; for without Me you can do nothing" (John 15:5). And Paul reminded us that we "can do all things through Christ who strengthens [us]" (Philippians 4:13), that "the excellence of the power [is] of God and not of us" (2 Corinthians 4:7), and that we are "strengthened with might through His Spirit in the inner man" (Ephesians 3:16).

Because of God's power, we can do whatever He asks of us—through Him. We base our confidence not in our own abilities, but in God's absolute promises.

So, today, with exceedingly more power than the little engine could ever muster, we can say, "I know I can. I know I can—because of Jesus."
—CHK

God gives to His servants this promise:
You'll not have to face life alone;
And when you grow weak in your struggle,
His strength will prevail—not your own. —Hess

God's requirements are met by God's enabling.

Tensile Strength

READ: 2 Corinthians 12:7–10

My grace is sufficient for you, for My strength is made perfect in weakness. —2 CORINTHIANS 12:9

When a new highway loop was being completed in West Michigan, a real danger was discovered. The bridges had been designed to bear their own weight, but not the traffic they were intended to carry. Before the highway could be opened, several bridges had to be re-engineered and rebuilt.

Engineers have to be especially concerned with the tensile strength of the material in their construction plans for structures that are required to bear large amounts of stress due to weight. Tensile strength is the maximum amount of stretching a material can withstand before it tears. If the engineer miscalculates, the structure may collapse under the pressure.

When we are under the weight of stress and hardship, we may wonder whether our Lord, who engineered us, has miscalculated our personal "tensile strength." We are certain that we are going to collapse under the weight of the trials, but our Designer knows exactly what we can handle by His grace. He knows our limits and will never permit more than we can bear. As Bible teacher Ron Hutchcraft said, "God may send a load, but He never sends an overload!"

Reinforced by the steel of God's provision, our tensile strength won't fail. —BC

Wait on the Lord from day to day,
Strength He provides in His own way;
There's no need for worry, no need to fear,
He is our God who is always near. —Fortna

Your problems can never exhaust God's provisions.

Indestructible!

READ: Hebrews 7:11–21

*[Christ] has come . . . according to the
power of an endless life.* —HEBREWS 7:16

The space shuttle reenters Earth's atmosphere at more than 25 times the speed of sound! Friction from wind resistance raises the space-craft's outer temperature to 3,000 degrees Fahrenheit. To keep the shuttle from burning up, 34,000 separate tiles protect its underbelly. These tiles must be virtually indestructible against high-speed friction.

In this world of death and decay, nothing is truly indestructible. Yet the Bible tells us of an indestructible life. Comparing the Lord Jesus to the works of the law, we are told, "[Christ] has come, not according to the law of a fleshly commandment, but according to the power of an endless life" (Hebrews 7:16). The Greek word translated "endless" is best rendered "indestructible."

The Messiah is our Great High Priest whose priestly duties required His own sacrificial death for our sins. His resurrection guarantees eternal redemption for all who repent and believe in Him.

The loss of health, relationships, or finances can make us feel as if our life has been destroyed. But for the believer, nothing could be further from the truth. Through our spiritual union with Christ, we have the promise that we'll share in His own indestructible life (John 14:19).

—DF

Marvelous day, all suffering ended,
Glorious bodies now like to His own;
We will be kings and priests in God's kingdom,
With glory and honor around the great throne. —Dixon

Nothing can shake those who are secure in God's hands.

Just Like David

READ: Psalm 51:1–12

I acknowledge my transgressions. —PSALM 51:3

The elderly woman didn't like the way her pastor prayed each Sunday morning, so she told him. It bothered her that before he preached he would confess to God that he had sinned the week before. "Pastor," she said, "I don't like to think my pastor sins."

We'd like to believe that our spiritual leaders don't sin. But reality tells us that no Christian is exempt from the burdens of the sinful nature. Paul told the believers at Colosse to "put to death, therefore, whatever belongs to your earthly nature" (Colossians 3:5 NIV). The problem is that sometimes we don't do that. We yield to temptation, and we're left with a mess.

But we are not left helpless. We have a pattern to follow for restoration.

That pattern comes from the heart and pen of King David, whose sin demonstrated the sad consequences of succumbing to temptation. Look closely at Psalm 51 as David owned up to his sin. First, he flung himself at God's feet, pleading for mercy, acknowledging his sin, and trusting in God's judgment (vv. 1–6). Next, he sought cleansing from the One who forgives and wipes the slate clean (vv. 7–9). Finally, David asked for restoration with the Holy Spirit's help (vv. 10–12).

Is sin stealing your joy and blocking your fellowship with the Lord? Like David, turn it over to Him. —DB

> *Our sinful ways can sap our joy*
> *And isolate us from the Lord;*
> *Confession and repentance, though,*
> *Provide the way to be restored.* —Sper

Repentance clears the way for us to walk with God.

Tell Your Story

READ: Mark 5:1–20

Go home to your friends, and tell them what great things the Lord has done for you, and how He has had compassion on you. —MARK 5:19

An organizational consultant in New York says that his graduate students typically recall only 5 percent of the main ideas in a presentation of graphs and charts, while they generally remember half of the stories told in the same presentation. There is a growing consensus among communication experts about the power of the personal touch in relating an experience. While facts and figures often put listeners to sleep, an illustration from real life can motivate them to action. Author Annette Simmons says, "The missing ingredient in most failed communication is humanity."

Mark 5:1–20 gives the dramatic account of Jesus setting a violent, self-destructive man free from the powerful demons that possessed him. When the restored man begged to stay with Jesus as He traveled, the Lord told him, " 'Go home to your friends, and tell them what great things the Lord has done for you, and how He has had compassion on you.' And he departed and began to proclaim in Decapolis all that Jesus had done for him; and all marveled" (vv. 19–20).

Knowledge and eloquence are often overrated in the process of communicating the good news of Jesus Christ. Never underestimate the power of what God has done for you, and don't be afraid to tell your story to others.   —DM

> *Take control of my words today,*
> *May they tell of Your great love;*
> *And may the story of Your grace*
> *Turn some heart to You above.* —Sees

Sharing the gospel is one person telling another good news.

Lament for a Friend

READ: 2 Samuel 1:11, 17–27

I am distressed for you, my brother Jonathan; you have been very pleasant to me. —2 SAMUEL 1:26

As a pastor, I was often asked to lead funeral services. Typically, the funeral director would give me a 3 x 5 index card with all the particulars about the deceased so I would be informed about him or her. I never got used to that, however. As practical and necessary as it may have been, it seemed a bit trite to take a person's earthly sojourn and reduce it to an index card. Life is too big for that.

After David received news of Jonathan's death, he spent time recalling the life of his friend—even writing a lament that others could sing as a way to respect Jonathan (2 Samuel 1:17–27). David recalled his friend's courage and skill, and honored his heroic life. For David, the loss of his friend Jonathan was an intense time of mourning and remembrance.

When we grieve for a loved one, it is vital to recall the cherished details and shared experiences of our lives together. Those memories flood our hearts with far more thoughts than an index card can hold. The day that grief visits our hearts is not a time for short summaries and quick snapshots of our loved one's life. It is a time to remember deeply, giving God thanks for the details, the stories, and the impact of an entire life. It's time to pause, reflect, and honor.   —BC

At journey's end, take a long look back
At the details of the story;
Take time to review the godly life
Of your loved one now in Glory. —Branon

Precious memories of life can temper the profound sadness of death.

The Importance of Theology

READ: 1 Kings 11:4–13

Do not be unequally yoked together with unbelievers.
—2 CORINTHIANS 6:14

When looking for a new car, potential buyers look at more than the exterior styling. They check out the inner workings that make it run smoothly and efficiently.

When choosing a spouse, however, some are not so careful. They discover too late that a beautiful body is camouflaging a defective mind and soul. Men and women both make this mistake, but author Carolyn Custis James was specifically concerned about men when she wrote: "[A] woman's interest in theology ought to be the first thing to catch a man's eye. . . . [Her] theology suddenly matters when a man is facing a crisis and she is the only one around to offer encouragement."

Solomon should have known this. He was, after all, the wisest man who ever lived (1 Kings 3:12; 4:29–34). But Solomon followed his own desires rather than God's command and married women whose allegiance was not to God (11:1–2). The results were disastrous. Solomon's wives turned his heart toward other gods, and God became angry with him (vv.3–4, 9). The kingdom of Israel was eventually divided and defeated (vv. 11–13).

Good theology is important for everyone. And it is difficult to make good decisions if our allegiance is to someone who does not know and love God.   —JAL

─────────── THINKING IT OVER ───────────
Why is it unwise for a follower of Christ to marry an unbeliever? What advice does Peter give to wives of unbelieving husbands? (See 1 Peter 3:1.)

Faulty beliefs about God lead to faulty decisions about people.

Light as a Feather

READ: 2 Samuel 6:12–23

A merry heart does good, like medicine. —PROVERBS 17:22

We Christians can sometimes be a joyless lot, preoccupied with maintaining our dignity. That's an odd attitude, though, since we're joined to a God who has given us His wonderful gift of joy and laughter.

It's okay to have fun! Each family expresses it in different ways, of course. I'm thankful that our house has been a house of laughter. Water fights, good-natured (albeit stiff) competition, gentle ribbing, and hilarity came easily to us. Laughter has been a gift of God's goodness that carried us through some of life's darkest days. The joy of the Lord has often been our refuge (Nehemiah 8:10).

When King David brought the ark of the covenant to Jerusalem from the house of Obed-Edom, he danced "with all his might" before the Lord (2 Samuel 6:14). The Hebrew word here that is translated as "danced" carries the idea of joyful exuberance and is akin to our expression "kick up your heels." In fact, in verse 16 it says that David was "leaping and whirling."

Michal, David's wife, felt that his antics were unbecoming to the dignity of a king and reacted with stern severity. David's response was to announce that he would become even more "undignified" (v. 22). His spirit was buoyant and he felt "as light as a feather."

Take time to laugh! (Ecclesiastes 3:4).   —DR

A merry heart does good, like medicine." —Proverbs 17:22

Wholesome laughter has great face value.

"Cast Down" Sheep

READ: Psalm 23

He restores my soul. —PSALM 23:3

In his classic book *A Shepherd Looks at Psalm 23,* Phillip Keller gives a striking picture of the care and gentleness of a shepherd. In verse 3 when David says, "He restores my soul," Keller writes, he uses language every shepherd would understand.

Sheep are built in such a way that if they fall over on their side and then onto their back, it is difficult for them to get up again. They flail their legs in the air, bleat, and cry. After a few hours on their backs, gas begins to collect in their stomachs, the stomach hardens, the air passage is cut off, and the sheep will eventually suffocate. This is referred to as a "cast down" position.

When a shepherd restores a cast down sheep, he reassures it, massages its legs to restore circulation, gently turns the sheep over, lifts it up, and holds it so it can regain its equilibrium.

What a picture of what God wants to do for us! When we are on our backs, flailing because of guilt, grief, or grudges, our loving Shepherd reassures us with His grace, lifts us up, and holds us until we've gained our spiritual equilibrium.

If you've been cast down for any reason, God is the only one who can help you get on your feet again. He will restore your confidence, joy, and strength.   —MW

This Shepherd of mine knows each trial, each snare,
And at just the right moment my Lord will be there,
On His shoulders to carry each burden for me—
Yes, the Lord is my Shepherd, and always shall be. —Henry

The weak and the helpless are in the Good Shepherd's special care.

The Power of Love

READ: Zephaniah 3:14–20

The Lord your God in your midst, the Mighty One, will save; He will rejoice over you with gladness, He will quiet you with His love.
—ZEPHANIAH 3:17

The documentary film *Young@Heart* gives a rollicking look at a senior chorus of twenty-four singers whose average age is eighty. Filled with humor and poignant moments, the film includes this remarkable singing group's deeply moving performance at a New England prison. When the concert concludes, the singers walk into the audience, greeting the surprised prisoners with handshakes and hugs.

The inmates' amazement at this unexpected personal touch reminds me of the book of Zephaniah, in which the prophet brings a powerful message of God's presence and love to His people during a dark time: "The Lord your God in your midst, the Mighty One, will save; He will rejoice over you with gladness, He will quiet you with His love, He will rejoice over you with singing" (3:17).

According to Bible teacher Henrietta Mears, Zephaniah "begins with sorrow but ends with singing. The first of the book is full of sadness and gloom, but the last contains one of the sweetest songs of love in the Old Testament."

God's love for us is always astonishing, especially when it touches us at a low ebb of life. During our darkest times, the Lord comes to us with His joy, His love, and His song.　　　　　　　　　—DM

If your heart is filled with sadness,
Or you struggle with despair,
Turn to God, who'll bring you gladness
When you sense His love and care. —Sper

In God's garden of love, you are His forget-me-not.

Like a Diamond in the Sky

READ: Psalm 8

You have crowned him with glory and honor. —PSALM 8:5

Astronomers discovered a star in the sky that has cooled and compressed into a giant diamond. The largest rough gem-quality diamond ever found on Earth is the Cullinan Diamond—at over 3,100 carats. So how many carats are in the cosmic diamond? Ten billion trillion trillion carats!

In our world, diamonds are prized for their rarity, beauty, and durability, and we often hear it said, "Diamonds are forever." But God isn't enamored with diamonds. To Him there is something far more precious.

Thousands of years ago, David marveled at the great value God had set on human beings: "What is man that You are mindful of him, and the son of man that You visit him? For You have made him a little lower than the angels, and You have crowned him with glory and honor" (Psalm 8:4–5).

In fact, God placed such a high value on us that it cost Him dearly to buy our redemption. The purchase price was the precious blood of His Son, Jesus Christ (1 Peter 1:18–19).

If God places such a high value on us, we should also place a high value on the people He has brought into our lives. Bring them before the Lord in prayer. Ask Him to show you how each person is more priceless than the most costly jewel in the universe.   —DF

> *Oh, teach me what it cost Thee*
> *To make a sinner whole;*
> *And teach me, Savior, teach me*
> *The value of a soul! —Bennett*

We are more precious to Jesus than the costliest diamond.

Reminders of Love

READ: John 19:1–7, 16–18

God is love. —1 JOHN 4:8

After the US entered World War II in 1941, Estelle tried to talk her boyfriend Sidney out of joining the Army. But he enlisted and began his training in April of the following year. For the next three years he wrote her love letters—525 in all. Then in March 1945, she learned that her beloved fiancé had been killed in combat.

Although Estelle did eventually marry, the memories of her first love lived in her heart. To honor that love, she published a book of Sidney's wartime correspondence more than sixty years later.

Like those letters, the Lord has left us with reminders of His love—the Scriptures. He says: "I have loved you with an everlasting love; therefore with lovingkindness I have drawn you" (Jeremiah 31:3). "As the Father loved Me, I also have loved you; abide in My love" (John 15:9).

The Bible also tells us that "Christ . . . loved the church and gave Himself for her" (Ephesians 5:25). "[Jesus] gave Himself for us, that He might redeem us" (Titus 2:14). And, "God is love" (1 John 4:8).

Read God's Word often and be reminded that Jesus loves you and died for you. —AC

> *With lovingkindness I have drawn you,*
> *Proving that My love is true;*
> *Do not neglect to read of that love,*
> *Written in My Word for you.* —Verway

Nothing can compare to the love of God.

Running a Marathon

READ: Philippians 3:12–21

I press toward the goal for the prize of the upward call of God in Christ Jesus. —PHILIPPIANS 3:14

The Comrades Marathon, which began in 1921, is the oldest ultra-marathon. Covering 90 km (56 miles), it is held annually in South Africa. Bruce Fordyce completely dominated this marathon in the 1980s, winning it nine times between 1981 and 1990. His 1986 record of 5 hours 24 minutes and 7 seconds stood for 21 years before it was finally broken in 2007. It's amazing to me that he has continued to run in this race every year.

In a sense, we as Christians are all in a marathon. It takes endurance to run and finish the race of life. When the apostle Paul wrote his letter to the Philippians, he spoke of how he was "reaching forward to those things which are ahead" (3:13) and pressing on "toward the goal for the prize of the upward call of God in Christ Jesus" (v. 14).

Our Lord Jesus has set an example of how to run life's marathon. The Bible tells us that Jesus "for the joy that was set before Him endured the cross, despising the shame, and has sat down at the right hand of the throne of God" (Hebrews 12:2). Despite "hostility from sinners," He completed His race (v. 3).

The secret to finishing well is to look forward to the joy that awaits us after life's race—eternal life with Him. —CPH

I ran to meet Him when I heard His call—
The Savior's arms were open to receive;
And I'm still running since I gave my all,
Inviting others also to believe. —Hess

The Christian's race is not a
competitive event but an endurance run.

Patience in Prison

READ: Genesis 40:1–14, 23

[God] Himself has said, "I will never leave you nor forsake you." —HEBREWS 13:5

Have you ever noticed that other people's forgetfulness can try your patience? As a college professor, I find my patience stretched when a student forgets to do an assignment that's clearly spelled out in the syllabus.

In the Old Testament story of Joseph, we see a far worse example of forgetfulness, and we can only imagine how Joseph struggled to be patient as a result.

While in prison, Joseph interpreted a dream for the king's butler, which led to the man's release. Joseph told him, "Remember me when it is well with you, and please show kindness to me; make mention of me to Pharaoh, and get me out of this house" (Genesis 40:14). It would seem that after Joseph had helped the butler gain freedom, remembering him would have been high on the man's "to do" list. But it was two years before the butler spoke to Pharaoh about Joseph (41:9). Then, finally, Joseph was freed.

Imagine the impatience Joseph felt as he waited each day in that dungeon, perhaps thinking his only chance at freedom had passed (40:15). Yet Joseph had a resource: He had God's presence (39:21), as do we (Hebrews 13:5).

When you're feeling impatient, lean on the God who is always with you. He'll turn your impatience into patient trust. —DB

Tune your anxious heart to patience,
Walk by faith where sight is dim;
Loving God, be calm and trustful
And leave everything to Him. —Chambers

Patience means waiting for God's time without doubting God's love.

Journeys

READ: Philippians 1:8–18

I want you to know, brethren, that the things which happened to me have actually turned out for the furtherance of the gospel.
—PHILIPPIANS 1:12

On a map in the back of my Bible, each of Paul's missionary journeys is shown by a colored line with arrows indicating his direction of travel. On the first three, the arrows lead away from his place of departure and back to a point of return. On the fourth journey, however, Paul was traveling as a prisoner, bound for trial before Caesar, and the arrows point only one direction, ending in Rome.

We might be tempted to call this an unfortunate time in Paul's life, if it were not for his view that God was leading and using him just as much on this journey as He did on the previous three.

He wrote: "I want you to know, brethren, that the things which happened to me have actually turned out for the furtherance of the gospel, so that it has become evident to the whole palace guard, and to all the rest, that my chains are in Christ; and most of the brethren in the Lord, having become confident by my chains, are much more bold to speak the Word without fear" (Philippians 1:12–14).

Even when our journey in life is marked by confinement and limitations, we can be sure that the Lord will encourage others through us as we speak His Word and trust in Him.   —DM

The journeys that we take in life,
Though unexpected they may be,
If we commit to follow Christ,
His work through us the world will see. —Sper

For the Christian, what looks like a
detour may actually be a new road to blessing.

Einstein's God

READ: Psalm 19:1–6

The heavens declare the glory of God; and the firmament shows His handiwork. —PSALM 19:1

When the great physicist Albert Einstein was asked if he believed in God, he responded: "We are in the position of a little child entering a huge library filled with books in many languages. The child knows someone must have written those books. It does not know how. . . . That, it seems to me, is the attitude of even the most intelligent human beings toward God. We see the universe marvelously arranged and obeying certain laws but only dimly understand these laws." Although Einstein marveled at the design he saw in nature, he did not believe in a personal Creator.

The psalmist shared Einstein's sense of awe about nature but took the next step and believed in the Designer behind the design: "The heavens declare the glory of God; and the firmament shows His handiwork" (Psalm 19:1).

The wonder we feel as we behold our universe should serve as a road sign pointing to the One who created it. The Scriptures tell us, "All things were made through [Christ], and without Him nothing was made that was made" (John 1:3).

Are you struggling in your beliefs? Look up at the stars tonight. In the sky is crafted an amazing road sign pointing to the Designer behind the design. —DF

> *God wrote His autograph*
> *Upon the sky last night,*
> *In the stars I never saw*
> *A signature so bright!* —Schoeberlein

Creation's design points to the Master Designer.

Life Is Good

READ: Romans 8:31–39

I am persuaded that [nothing] shall be able to separate us from the love of God which is in Christ Jesus our Lord. —ROMANS 8:38–39

While shopping in a nearby tourist town, I wandered into a small store stuffed with clothing and other items all marked with the slogan "Life is good." Sometimes we need to remind ourselves of that simple truth.

When the work of earning a living, raising a family, maintaining health and fitness, and managing relationships starts to overwhelm us, it's good to think about how small our part in the universe really is.

While we obsess over our work, God quietly does His. He keeps the earth rotating, the planets revolving, and the seasons changing. Without any help from us, He makes the sun rise every morning and set every evening. Every night He changes the pattern of lights in the sky. He turns out the light so we can sleep, and turns it on again so we can see to work and play. Without lifting a finger, we get to enjoy sunrises and sunsets. Every year the seasons change on schedule. We don't need to pray about it or tell God that it's time to send spring. And all that He does reminds us He is good (Acts 14:17).

Life will at times be difficult, often it is painful, and for now it is imperfect. But still it is good, for in all these things nothing can separate us from God's lavish expressions of love (Romans 8:39).   —JAL

Thank you, loving Father, for the good gift of life. Forgive me for making it complicated for myself and others. I thank you and praise you for all you do so that I can enjoy so much. Amen.

God's grace is immeasurable, His mercy
inexhaustible, His peace inexpressible.

Prelude of Praise

READ: Psalm 150

I will sing praise to Your name forever, that
I may daily perform my vows. —Psalm 61:8

We enter a concert hall, find our seats, and listen with anticipation as the members of the orchestra tune their instruments. The sound is discordant, not melodic. But the tuning is simply a prelude to the symphony.

C. S. Lewis suggested that's how it is with our devotional practices and even our worship services. Sometimes they sound discordant, but God hears our prayers and praises with fatherly delight. We are really preparing for participation in the glorious symphony of heaven. Now we are making a minuscule contribution to the harmonies of angelic and redeemed hosts. But our adoration, though feeble, pleases the heart of the Divine Listener more than the finest rendition of earth's greatest orchestra.

Are we eagerly awaiting our participation in heaven's symphony of praise? Are we joyfully participating in the adoration that delights the heart of God? Or do we regard devotion as more of a discipline than a delight?

Our attitudes will be transformed when we realize that praise delights God's heart. Praise helps us to tune our lives to heavenly harmonies. Praise is an indispensable preparation for the worship that will be our eternal joy.

"Let everything that has breath praise the Lord" (Psalm 150:6).
—VG

Joyfully, heartily resounding,
Let every instrument and voice
Peal out the praise of grace abounding,
Calling the whole world to rejoice. —Routley

The heart filled with praise brings pleasure to God.

Unanswered Prayers

READ: Luke 7:1–10

*[Jesus said], "I have not found such great
faith, not even in Israel!"* —LUKE 7:9

An explanation we often hear for "unanswered" prayers is that we don't have enough faith. But Jesus said that if we have faith the size of a mustard seed, we can command a mulberry tree to be uprooted and planted in the sea and it will obey us (see Luke 17:6). In other words, the effectiveness of our prayers depends not on how much faith we have but on whether we even have faith.

Luke tells of a Roman centurion with "great faith" (7:9). His faith was expressed first as an appeal to Jesus to heal his dying servant. Then it was expressed as an acknowledgment that Jesus could heal his servant anytime, anywhere. The centurion did not ask Jesus to do things his way.

Faith has been described as "trusting God's heart and trusting God's power." Some prayers that seem to go unanswered are simply instances in which God has lovingly overruled our wishes. He knows that what we have asked for is not best. Or it may be that our timing is not His timing, or He has some far greater purpose in mind. Let us remember, even Jesus prayed to His heavenly Father, "Nevertheless not My will, but Yours" (Luke 22:42).

Do we have the centurion's great faith—a faith that trusts God to do His work, in His way?   —CPH

Unanswered prayers are answered still
As part of God's great master plan;
They help to carry out His will
To demonstrate God's love for man. —D. DeHaan

God's answers are wiser than our prayers.

Comforted to Comfort

READ: 2 Corinthians 1:3–11

[God] comforts us . . . that we may be able to comfort [others]
with the comfort with which we ourselves are comforted by God.
—2 CORINTHIANS 1:4

While speaking to a group of Christian athletes, I asked them how they normally responded to hardships. Their responses included fear, anger, self-pity, aggression, despair, abusive behavior, apathy, and turning to God. I encouraged them to trust that God would comfort them and then use them to comfort others.

Just as I encouraged those athletes, Paul encouraged a group of believers in a town called Corinth. He reminded them that afflictions were inevitable for the follower of Jesus. Many of the Corinthians were being persecuted, imprisoned, and oppressed—all because of their relationship with Jesus—and Paul wanted them to know that in the midst of their trouble God was their source of help. He would come to their side and help them to have godly responses. Then Paul gave one of the reasons God allowed their suffering and brought divine comfort: so that the Corinthians might have the empathy to enter into other people's sorrow and comfort them (2 Corinthians 1:4).

When we suffer, let us remember that God will bring comfort to us through His Word, by the Holy Spirit, and through fellow believers. God does not comfort us so that we'll be comfortable; we are comforted by God so that we might be comforters. —MW

When you receive God's comfort,
Be sure to pass it on,
Then give to God the glory
From whom the comfort's drawn. —Hess

When God permits trials, He also provides comfort.

How to Become Rich

READ: Luke 12:13–21

Take heed and beware of covetousness, for one's life does not consist in the abundance of the things he possesses. —LUKE 12:15

I find it interesting that Jesus often taught about money. And He wasn't trying to ratchet up the treasury. As far as we know, He never even asked for an offering. The reason He taught extensively on the subject is that nothing clogs our spiritual arteries more quickly than money—either working to have a lot of it or wishing that we had.

Think of the man who brazenly asked Jesus, "Teacher, tell my brother to divide the inheritance with me" (Luke 12:13). Amazing! He had an opportunity to "go deep" with Jesus, but instead he wanted deep pockets.

Jesus responded with a stunning, counterintuitive statement: "Beware of covetousness, for one's life does not consist in the abundance of the things he possesses" (v. 15). He then went on to tell the parable of a rich man who was wildly successful from a worldly standpoint—having so many crops that he had to keep building bigger barns—but who, in God's eyes, was actually a "fool." Not because he was rich, but because he was not rich toward God.

You'll hear a lot of advice about how to become rich. But only Jesus tells it to us straight. It's not about the money. It's about the richness of our relationship with Him and the joy of turning our greed into generosity. —JS

> *The riches of this world are vain,*
> *They vanish in a day;*
> *But sweet the treasures of God's love—*
> *They never pass away.* —Bosch

Learning how to be rich toward God yields eternal dividends.

Untended Places

READ: Psalm 119:9–16

*Your Word I have hidden in my heart, that
I might not sin against You.* —PSALM 119:11

Our family had just arrived at the lake cottage we had rented for a week of much-anticipated vacation when my wife discovered the unmistakable evidence of spiders and mice in the house. It wasn't that we had never encountered such things, but that we had expected the cottage to be cleaned and prepared for our stay there. Instead, the counters, cabinets, and beds were littered with the residue of infestation, requiring much cleaning before we settled in. It wasn't a bad house; it had just been left untended.

We might be guilty of dealing with our hearts the way that cottage was managed. Our "untended places" can become breeding grounds for infestations of wrong thinking, poor attitudes, or sinful behavior—creating problems that require significant attention to correct. The wise path is to recognize our need to tend our hearts by staying in God's Word and embracing its truths.

In Psalm 119:11, the psalmist recognized the danger of not building our lives on the Scriptures. He said, "Your Word I have hidden in my heart, that I might not sin against You."

With a focus on the Word, we can build strong spiritual lives that will help us avoid the dangers that inevitably grow in untended places.
—BC

*Give me, O Lord, a strong desire
To look within Your Word each day;
Help me to hide it in my heart,
Lest from its truth my feet would stray.* —Branon

To grow spiritually strong, read the Word.

How Honest Are You?

READ: Acts 5:1–11

Those who deal truthfully are [God's] delight.
—PROVERBS 12:22

Woman's Day magazine surveyed more than 2,000 people to check out their honesty level. When asked, "How honest are you?" 48 percent said very honest, 50 percent said somewhat honest, and the other 2 percent said not very honest.

In the same survey, 68 percent of respondents confessed that they had taken office supplies from their job for personal use. And 40 percent admitted that they would cheat on their taxes if they knew they wouldn't get caught.

Ananias and Sapphira must have thought they could get away with lying (Acts 5:1–11). But they quickly found out differently when Peter confronted them and told them that they had lied to the Holy Spirit. Immediately they were struck dead (vv. 5, 10). The Lord's desire was to keep His new church pure so He could use the believers in the lives of others.

As Bible teacher G. Campbell Morgan said, "The church pure is the church powerful. . . . The only power [able to make] a church pure is that of the indwelling Spirit of God." The purity of the church led to the testimony of believers spreading, and "believers were increasingly added to the Lord" (v. 14).

Let's be the kind of people who "deal truthfully" (Proverbs 12:22) so we can be used by the Lord.   —AC

Lord, by Your Spirit grant that we
In word and deed may honest be;
All falsehood we would cast aside,
From You, O Lord, we cannot hide. —D. DeHaan

There are no degrees of honesty.

Lateral Violence

READ: Matthew 20:20–28

Whoever desires to become great among you,
let him be your servant. —MATTHEW 20:26

An intriguing article in *Michigan Nurse* magazine called attention to "nursing's dirty little secret"—the incivility and verbal abuse that occurs among some nurses. This peer-level bullying (also known as lateral violence) takes the form of backstabbing, innuendo, infighting, sabotage, verbal affronts, failure to respect privacy, and others.

Not only is lateral violence occurring among nurses, it's a growing problem in a host of other work environments. This bullying always includes an imbalance of power, an intent to harm, and the threat of further aggression.

Of course, this would never occur in the church—or would it? Think about the personal interaction in deacon and elder boards, church office staffs, Bible study groups, and youth ministries. Are they ever marked by the kinds of behavior that harm, denigrate, or intimidate others? And what about in our families?

When the disciples were jockeying for position in the coming kingdom, Jesus rebuked them and said, "Whoever desires to become great among you, let him be your servant" (Matthew 20:26). With that attitude in all our relationships, bullying will never be found among us.
　　　　　　　　　　　　　　　　　　　　　　　　　　　　　—DE

> *Lord, may we have a servant's heart*
> *In all we say and do*
> *By placing others' needs above*
> *What we want to pursue.* —Sper

Only the one who serves is qualified to lead.

Mell's Smiley Face

READS: Romans 5:1–5

We also glory in tribulations, knowing that
tribulation produces perseverance. —ROMANS 5:3

Some people think you shouldn't draw in your Bible, but I'm glad my daughter Melissa drew in hers. In the margin next to Romans 5, she used a green ink pen to draw a small, simple smiley face, and circled verse 3.

How could she have known that her family and friends would need this passage when she left us so suddenly in a car accident at age seventeen? How could she know that these verses would tell her story, while guiding our lives and the lives of others over the past ten years?

Romans 5 begins by explaining our justification through faith, which gives us peace with God through Jesus (v. 1). Melissa had that peace. And right now she is enjoying the fruits of her faith, as verse 2 describes: We "rejoice in hope of the glory of God." Imagine the smiley face she could draw now!

And for the rest of us—all of us left behind when loved ones precede us in death? Somehow, we "rejoice in our sufferings." Why? Because our suffering brings perseverance, which brings character, which brings us hope (vv. 3–4).

We feel helpless in times of tragedy, but we are never hopeless. God pours His love into our hearts, and with it the great hope of His glory. It's all part of God's mysterious yet marvelous plan.   —DB

God often digs wells of joy with the spade of sorrow.

Leaving a Legacy

READ: Deuteronomy 6:4–9

You shall teach them diligently to your children . . . when you sit in your house, when you walk by the way. —DEUTERONOMY 6:7

Recently my grandson Alex accompanied me as I ran errands. Unexpectedly he asked, "So, Grandpa, how did you receive Christ as your Savior?" Touched, I told him about my childhood conversion. Alex was still interested, so I described how his great-grandfather had come to faith. This included a brief overview of how he survived World War II, his initial resistance to the gospel, and how his life changed after becoming a Christian.

Later I was reminded of our conversation when I read a Bible passage that speaks of faith being passed down through the generations. Moses instructed the Israelites to take to heart God's truths and share them with the next generation as a way of life: "These words which I command you today shall be in your heart. You shall teach them diligently to your children, and shall talk of them when you sit in your house, when you walk by the way, when you lie down, and when you rise up" (Deuteronomy 6:6–7).

Biblical parenting is not a guarantee of having godly offspring. But when we see spiritual interest in the next generation, we can cultivate vital conversations about God's Word. This can be one of a parent's, or grandparent's, greatest legacies.   —DF

> *God gives us children for a time,*
> *To train them in His way,*
> *To love them and to teach them how*
> *To follow and obey.* —Sper

The richest legacy a parent can leave a child is a godly example.

Letting Go

READ: Philippians 3:3–11

*What things were gain to me, these I have
counted loss for Christ.* —PHILIPPIANS 3:7

It has been said that "one person's junk is another's treasure." When David Dudley tried to help his parents clear their house of "unnecessary items" before they moved to a smaller home, he found it very difficult. He was often angered by his parents' refusal to part with things they had not used for decades. Finally, David's father helped him understand that even the worn-out, useless items were tied to close friends and important events. Clearing the clutter felt like throwing away their very lives.

A spiritual parallel to our reluctance to let go of the clutter in our homes may be our inability to clear our hearts of the attitudes that weigh us down.

For many years, Saul of Tarsus clung to the "righteousness" he had earned by obeying God's law. His pedigree and performance were prized possessions until he encountered Jesus in a blinding moment on the Damascus Road (Acts 9:1–8). Face to face with the risen Savior, he let go of his cherished self-effort and later wrote, "But what things were gain to me, these I have counted loss for Christ" (Philippians 3:7).

When the Holy Spirit urges us to release our grip on any attitude that keeps us from following Christ, we find true freedom in letting go.
—DM

*Speak to us, Lord, till shamed by Thy great giving
Our hands unclasp to set our treasures free;
Our wills, our love, our dear ones, our possessions,
All gladly yielded, gracious Lord, to Thee.* —Anonymous

Through Christ we have the freedom to let go.

Things Said in Secret

READ: Ephesians 4:25–32

The words of a wise man's mouth are gracious.
—ECCLESIASTES 10:12

Some say that anonymity is the last refuge for cowards. Judging from mail and comments I've read that have been submitted anonymously, I would agree. People hiding behind the screen of anonymity or a false identity feel the freedom to launch angry, hurtful tirades. Anonymity allows them to be unkind without having to take responsibility for their words.

Whenever I am tempted to write something anonymously because I don't want to be identified with my own words, I stop and reconsider. If I don't want my name attached to it, I probably shouldn't be saying it. Then I do one of two things: I either toss it out or I rewrite it in a way that makes it helpful rather than hurtful.

According to Ephesians, our words should edify and impart grace (4:29). If I'm unwilling to use my name, there's reason to believe that my motive is to hurt, not to help.

Whenever you're tempted to say something in secret—perhaps to a family member, co-worker, or your pastor—consider why you don't want your name to be identified with your words. After all, if you don't want to be identified with your words, God probably doesn't either. He is gracious and slow to anger (Exodus 34:6), and we should be the same.
—JAL

O Lord, help us to turn aside
From words that spring from selfish pride,
For You would have Your children one
In praise and love for Your dear Son. —D. DeHaan

Anonymity can be a coward's way of hiding behind hurtful words.

The Thinking Christian

READ: 2 Corinthians 10:1–11

Casting down arguments and . . . bringing every thought into captivity to the obedience of Christ. —2 CORINTHIANS 10:5

David McCullough's biography of John Adams, one of America's founding fathers and early presidents, describes him as "both a devout Christian and an independent thinker, and he saw no conflict in that." I am struck by that statement, for it carries a note of surprise, suggesting that Christians are somehow naïve or unenlightened, and that the idea of a "thinking Christian" is a contradiction.

Nothing could be further from the truth. One of the great benefits of salvation is that it causes the believer's mind to be guarded by the peace of God (Philippians 4:7), which can foster clear thinking, discernment, and wisdom. Paul described this in his second letter to Corinth when he wrote that in Christ we are equipped for "casting down arguments and every high thing that exalts itself against the knowledge of God, bringing every thought into captivity to the obedience of Christ" (2 Corinthians 10:5).

To sift through an argument wisely, to embrace the clarity of the knowledge of God, and to align our thinking with the mind of Christ are valuable skills when living in a world lacking in discernment. These skills enable us to use our minds to represent Christ. Every Christian should be a thinking Christian. Are you?   —BC

If you grasp the message of God's Word,
If you've learned to think things through,
Then you can defend the Christian faith
With wise words both clear and true. —Branon

Faith was never intended as a substitute for intelligence.

Later On

READ: Genesis 13:10–18

I consider that the sufferings of this present time are not worthy to be compared with the glory which shall be revealed in us.
—ROMANS 8:18

It seems there are two kinds of people in this world: those who have an eternal perspective and those who are preoccupied with the present.

One is absorbed with the permanent; the other with the passing. One stores up treasure in heaven; the other accumulates it here on earth. One stays with a challenging marriage because this isn't all there is; another looks for happiness in another mate, believing this life is all there is. One is willing to suffer poverty, hunger, indignity, and shame because of "the glory which shall be revealed" (Romans 8:18); another believes that happiness is being rich and famous. It's all a matter of perspective.

Abraham had an "other world" perspective. That's what enabled him to give up a piece of well-watered land by the Jordan (Genesis 13). He knew that God had something better for him later on. The Lord told him to look in every direction as far as he could see and then said that his family would someday have it all. What a land grant! And God promised that his descendants would be as numerous "as the dust" (v. 16).

That's an outlook many people can't understand. They go for all the gusto right now. But God's people have another point of view. They know that God has something better later on! —DR

I'd rather have Jesus than silver or gold;
I'd rather be His than have riches untold;
I'd rather have Jesus than anything
This world affords today. —Miller

Live for Jesus, and you'll live for eternity.

A Much Greater Plan

READ: Luke 5:1–11

Jesus said to Simon, "Do not be afraid.
*From now on you will catch men." —*LUKE 5:10

Recently our family was in Erie, Pennsylvania, visiting a relative. While there, we had a chance to swim in the community swimming pool. It was fun, but our host wanted to take us to Lake Erie to enjoy the sandy beaches, the cresting waves, and the beauty of the setting sun. My children protested because they wanted to swim in the pool. But I tried to get them to see that going to the beaches of Presque Isle would be a much greater plan.

I believe Jesus wanted Simon Peter to see that He had something much greater in mind for him—he would "catch men" instead of fish (Luke 5:10). Jesus told Peter to go to the deeper water and let down his nets for a catch (v. 4). Peter had just returned from an unsuccessful night of fishing, but at Jesus' command he obeyed and said, "Master, we have toiled all night and caught nothing; nevertheless at Your word I will let down the net" (v. 5). Humbled by the miraculous catch of fish, Peter bowed in awe before the Lord, who then told him that from that point on He wanted him to fish for men. Peter left everything and followed Him.

God's greater plan for us may not be to leave our occupation. But it's His plan that we use our time, resources, and careers to bring others into the kingdom.   —MW

The next person you meet may need to meet Christ.

The Others

READ: Hebrews 11:32–40

Blessed are you when they revile and persecute you, and say all kinds of evil against you falsely for My sake. . . . Great is your reward in heaven. —MATTHEW 5:11–12

When I was growing up, I often spent a week each summer with my grandparents. Many afternoons I would lie in the backyard hammock and read books I found in Grandpa's bookcase. One was *Foxe's Book of Martyrs*. It was heavy reading for a young girl, but I was absorbed by the detailed accounts of Christian martyrs, believers who were told to deny their faith in Christ but refused—and thus suffered horrific deaths.

Hebrews 11 tells similar stories. After listing the familiar names of those who demonstrated immense faith in God, the chapter tells of the torture and death of people referred to simply as "others" (vv. 35–36). While their names are not mentioned, this tribute is paid to them: "The world was not worthy" of them (v. 38). They died boldly for their faith in Jesus.

Today, we hear of persecuted Christians around the world, yet many of us have not been tested to that extent. When I examine my own faith, I wonder how I would respond to the prospect of martyrdom. I hope I would have the attitude of Paul, who said that although "chains and tribulations" awaited him, he looked forward to finishing life's race "with joy" (Acts 20: 23, 24).

Are we facing life with that kind of trusting attitude?   —CHK

> *When pressures mount because we walk*
> *The path of truth and right,*
> *We can rejoice to know that we*
> *Are pleasing in God's sight.* —D. DeHaan

The way to have joy in persecution is to find your joy in Jesus.

Mixing-Bowl Musings

READ: Luke 18:18–27

The things which are impossible with men are possible with God. —LUKE 18:27

Countless times I've heard myself say, "I'm going to bake a cake." Then one day I realized that I've never baked a cake in my life— only my oven can do that. I simply mix the right ingredients and allow the oven to do its part. Through that division of labor, I have the joy of seeing others taste and enjoy delicious cake.

God used my mixing-bowl musings to clarify a dilemma I once had after starting a neighborhood Bible study. It was one thing to bring my neighbors together to study the Bible, but seeing them believe and follow Christ was another. I felt powerless. Suddenly I saw the obvious. Like baking cakes, making Christians was impossible for me, but not for God. I had blended the right ingredients—an open home, friendship, and love. Now I had to trust the Holy Spirit, through His Word, to do His work. When I cooperated with that division of labor, I had the joy of seeing others taste of God's goodness.

In Luke 18:18–27, Jesus so vividly described some hindrances to saving faith that His listeners began to wonder if anyone could be saved. Do you feel that way about someone? Be encouraged by the Lord's strong reminder that there are some things that only God can do. Saving people is one of them. —JY

> *The Lord's the only one who can*
> *Transform a person's heart;*
> *But when we share God's saving truth,*
> *We play a crucial part.* —Sper

We sow the seed, but God brings the harvest.

Everyone Sings!

READ: Revelation 5:8–14

Blessing and honor and glory and power be to Him who sits on the throne, and to the Lamb, forever and ever! —REVELATION 5:13

Each summer I enjoy attending many of the free outdoor concerts presented in our city. During one performance by a brass band, several of the members briefly introduced themselves and told how much they enjoyed practicing and playing together.

The pleasure of sharing music in community has drawn people together for centuries. As followers of Christ, whether we are in small groups, choirs, or congregations, bringing praise to God is one of the key elements in our own expression of faith. And one day, we'll be singing in a concert that defies imagination.

In a sweeping vision of the tumultuous events at the end of time, John records a chorus of praise that begins with a few and swells to a company beyond number. In honor of the Lamb of God, who with His blood has redeemed people from every tribe and nation (Revelation 5:9), the song begins at the throne of God, is joined by multiplied thousands of angels, and finally includes every creature in heaven, earth, and sea. Together we will sing, "Blessing and honor and glory and power be to Him who sits on the throne, and to the Lamb, forever and ever!" (v. 13).

What a choir! What a concert! What a privilege to start rehearsing today! —DM

> *Give me a spirit of praise, dear Lord,*
> *That I may adore Your name,*
> *Sing praises from a grateful heart*
> *To the One who is always the same.* —Dawe

Those who know Christ now will sing His praise forever.

Julie's Prayer

READ: John 14:12–14

Whatever you ask in My name, that I will do, that the Father may be glorified in the Son. —JOHN 14:13

In 2008, the *Day of Discovery* film crew traveled to China on a special assignment—to retrace the life of missionary Eric Liddell, the 1924 Olympic gold medalist whose story was told in the movie *Chariots of Fire*. The crew took with them Eric's three daughters—Patricia, Heather, and Maureen—allowing them to revisit some of the places where the two older sisters had lived in China. Also along on the trip was their elderly Aunt Louise.

On one occasion, after the entourage had arrived in Beijing, they had to walk quite a distance with their luggage. As they did, Aunt Louise grew short of breath. Julie Richardson, a *Day of Discovery* crew member, sat down beside her, put her hand on her knee, and prayed simply, "Dear Jesus, help Aunt Louise to breathe." Immediately, she began to catch her breath.

Later, Heather retold the story and shared that Julie's prayer had rekindled her faith. Julie's simple act of faith reminded Heather of the continual connection we have with Jesus, a reality she had set aside in her life.

Sometimes we need reminders that God is near. When trials come and God seems far away, remember Julie's prayer and the truth that we are just one prayer from connecting with the God of the universe (John 14:13). —DB

God answers prayer, it is His sovereign way
To freely give His blessings day by day;
One earnest plea and lo! from heaven's throne
The answer comes, for God has heard His own. —*Anonymous*

God delights in the earnest prayers of His people.

Contentment

READ: Matthew 6:24–34

No one can serve two masters. —MATTHEW 6:24

A gripping photograph of an old woman sitting in a pile of garbage made me ponder. She was smiling as she ate a packet of food she had foraged from the garbage dump. It took so little for the woman to be satisfied.

There is much concern about a struggling economy and the cost of living going higher. And many are getting increasingly anxious about their livelihood. In this environment, is it possible to heed our Lord Jesus' teaching in Matthew 6:25, "Do not worry about your life, what you will eat or what you will drink; nor about your body, what you will put on"?

Our Lord was not saying that we don't need to work, that we don't need to eat, or that we shouldn't bother about how we dress. He was warning against those things becoming so important that we become slaves of money instead of trusting Him. "No one can serve two masters," He said (v. 24).

Seeking first "the kingdom of God and His righteousness" (v. 33) is recognizing that no matter how much effort we expend to make a better life for ourselves and our families, ultimately it is the Lord who takes care of our needs. And since God is our heavenly Father, we will have enough. —CPH

> *Hidden in the hollow of His blessed hand,*
> *Never foe can follow, never traitor stand;*
> *Not a surge of worry, not a shade of care,*
> *Not a blast of hurry touch the spirit there.* —Havergal

Money serves us well if we receive it as God's provision.

The Teacher as a Midwife

READ: Galatians 4:12–20

My little children, for whom I labor in birth again
until Christ is formed in you. —GALATIANS 4:19

The mother of the ancient Greek philosopher Socrates was a midwife. So Socrates grew up observing that she assisted women in bringing new life into the world. This experience later influenced his teaching method. Socrates said, "My art of midwifery is in general like theirs; the only difference is that my patients are men, not women, and my concern is not with the body but with the soul that is in travail of birth."

Instead of just passing information on to his students, Socrates used the sometimes painful process of asking probing questions to help them arrive at their own conclusions. Teaching them to think seemed at times like the travail of childbirth.

Paul expressed a similar idea in discipling believers in the faith when he said, "My little children, for whom I labor in birth again until Christ is formed in you" (Galatians 4:19). Paul was concerned that each believer grow to spiritual maturity in Christlikeness (Ephesians 4:13).

Becoming like Christ is a lifelong experience; therefore, we need patience with others and ourselves. All of us will have challenges and disappointments along the way. But if we put our trust in Him, we'll grow spiritually and have character qualities that will radiate new life.
—DF

Lord, help us see how much we need each other
As we walk along the Christian way;
In fellowship with sister and with brother,
You will keep us growing day by day. —Hess

Conversion is the miracle of a moment; maturing takes a lifetime.

Love Believes All Things

READ: 1 Corinthians 13

[Love] believes all things, hopes all things.
—1 CORINTHIANS 13:7

It was forty years ago or more that I observed a friend of mine showing great affection for someone I considered unworthy of love. I thought my friend was being taken in, and I was afraid he would be disillusioned and saddened in the end. When I expressed my concern, he replied, "When I stand before my Lord, I hope He'll say of me that I've loved too many, rather than too few." I've never forgotten his words.

Paul insists that "[love] believes all things" (1 Corinthians 13:7). Love "believes" in people. It can see the potential in them. It believes that God can take the most unattractive and unworthy individual and turn that person into a masterpiece of beauty and grace. If love errs, it must err in the way of trustfulness and hopefulness.

Certainly, we must be aware of danger when we see it coming, and become "as wise as serpents" (Matthew 10:16). Tough love may be the best response to irresponsible and foolish people. But we can be too guarded, too wary and distrustful.

It's better to believe in someone and have your heart broken than to have no heart at all. British poet Alfred Tennyson wrote, " 'Tis better to have loved and lost than never to have loved at all." I agree.   —DR

Lord, help us to believe in people
And all that in them You can do,
So we can say we've loved too many,
Rather than too few. —Sper

Love looks beyond what people are to what they can become.

Nailed to the Cross

READ: Colossians 2:9–17

[Jesus] has made [you] alive together with Him,
having forgiven you all trespasses. —COLOSSIANS 2:13

It was a touching church service. Our pastor talked about Jesus taking our sins upon himself and dying in our place to take our punishment. He asked if anyone still felt guilt over confessed sins and was therefore not enjoying the forgiveness of God.

We were to write the sin or sins on a piece of paper, walk to the front of the church, and nail the paper to the cross that was placed there. Many went forward, and you could hear the pounding of nails for several minutes. That act didn't give us forgiveness, of course, but it was a physical reminder that Jesus had already taken those sins on himself as He hung on the cross and died.

That's what the apostle Paul taught the church at Colosse. The people were being influenced by false teachers who presented Christ as less than adequate for their needs. But Paul explained that Jesus paid the price for our sins. He said, "The handwriting of requirements that was against us, . . . He has taken it out of the way, having nailed it to the cross" (Colossians 2:14).

If we confess our sin to God, seeking His cleansing, He will forgive (1 John 1:9). We don't need to hold on to the guilt. Our sins have been nailed to the cross; they've been taken away. Jesus has forgiven them all.

—AC

Lord, give me courage to confess,
To bare my sinful heart to Thee;
Thy full forgiveness I would know
And from this weight of guilt be free. —D. DeHaan

Guilt is a burden God never intended His children to bear.

Beware of Jumping to Conclusions

READ: Joshua 22:10–34

Do not hasten in your spirit to be angry, for anger rests in the bosom of fools. —ECCLESIASTES 7:9

The e-mail contained nothing but Bible verses, and it came from someone I didn't know very well at a time when there was disagreement among members of a church committee I was on. I assumed that the verses were aimed at me in an accusing way, and I was angry that someone who didn't know all the issues involved would use Scripture to attack me.

Before I could retaliate with a response, my husband, Jay, suggested I give the person the benefit of the doubt instead of assuming the worst. "Perhaps there's an innocent explanation," he said. I couldn't imagine what it would be, but I followed his advice and called the person.

"Thank you so much for calling," she said. "My computer has a virus and it spewed out e-mails using pieces of our Sunday school lesson to random people in my address book." Gulp. I'm thankful that God used Jay to keep me from creating a problem where none existed.

By jumping to a conclusion that was logical but untrue, I came dangerously close to unnecessary conflict. The Israelites did the same thing. They were ready to go to war because they wrongly assumed that the altar built by their brothers was a sign of rebellion against God (Joshua 22:9–34).

To avoid making wrong judgments, we must be careful to get the facts right. —JAL

When you're forming your opinions,
Do it carefully—go slow;
Hasty judgments oft are followed
By regretting—that I know. —Anonymous

To avoid an embarrassing fall, don't jump to a wrong conclusion.

Struggling to Kneel

READ: Colossians 4:1–12

Always laboring fervently for you in prayers, that you may stand perfect and complete in all the will of God. —COLOSSIANS 4:12

Just before John Ashcroft was being sworn in as a US senator, he met with family and friends for prayer. As they gathered around him, he saw his dad trying to get up from the couch where he sat. Since his father was in frail health, Ashcroft told him, "That's okay, Dad. You don't have to stand up to pray for me."

His father replied, "I'm not struggling to stand up. I'm struggling to kneel."

His father's effort reminds me of the exertion it sometimes takes to intercede for a fellow believer. In Colossians, Paul refers to Epaphras as a bondservant who is "always laboring fervently for you in prayers, that you may stand perfect and complete in all the will of God" (4:12). "Laboring fervently" is the translation of a Greek word from which we get our word *agony*. It was used of wrestlers who in the Greek gymnastic games strained to overcome an opponent.

Epaphras interceded for other believers to become mature in their walk with the Savior. Asking God to overcome obstacles to spiritual growth in the lives of others requires our concentration and discipline. Are we willing to labor "fervently" in prayer to ask God to meet the needs of our loved ones?   —DF

> There's a holy, high vocation
> Needing workers everywhere;
> 'Tis the highest form of service,
> 'Tis the ministry of prayer. —Woodworth

Intercessory prayer is life's real work.

The Measure of Love

READ: John 15:9–17

Greater love has no one than this, than to lay down one's life for his friends. —JOHN 15:13

On October 2, 1954, First Lieutenant James O. Conway was taking off from Boston Logan Airport, flying a plane that carried a load of munitions. When his plane became airborne, he suddenly lost power over Boston's bay. In an instant, Conway faced a brutal choice: He could eject from the plane and save his own life, or crash the plane into the bay causing his own death. If he ejected, however, the plane would crash into an East Boston neighborhood filled with homes and families. Conway chose to crash the plane into the bay, giving his life for the lives of others.

In John 15:13, Jesus said, "Greater love has no one than this, than to lay down one's life for his friends." Conway was willing to make the ultimate sacrifice to protect others.

Someone once said that "the measure of love is what one is willing to give up for it." God the Father loved so much that He gave up His Son. Christ loved so much that He gave up His life—even taking our sins on himself and dying in our place.

The measure of God's love for you is great. Have you accepted His love personally? —BC

> *When Jesus gave His life for me,*
> *Enduring all the agony*
> *Upon the cross of Calvary,*
> *He showed the love of God.* —Sper

Nothing speaks more clearly of God's love than the cross of Christ.

Expectancy

READ: Matthew 7:7–11

*If you . . . know how to give good gifts to your children,
how much more will your Father who is in heaven give
good things to those who ask Him!* —MATTHEW 7:11

With a handful of Cheerios, I tiptoed across the deck in my back-yard trying to sneak up on the fish in the pond. Perhaps it was my shadow on the water, or maybe I wasn't as sneaky as I thought, because as I approached the railing, fifteen enormous goldfish raced toward me, their large mouths frantically opening and closing in eager anticipation of an expected treat.

So, why did the fish so furiously flap their fins? Because my mere presence set off a conditioned response in their tiny fish brains that told them I had something special to give them.

If only we always had such a response to God and His desire to give us good gifts—a response based on our past experience with Him that flows from a deep-seated knowledge of His character.

Missionary William Carey stated: "Expect great things from God. Attempt great things for God." God desires to equip us perfectly for what He wants us to do, and He invites us to "come boldly" to find mercy and grace in time of need (Hebrews 4:16).

When we as God's children are living in faith, we can have an exciting expectancy and a quiet confidence that God will give us exactly what we need, when we need it (Matthew 7:8–11).   —CHK

When with expectancy we pray
According to God's will,
We'll see Him working in our lives
His purpose to fulfill. —Sper

Prayer without expectancy is unbelief in disguise.

Music of the Soul

READ: Ephesians 5:15–21

Speaking to one another in psalms and hymns and spiritual songs, singing and making melody in your heart to the Lord.
—EPHESIANS 5:19

In his book *Musicophilia: Tales of Music and the Brain*, Oliver Sacks devotes a chapter to the therapeutic role of music with people suffering from Alzheimer's. He writes of watching people with advanced dementia respond to songs that bring back memories that had seemed lost to them: "Faces assume expression as the old music is recognized and its emotional power felt. One or two people, perhaps, start to sing along, others join them and soon the entire group—many of them virtually speechless before—is singing together, as much as they are able."

I have seen this occur at Sunday morning services in the Alzheimer's care facility where my wife's mother lives. Perhaps you've experienced it with a loved one whose mind is clouded, yet a song calls forth an awareness from deep within.

Paul encouraged the Christians in Ephesus to "be filled with the Spirit, speaking to one another in psalms and hymns and spiritual songs, singing and making melody in your heart to the Lord" (Ephesians 5:18–19). Songs that glorify God can reach the deepest level where the meaning never fades. More than words, harmony, or conscious thought, such music is good for the heart and soul.   —DM

> *There's wondrous music in my soul*
> *Since Jesus' blood has made me whole;*
> *Now my heart sings His songs of praise*
> *For all His blessings all my days.* —Hess

A heart in tune with God can't help but sing His praise.

Distortion

READ: 1 Corinthians 2

*Your faith should not be in the wisdom of men
but in the power of God.* —1 CORINTHIANS 2:5

Cartographers (mapmakers) must deal with the problem of distortion when they display the round shape of the earth on the flat surface of a map. Since there is no perfect way to do this, some world maps depict Greenland as larger than Australia.

Christians have to deal with the problem of distortion as well. When we try to understand the spiritual realm within the limitations of the physical world, we can end up exaggerating minor things and minimizing important things.

The New Testament often addresses the distortion that results when the ideas of popular teachers become more important to us than what God says. God's purpose, said the apostle Paul, is "love from a pure heart, from a good conscience, and from sincere faith" (1 Timothy 1:5). Sound teaching does not distort God's Word or divide the church. Rather, it unites believers and builds up the body of Christ to care for one another and to do the work of God in the world (1 Corinthians 12:25).

All human attempts to explain God are inadequate, and can even distort our priorities, confuse our thinking, and flatten our understanding of the spiritual life. To keep from distorting God's truth, we must rely on God's power rather than man's wisdom (1 Corinthians 2:5).

—JAL

This mortal life is far too brief,
Eternity too vast,
To follow human sophistries
And lose the soul at last. —*Clayburn*

To detect error, expose it to the light of God's truth.

Goats for Jesus

READ: 1 John 3:16–20

Whoever has this world's goods, and sees his brother in need, and shuts up his heart from him, how does the love of God abide in him?
—1 JOHN 3:17

When Dave and Joy Mueller felt God prompting them to move to Sudan as missionaries, all they knew was that they would be helping to build a hospital in that war-ravaged land. How could they know that goats would be in their future?

As Joy began working with the women, she discovered that many were widows because of the devastating civil war, and they had no way to earn a living. So Joy had an idea. If she could provide just one pregnant goat to a woman, that person would have milk and a source of income. To keep the program going, the woman would give the newborn kid back to Joy, but all other products from the goat would be used to support the woman's family. And the baby goat would eventually go to another family. The gift of goats given in Jesus' name would change the life of numerous Sudanese women—and open the door for Joy to explain the gospel.

What is your equivalent to goats? What can you give a neighbor, a friend, or even someone you don't know? Is it a ride? An offer to do yard work? A gift of material resources?

As believers in Christ, we have the responsibility to care for the needs of others (1 John 3:17). Our acts of love reveal that Jesus resides in our hearts, and giving to those in need may help us tell others about Him.
—DB

O Lord, my heart is filled with love
For others who have urgent needs
So help me share in every way
What I can give through words and deeds. —Hess

God gives us all we need, so let's give to others in their need.

Worth Dying For

READS: Philippians 1:19–26

For to me, to live is Christ, and to die is gain.
—PHILIPPIANS 1:21

Sophie Scholl was a young German woman during the 1940s. She saw the deterioration of her country under the iron rule of the Nazi regime, and she determined to make a difference. She and her brother, with a small group of friends, began to peacefully protest not only the actions but the values that the Nazis had forced upon the nation.

Sophie and others were arrested and executed for speaking out against the evil in their land. Although she wasn't anxious to die, she saw that the conditions in her country had to be addressed—even if it meant her death.

Sophie's story raises a critical question for us as well. What would we be willing to die for? Jim Elliot, Nate Saint, Pete Fleming, Roger Youderian, and Ed McCully gave their lives in the jungles of South America because they were committed to spreading the gospel. Elliot revealed the heart that drove such sacrifice when he wrote, "He is no fool who gives what he cannot keep to gain that which he cannot lose." The apostle Paul put it this way: "For to me, to live is Christ, and to die is gain" (Philippians 1:21).

Some things really are worth dying for—and in them we gain the reward of the One who declares, "Well done, good and faithful servant" (Matthew 25:21, 23).   —BC

> *Forbid it, Lord, that I should be*
> *Afraid of persecution's frown;*
> *For You have promised faithful ones*
> *That they shall wear the victor's crown.* —Bosch

Those who faithfully bear the cross in this
life will wear the crown in the life to come.

Are You Distracted?

READ: Luke 10:38–42

Martha was distracted with much serving.
—LUKE 10:40

In data collected from over 20,000 Christians in 139 countries, The Obstacles to Growth Survey found that, on average, more than 40 percent of Christians around the world say they "often" or "always" rush from task to task. About 60 percent of Christians say that it's "often" or "always" true that the busyness of life gets in the way of developing their relationship with God. It's clear that busyness does distract us from our fellowship with Him.

It seems that Martha too allowed busyness to distract her from spending time with Jesus. When she welcomed Him and His disciples into her home, she was occupied with preparing the food, washing their feet, and making sure they were comfortable. All of these things had to be done, but Luke seems to intimate that Martha's busyness in preparation degenerated into busywork that distracted her from reflecting on Jesus' words and enjoying time with Him (Luke 10:38–42).

What about us? Are we rushing from task to task, allowing the busyness of life and even work for Jesus to distract us from enjoying sweet fellowship with Him? Let's ask God to help us diminish our distractions by making Jesus our focus.   —MW

Lord, I don't want to miss out on moments of intimacy with you. Help me not to be so busy that I fail to devote time each day to prayer and reading your Word. Amen.

If you are too busy for God, you are too busy.

Understand One Another

READ: Proverbs 16:16–22

Counsel in the heart of man is like deep water, but a man of understanding will draw it out. —PROVERBS 20:5

One of the best ways for a man to love his wife is to understand her. Peter explains that it is imperative for a husband to "dwell with [his wife] with understanding" (1 Peter 3:7).

This principle works both ways. Husbands want to be understood as well. Actually, we all do. Everyone, married or not, longs to be understood by others at the deepest possible level. We're born with that need, and we never seem to outgrow it.

It's feeble avoidance to say we can't understand one another. We can and we must. It takes time—time spent in one another's presence asking questions, listening intently, then asking again. It's as simple and as difficult as that.

No one, of course, can fully plumb the mystery of another person's heart, but we can learn something new every day. The wise man of Proverbs called understanding "a wellspring of life" (16:22), a deep source of wisdom to all who seek it.

Again, I say, understanding takes time—one of the most precious gifts we can give to others. How we choose to spend our time is the surest indicator of how much we care for those we love.

Ask the Lord today to give you the grace to take the time to understand the important people in your life.   —DR

> *To those whose lives we touch in life,*
> *To whom our love we would impart,*
> *The greatest gift that we can give*
> *May be an understanding heart.* —Branon

Listening is an open door to understanding.

Déjà Vu All Over Again

READ: John 21:1–14

*After these things Jesus showed Himself again to
the disciples at the Sea of Tiberias.* —JOHN 21:1

Baseball legend Yogi Berra is known for his oft-repeated quips like, "It ain't over till it's over" and "It's like déjà vu all over again!"

I wonder if the disciples felt déjà vu when they saw Jesus standing by the shore (John 21). Discouraged and distracted by their own needs in the shadow of Peter's denial and their desertion of Jesus, they had abandoned their calling to follow Jesus and returned to their previous occupation—fishing.

Then, after a fruitless night of fishing, a voice from the shore called out, "Cast the net on the right side of the boat, and you will find some" (21:6). When they did, the nets were so full that they couldn't be dragged in. No doubt their minds raced back to their first encounter with Jesus—when He showed up on the shore of their careers and, after another miraculous catch of fish, called them to leave their nets and follow Him (Luke 5:1–11).

Like the disciples, we may want to return to our own agendas when we get discouraged in our walk with Jesus. But then Jesus shows up again on the shore of our lives to extend forgiveness and to draw us back to those moments when He first called us.

It's like déjà vu all over again! —JS

*Son of the living God! Oh, call us
Once and again to follow Thee;
And give us strength, whate'er befall us,
Thy true disciples still to be.* —Martin

Jesus calls us to follow Him—and repeats His call when necessary.

Sorry About the Tears

READ: John 11:32–44

[Jesus] groaned in the spirit and was troubled.
—JOHN 11:33

My friend was making a major change in her life. She was leaving her employer of fifty years for a new venture. She cried when she said her goodbyes. And as she did, she frequently said, "Sorry about the tears."

Why do we sometimes feel the need to apologize for crying? Perhaps we look at tears as showing a weakness in our character or a vulnerability we don't like. Maybe we're uncomfortable or think our tears are making others uncomfortable.

Our emotions, however, are God-given. They're a characteristic of our having been made in God's image (Genesis 1:27). God grieves. God was sorrowful and angry about His people's sin and the separation it caused between Him and them (Genesis 6:6–7). Jesus, God in the flesh, joined His friends Mary and Martha in grieving over the loss of their brother Lazarus (John 11:28–44). "He groaned in the spirit and was troubled" (v. 33). He "wept" (v. 35). "Jesus, again groaning in Himself, came to the tomb" (v. 38). I doubt that He apologized.

Someday when we get to heaven, there will be no more sorrow or separation or pain, and God will wipe away every tear from our eyes (Revelation 21:4). In the meantime, the tears may flow. No apologies needed.　　　　　　　　　　　　　　　　　　　　　　—AC

> *He knows our burdens and our crosses,*
> *Those things that hurt, our trials and losses,*
> *He cares for every soul that cries,*
> *God wipes the tears from weeping eyes.* —Brandt

If you doubt that Jesus cares, remember His tears.

Speaking the Truth

READ: 2 Chronicles 24:15–22

He sent prophets to them, . . . but they
would not listen. —2 CHRONICLES 24:19

In the novel *To Kill a Mockingbird*, Atticus Finch is a respected small-town lawyer in the segregated South during the 1930s. When he takes on a case that pits an innocent black man against two dishonest white people, Atticus knows he will face terrible prejudice from the jury. But his conscience compels him to speak the truth boldly in the face of opposition.

The Old Testament prophets were often sent to preach the truth to a stubborn people. "[God] sent prophets to them, to bring them back to the Lord; and they testified against them, but they would not listen" (2 Chronicles 24:19). Their message often resulted in persecution and sometimes even death (Hebrews 11:32–38).

During Christ's ministry on earth, His message also resulted in angry opposition (Luke 4:21–30). Yet, in the sovereignty of God, the terrible miscarriage of justice that sentenced Jesus to death on the cross purchased our redemption.

Now, as representatives of the risen Christ in this world, we are to promote reconciliation, justice, and integrity (Micah 6:8; 2 Corinthians 5:18–21). And in so doing, this may mean speaking the truth in the face of opposition. This is the charge to every believer until that day when Christ sets all things right (Revelation 20:11–15). —DF

The life that counts must toil and fight,
Must hate the wrong and love the right;
Must stand for truth, by day, by night—
This is the life that counts. —Anonymous

It's better to declare the truth and be rejected
than to withhold the truth just to be accepted.

Go Beyond Reading

READ: Colossians 3:12–17

As the elect of God, holy and beloved, put on tender mercies, kindness . . . longsuffering. —COLOSSIANS 3:12

"Pastor, where are the *Our Daily Bread* devotionals?" The words came harshly—almost in anger. The latest edition had not yet been placed in the rack outside the church auditorium. This led at least one reader to confront the pastor about their absence. Although it was not the pastor's responsibility to distribute the booklets, he felt terrible about the way this parishioner had reprimanded him for not making sure the devotional guides were there on time.

When I heard this, I was struck by the irony of this situation. Devotional booklets are meant to encourage Christian growth and godly grace. And as followers of Christ who read devotional materials, we hope we are moving toward spiritual maturity that leads to "tender mercies, kindness, humility, meekness, longsuffering"—qualities Paul says we should "put on" (Colossians 3:12).

Our spiritual disciplines—reading God's Word along with accompanying study or devotional materials, prayer, and worshiping together—should not be ends in themselves. Instead, those actions are means to becoming more Christlike, more godly, more Spirit-led. Our spiritual practice should lead to having the "Word of Christ dwell in [us] richly" (3:16). That will show in everything we do and say.   —DB

> *I want my heart to be in tune with God,*
> *In every stage of life may it ring true;*
> *I want my thoughts and words to honor Him,*
> *Exalting Him in everything I do.* —Hess

Bible study is not merely to inform us; it's meant to transform us.

Details, Details

READ: Philemon 1:4–16

In everything give thanks. —1 THESSALONIANS 5:18

Details make a difference. Ask the man from Germany who planned to visit his fiancée for Christmas but ended up in snowy Sidney, Montana, instead of sunny Sydney, Australia.

Prepositions in our language seem like insignificant details, but they can make a big difference. The words "in" and "for" are an example.

The apostle Paul wrote, "*In* everything give thanks" (1 Thessalonians 5:18). That doesn't mean we have to be thankful *for* everything. We need not be thankful *for* the bad choices someone makes, but we can be thankful *in* the circumstances because the Lord can use the resulting difficulties for good.

The letter to Philemon illustrates this idea. Paul was imprisoned with Onesimus, a runaway slave. He certainly didn't have to give thanks for his bad situation. Yet his letter is full of gratitude because he knew that God was using it for good. Onesimus had become something more than a slave; he was now a beloved brother in the Lord (v. 16).

Knowing that God can use all things for good is more than enough reason to give thanks in everything. Giving thanks in difficult circumstances is a small detail that makes a big difference.   —JAL

Father, thank you that in every trial, challenge, and difficulty, you are behind the scenes working things out for our good. Help us to see your hand in everything. Amen.

God has not promised to keep us from life's
storms, but He will keep us through them.

Olympic Extravaganza

READ: 1 Kings 10:4–10

Let your light so shine before men, that they may see your
good works and glorify your Father in heaven. —MATTHEW 5:16

The opening ceremony of the Beijing Summer Olympics on August 8, 2008, impressed the world. I saw it on TV as more than 90,000 people watched it live in the Bird's Nest Stadium in Beijing. It was inspiring to hear about China's 5,000 years of history and the inventions she had contributed to the world: papermaking, movable-type printing, the compass, and fireworks.

The Queen of Sheba was greatly impressed by what she saw during her visit with Solomon (1 Kings 10:4–5). The sights of Jerusalem so overwhelmed her that she exclaimed, "The half was not told me" (v. 7). Above all, she was impressed with Solomon's wisdom (vv. 6–7). She was convinced that the people in Solomon's kingdom were happy because they continually stood before him and heard his wisdom (v. 8). She concluded by praising Solomon's Lord for making him king so he would "do justice and righteousness" (v. 9).

Solomon's impact on his people makes me wonder about our contribution to the world. Do we want to make a difference in the lives of others? What if we did just one thing today that would cause someone to praise the Lord? —CPH

This is the wish I always wish,
The prayer I always pray:
Lord, may my life help others
It touches on the way. —Anonymous

Christians are windows through which Jesus can shine.

Be Still

READ: Psalm 46

Be still, and know that I am God; I will be exalted among the nations, I will be exalted in the earth! —PSALM 46:10

As I sat in the dentist's chair, I braced myself for the drilling that would begin my root canal. I was ready for the worst, and my body language and facial expression exposed my sense of dread. The dentist looked at me and smiled, saying, "It's okay, Bill. Try to relax."

That isn't easy to do. It is actually very difficult *to try* (requiring effort and exertion) *to relax* (requiring an absence of effort and exertion). *Try* and *relax* just don't seem to fit together—not only in the dentist's chair, but in the spiritual realm as well.

Far too often I don't limit my efforts of resistance to visits at the dentist's office. In my relationship with Christ, I find myself not pressing for God's purposes but for my own interests. In those moments, the hardest thing for me to do is "try to relax" and genuinely trust God for the outcome of life's trials.

In Psalm 46:10 we read, "Be still, and know that I am God; I will be exalted among the nations, I will be exalted in the earth!" In the moments when my heart is anxious, this verse reminds me to "be still, and know." Now, if I can only put that into practice and rest confidently in His care, I'll be at peace.   —BC

Lord, we know that true rest can be found only in you. Help us to end our striving and to trust that you will provide. In your loving arms we find rest. Amen.

God knows the future, so we are safe in His hands.

Conflict Resolution

READ: Philippians 4:1–9

*I implore Euodia and I implore Syntyche to be
of the same mind in the Lord.* —PHILIPPIANS 4:2

The third Thursday of October is observed in many countries as International Conflict Resolution Day. Its purpose is to encourage people to use mediation and arbitration rather than the legal system to settle their differences. Because we as followers of Christ are not immune to conflict, we need to learn how to resolve our disagreements in ways that honor the Lord.

It has been said that "church fights are the worst fights," perhaps because they break out among people who profess to believe in unity and love. Many Christians have been so hurt by fellow believers that they walk away from the church and never return.

Euodia and Syntyche are mentioned by name in the Bible and urged to resolve their differences: "Be of the same mind in the Lord" (Philippians 4:2). Instead of leaving them alone to settle their dispute, Paul appealed to a trusted fellow worker to "help these women who labored with me in the gospel" (v. 3). In this same context, Paul urged the Philippians to bring their requests to God, noting that prayer brings the peace of God (v. 7) and a sense of His abiding presence (v. 9).

Fractured relationships in a Christian community are a community responsibility. In the midst of hurts and differences, we can encourage, listen, and pray. —DM

Forgiveness is the glue that repairs broken relationships.

OCTOBER 16

The Defeat of Death

READ: 1 Thessalonians 4:15–18

Thanks be to God, who gives us the victory through our Lord Jesus Christ. —1 CORINTHIANS 15:57

Christian faith ought to make a difference in how we live from day to day. But the final test of our trust in the gospel is how we react in the face of death. When we attend a memorial service for a departed friend who loved the Lord Jesus, we gather to honor a believer whose stalwart trust has richly blessed the lives of those who knew him. The words spoken are more an expression of praise to God than a tribute to an admired fellow pilgrim. The service is a God-glorifying testimony to our Savior's victory over death and the grave (1 Corinthians 15:54–57).

How different from the funeral service of Charles Bradlaugh, a belligerent British atheist. Writer Arthur Porritt recalls: "No prayer was said at the grave. Indeed, not a single word was uttered. The remains, placed in a light coffin, were lowered into the earth in a quite unceremonious fashion as if carrion were being hustled out of sight. . . . I came away heart-frozen. It only then dawned on me that loss of faith in the continuity of human personality after death gives death an appalling victory."

Christians, however, believe in a face-to-face fellowship with our Lord after death and the eventual resurrection of our bodies (1 Corinthians 15:42–55; 1 Thessalonians 4:15–18). Does your faith rejoice in victory over death? —VG

(Dr. Vernon Grounds entered the Lord's presence on September 12, 2010, at the age of 96.)

From earth's wide bounds and ocean's farthest coast,
Through gates of pearl stream in the countless host,
Singing to Father, Son, and Holy Ghost—
Alleluia! Alleluia! —How

Because Christ is alive, we too shall live.

On Shoulders of Giants

READ: Joshua 1:1–9

As I was with Moses, so I will be with you. —JOSHUA 1:5

Giants hold a special place in our lore, both historical and literary. From the real giant Goliath to the fictional giant of *Jack and the Beanstalk* fame, we are fascinated by these larger-than-life characters.

Sometimes we use the word giant to honor ordinary-size people who have done extraordinary things. One example is the seventeenth-century physicist Sir Isaac Newton. A committed Christian, he credited his success to other "giants" who had gone before. "If I have seen a little further," he said, "it is by standing on the shoulders of giants." Indeed, Newton became a giant on whose shoulders later scientists stood—even as they used his observations in the conquest of space flight.

When God commanded Joshua to lead the Israelites into the Promised Land, Joshua certainly had a giant's shoulders to stand on. He had watched Moses' leadership for forty years, and now he would put what he had learned into action.

Joshua had another advantage: his walk with God sustained his life's mission. Therefore, he had both Moses' example and God's promised presence as he led Israel.

Looking for help as you face the future? Look for a giant to follow. And never underestimate the importance of your walk with God.

—DF

There is a destiny that makes us brothers:
None goes his way alone;
All that we send into the lives of others
Comes back into our own. —Markham

A good example is someone who knows
the way, goes the way, and shows the way.

Teach Your Children Well

READ: Deuteronomy 11:13–21

You shall teach [God's Word] to your children . . . when you sit in your house, when you walk by the way, when you lie down, and when you rise up. —DEUTERONOMY 11:19

The *Sleeping Beauty Waltz*, the *1812 Overture*, and *The Nutcracker Suite* were all part of the music of my childhood. Sometimes a narrator told stories or, as in the case of *Tubby the Tuba* and *Peter and the Wolf*, introduced my sisters and me to the sounds of different instruments. In their desire to pass on their love for music, my parents used this method as a teaching tool. It worked! Weaving the classic tales with classical tunes made a powerful impact on us.

When an adult wants to impart important information to a child, it's often best related in a story because it is more easily understood and enjoyed. Telling children the stories in God's Word is especially crucial because the Bible's enduring truth can shape character and show consequences of actions (1 Corinthians 10:11). Tiny seeds of faith can be cultivated in fertile soil and help children to see how God has worked in the lives of His followers throughout history. Bible stories also show how God is intimately involved in our lives.

What we have seen God do for us and what He has done for His people throughout history must be passed on to the next generation (Deuteronomy 11:1–21). Their future depends on it. Teach your children well. —CHK

Tell me the story of Jesus,
Write on my heart every word;
Tell me the story most precious,
Sweetest that ever was heard! —Crosby

The character of your children tomorrow
depends on what you put into their hearts today.

Retirement Time

READ: Matthew 16:24–28

Whoever loses his life for My sake will find it.
—MATTHEW 16:25

After working for forty years as a teacher, Jane Hanson retired. She and her husband were looking forward to the arrival of their first grandchild.

Retirement is that time of life when many people simply relax, travel, or enjoy hobbies. But Jane heard about a ministry to at-risk youth in a city near her home, and she knew she had to get involved. "I realized there are kids just waiting, and I could make a difference," she said. She began teaching English to a young Liberian man who had been forced to flee his home country because of civil war. Though he was in a safe environment, he didn't understand the new language. Of this ministry opportunity, Jane said with a smile, "I could just go shopping to stay busy, but what fun would that be?"

Jane is making a difference. Perhaps she has learned a little of what Jesus meant when He said, "Whoever desires to save his life will lose it, but whoever loses his life for My sake will find it" (Matthew 16:25). Giving ourselves to the Lord through helping others takes self-denial, yet one day Jesus will reward that effort (v. 27).

Let's follow Jane's example of love for God and others, no matter what our stage of life may be. —AC

> *Oh, let us be faithful to Jesus,*
> *The faith we confessed let's renew,*
> *And ask Him this question each morning:*
> *"Lord, what will You have me to do?"* —Pangborn

Work for the Lord—His retirement plan is out of this world.

Peace in the Storm

READ: Isaiah 26:1–4

You will keep him in perfect peace, whose mind is stayed on You, because he trusts in You. —ISAIAH 26:3

Life can seem unbearable at times. Physical pain, difficult decisions, financial hardships, the death of a loved one, or shattered dreams threaten to engulf us. We become fearful and perplexed. Plagued by doubts, we may even find it difficult to pray.

Nevertheless, those of us who know the Lord through personal faith in Christ have in Him a calm retreat in the storms of life, even while the howling winds of trial are sweeping over us. We can experience peace of mind and calmness of spirit.

Richard Fuller, a nineteenth-century minister, told of an old seaman who said, "In fierce storms, we must put the ship in a certain position and keep her there." Said Fuller, "This, Christian, is what you must do. . . . You must put your soul in one position and keep it there. You must stay upon the Lord; and, come what may—winds, waves, cross seas, thunder, lightning, frowning rocks, roaring breakers—no matter what, you must hold fast your confidence in God's faithfulness and His everlasting love in Christ Jesus."

Do you feel overwhelmed by your troubles? Learn a lesson from that old sailor. Fix your mind on the Lord. Ask for His help. Then trust Him to give you peace in your storm (Philippians 4:6–7).   —RD

> *Stayed upon Jehovah,*
> *Hearts are fully blest—*
> *Finding, as He promised,*
> *Perfect peace and rest.* —Havergal

The secret of peace is to give every anxious care to God.

Who Goes There?

READ: John 10:1–6

When he brings out his own sheep, he goes before
them; and the sheep follow him. —JOHN 10:4

Last fall my wife, Carolyn, and I were driving up a winding mountain road near our home in Idaho when we came across a large flock of sheep moving down the road toward us. A lone shepherd with his dogs was in the vanguard, leading his flock out of summer pasture into the lowlands and winter quarters.

We pulled to the side of the road and waited while the flock swirled around us. As we watched them until they were out of sight, I wondered: *Do sheep fear change, movement, new places?*

Like most older folks, I like the "fold"—the old, familiar places. But all is shifting and changing these days; I'm being led out, away from familiar surroundings and into a vast unknown. What new limits will overtake me in the coming days? What nameless fears will awaken? Jesus' words from John 10 come to mind: "When he brings out his own sheep, he goes before them" (v. 4).

We may well be dismayed at what life has for us this year or next, but our Shepherd knows the way we're taking. And He goes before. He will not lead us down paths too dangerous or too arduous where He cannot help us. He knows our limits. He knows the way to green pasture and good water; all we have to do is follow. —DR

Child of My love, fear not the unknown morrow,
Dread not the new demand life makes of thee;
Thy ignorance doth hold no cause for sorrow
Since what thou knowest not is known to Me. —Exeley

Our unknown future is secure in the hands of our all-knowing God.

Failing Memory

READ: Psalm 119:33–40

Turn away my eyes from looking at worthless things, and revive me in Your way. —PSALM 119:37

A *New York Times* article linked the increase of computer storage with the decrease of data in the human mind. Our electronic aids now remember phone numbers, driving directions, and other information we used to learn by repeated use. In schools, memorization and oral recitation are disappearing from the curriculum. We have become, according to the *Times*, "products of a culture that does not enforce the development of memory skills."

Yet never have we as followers of Christ been in greater need of hiding God's Word in our hearts (Psalm 119:9–11). Scripture memory is more than a helpful mental exercise. The goal is to saturate our minds with God's truth so that our lives will conform to His ways. The psalmist wrote: "Teach me, O Lord, the way of Your statutes, and I shall keep it to the end. . . . Turn away my eyes from looking at worthless things, and revive me in Your way" (33, 37).

Why not begin committing Scripture to memory? Daily consistency and review are keys to success. And just like physical exercise, this spiritual discipline is enhanced when done with a small group or with a friend.

Let's not forget to remember and follow the life-giving wisdom of God's Word.   —DM

> *God's Word will change your life*
> *If you will do your part*
> *To read, to study, and obey,*
> *And hide it in your heart.* —Sper

Let the Bible fill your mind, rule your heart, and guide your life.

Close on His Heels

READ: Matthew 4:18–25

Follow Me, and I will make you fishers of men.
—MATTHEW 4:19

Stan and Jennifer were speaking at a mission conference in Marion, North Carolina, after their first term of service on the field.

Jennifer told of a Bible study she had held with one woman. The two were discussing Matthew 4:19, and the woman told Jennifer about a word in her native language which means "follow." She said, "It is the word for following closely, not at a distance."

To illustrate, Jennifer held up slippers used by the native women, showing one far behind the other. Then she moved one slipper right up against the back of the other one and said that the word means "to follow right on one's heels." It suggests that we are to follow Jesus as closely as possible.

Later, when Jennifer was reading over the journal she had been keeping, she was surprised to see that she had often questioned, "Is Jesus enough?" She had been working her way through culture shock, loneliness, illness, and childlessness. At times she had felt far from Christ. But when through prayer and faith she had drawn as close to Him as she could, walking "right on His heels," He had calmed her soul, restored her strength, and given her peace.

Are you feeling far from the Lord—empty, weak, and afraid? It's time to follow close on His heels. —DE

God, give me the faith of a little child!
A faith that will look to Thee—
That never will falter and never fail,
But follow Thee trustingly. —Showerman

The closer we walk with God, the clearer we see His guidance.

Secrets Exposed

READ: Psalm 32:1–7

I acknowledged my sin to You, and my iniquity I have not hidden. . . . And You forgave the iniquity of my sin.
—PSALM 32:5

For many years, Lake Okeechobee hid its secrets in thick waters and layers of muck. But in 2007, drought shrank the Florida lake to its lowest level since officials began keeping records in 1932, unveiling hundreds of years of history. Raking through the bottom of the lake, archaeologists found artifacts, pottery, human bone fragments, and even boats.

After King David committed adultery with Bathsheba and planned the death of her husband, Uriah, he covered his sins by denying them and not confessing them. He probably went many months conducting business as usual, even performing religious duties. As long as David cloaked his sinful secrets, he experienced God's crushing finger of conviction and his strength evaporated like water in the heat of summer (Psalm 32:3–4).

When the prophet Nathan confronted David about his sin, God's conviction was so great that David confessed his sins to God and turned away from them. Immediately the Lord forgave David and he experienced God's mercy and grace (2 Samuel 12:13; Psalm 32:5; Psalm 51).

Let's be careful not to hide our sin. When we uncover our sins by confessing them to God, we are covered with His forgiveness. —MW

Lord, help me to expose my sin,
Those secret faults that lurk within;
I would confess them all to Thee;
Transparent I would always be. —D. DeHaan

Give God what He desires most—a broken and repentant heart.

Five People You Meet In Heaven

READ: 2 Corinthians 5:6–11

We must all appear before the judgment seat of Christ. —2 CORINTHIANS 5:10

Mitch Albom, author of *The Five People You Meet in Heaven*, said that he got the idea for his book when he speculated: What would heaven be like if it were a place where some of the people you impacted on earth explained your life when you met them in heaven?

Albom's book does give insight into how we unintentionally affect others' lives. But for the Christian, our ultimate joy in eternity does not stem from other people but from our Lord and Savior. Heaven is a real place that Jesus is now preparing for us. And when we get there, we'll rejoice to meet the living Christ (John 14:2–3; 2 Peter 3:13).

This encounter with Jesus, however, will also include accountability for the life we lived on earth. Believers are told: "We must all appear before the judgment seat of Christ, that each one may receive the things done in the body, according to what he has done, whether good or bad" (2 Corinthians 5:10). His wise and just evaluation will show us how well we have loved God and our neighbor (Matthew 22:37–40).

We don't know who will be the first five people we meet in heaven. But we do know who the first One will be—the Lord Jesus.   —DF

When we stand with Christ in glory,
Looking o'er life's finished story,
Then, Lord, shall I fully know—
Not till then—how much I owe. —McCheyne

To be with Jesus forever is the sum of all happiness.

Is That Jesus?

READ: Romans 8:26–29

Whom He foreknew, He also predestined to be conformed to the image of His Son, that He might be the firstborn among many brethren.
—ROMANS 8:29

As I walked into church one Sunday morning, a little boy looked at me and said to his mother, "Mom, is that Jesus?" Needless to say, I was curious to hear her response. "No," she said, "that's our pastor."

I knew she would say no, of course, but I still wished she could have added something like, "No, that's our pastor, but he reminds us a lot of Jesus."

Being like Jesus is the purpose of life for those of us who are called to follow Him. In fact, as John Stott notes, it is the all-consuming goal of our past, our present, and our future. Romans 8:29 tells us that in the past we were "predestined to be conformed to the image of His Son." In the present we "are being transformed into the same image" (the likeness of Christ) as we grow from "glory to glory" (2 Corinthians 3:18). And in the future "we shall be like Him, for we shall see Him as He is" (1 John 3:2).

Being like Jesus is not about keeping the rules, going to church, and tithing. It's about knowing His forgiveness, and committing acts of grace and mercy on a consistent basis. It's about living a life that values all people. And it's about having a heart of full surrender to the will of our Father.

Be like Jesus. You were saved for it!   —JS

> *Be like Jesus—this my song—*
> *In the home and in the throng;*
> *Be like Jesus all day long!*
> *I would be like Jesus.* —Rowe

Live in such a way that others see Jesus in you.

"Light" of Creation

READ: Job 37:1–18

[God] does great things, and unsearchable,
marvelous things without number. —Job 5:9

Among the wonders of Jamaica is a body of water called Luminous Lagoon. By day, it is a nondescript bay on the country's northern coast. By night, it is a marvel of nature.

If you visit there after dark, you notice that the water is filled with millions of phosphorescent organisms. Whenever there is movement, the water and the creatures in the bay glow. When fish swim past your boat, for example, they light up like waterborne fireflies. As the boat glides through the water, the wake shines brightly.

The wonder of God's creation leaves us speechless. And this is just a small part of the total mystery package of God's awesome handiwork as spelled out in Job 37 and 38. Listen to what the Lord's role is in nature's majesty: "Do you know how God controls the clouds and makes His lightning flash?" (37:15 NIV); "What is the way to the abode of light? And where does darkness reside?" (38:19 NIV).

God's majestic creations—whether dazzling lightning or glowing fish—are mysteries to us. But as God reminded Job, all of the wonders of our world are His creative handiwork.

When we observe God's amazing creation, our only response can be that of Job: These are "things too wonderful for me" (42:3).   —DB

All things bright and beautiful,
All creatures great and small,
All things wise and wonderful;
The Lord God made them all.   —Alexander

When we cease to wonder, we cease to worship.

Almost-Perfect Disguise

READ: Revelation 12:7–12

The accuser of our brethren, who accused them before our God day and night, has been cast down. —REVELATION 12:10

Radovan Karadzic, once the leader of the Bosnian Serbs and accused of genocide, had been one of the most wanted men in the world. By growing a long, white beard, carrying false papers, and practicing alternative medicine, he fooled everyone—for a while. After thirteen years in hiding, he was finally arrested.

The Bible tells us that Satan is also in the business of fooling people with disguises. Right from the beginning of human history, he pretended to be an enlightened advisor, telling Eve that God was not honest with her (Genesis 3:4). He "masquerades as an angel of light" (2 Corinthians 11:14 NIV), but the Lord Jesus Christ has unmasked him as "a liar and the father of it" (John 8:44).

People often err at two extremes in their view of Satan. Some dismiss him while others attribute more power to him than he deserves. Let us not be deceived. Satan is powerful as the "god of this age" (2 Corinthians 4:4). But Christians need not cower before him in fear, because "He who is in you is greater than he who is in the world" (1 John 4:4). The day is coming when Satan will be cast into the lake of fire (Revelation 20:10).

Until that day, let's not be deceived. Let's live godly lives that reflect the image of Christ, for He is "a man of truth; there is nothing false about Him" (John 7:18 NIV). —CPH

In our day-to-day existence,
Evil often wears a mask;
Trust the Lord for true discernment—
He gives wisdom when we ask. —Hess

Satan offers nothing but tricks and deceit.

Lost and Found

READ: Luke 15:4–24

This my son was dead and is alive again;
he was lost and is found. —LUKE 15:24

A *Wall Street Journal* article by Jennifer Saranow chronicled the extraordinary efforts of middle-aged American men who are trying to find the favorite car they once owned and loved, but lost. They are searching on-line car ads, phoning junkyards, and even hiring specialists who charge $400 an hour to help them search for an automobile that once symbolized their youth. These men want the actual car they owned, not one just like it.

Some would call their efforts frivolous—a waste of time and money. But the value of a car, like many things, is in the eye of the beholder.

In Luke 15, people who were despised by their society came to hear Jesus. But some religious leaders complained, "This Man receives sinners and eats with them" (v. 2). To affirm how valuable these "sinners" are to God, Jesus told three memorable stories about a lost sheep (vv. 4–7), a lost coin (vv. 8–10), and a lost son (vv. 11–32). Each parable records the anguish of losing, the effort of searching, and the joy of finding something of great worth. In every story, we see a picture of God, the loving Father, who rejoices over every lost soul who is found.

Even if you feel far from God today, you are highly valued by Him. He's searching for you.   —DM

I once was lost, but now I'm found;
Praise God! Christ died for me;
He valued me, redeemed my soul;
From sin, He set me free. —Sper

Those who have been found should seek the lost.

Be a Stander

READ: 2 Timothy 4:9–18

A friend loves at all times, and a brother is born for adversity. —PROVERBS 17:17

Western novelist Stephen Bly says that in the days of America's Old West there were two types of friends (and horses): runners and standers. At the first sign of trouble, the runner would bolt, abandoning you to whatever peril you were facing. But a stander would stick with you no matter the circumstances. Unfortunately, you wouldn't know which kind of friend you had until trouble came. And then it was too late—unless your friend was a stander.

Rather than being concerned with what kind of friends we *have*, however, we ought to consider what kind of friends we *are*. In the final days of Paul's ministry, as he awaited death, some who had ministered with him turned into runners and abandoned him to face execution alone. In his last letter, he listed some (like Demas) who had run off, then simply stated, "Only Luke is with me" (2 Timothy 4:11). Luke was a stander. While undoubtedly disappointed by those who had deserted him, Paul must have been deeply comforted to know he was not alone.

Proverbs tells us that "a friend loves at all times" (17:17). During times of adversity, we need friends we can rely on.

When the people we know face trouble, what kind of friend will we be—a runner or a stander?　　　　　　　　　　　　　　　　　—BC

Dear Lord, help us to be the kind of friend who doesn't run when our friends are in need. Give us the courage to stand by them, the wisdom to know what to say, and the ability to serve them. Amen.

A true friend stands with us in times of trial.

Hallowing Halloween

READ: 2 Timothy 2:19–26

He will be a vessel for honor, sanctified and useful for the Master, prepared for every good work. —2 TIMOTHY 2:21

The word hallow isn't used much anymore, and when it is, the uses have a broad range of meaning. Christians use the word when we say the Lord's Prayer, as in "Hallowed be Thy name." And often the word is associated with the last day of October, which we in the US refer to as Halloween, a shortened form of All Hallows' Eve.

In Scripture, the word *hallow* is a synonym for the word *sanctify*. When we hallow or sanctify something, we set it apart as being holy.

The name of God is not the only thing that we are to hallow. We too are to be hallowed. Paul urged Timothy to be a vessel sanctified and useful for God by pursuing "righteousness, faith, love, [and] peace with those who call on the Lord out of a pure heart" and by avoiding "foolish and ignorant disputes, knowing that they generate strife" (2 Timothy 2:21–23).

On this last day of October, many children in the US will be carrying bags filled with sweets. Thinking of them can remind us to ask: "What is filling the vessel of my life? Is it a bitter attitude that leads to foolish disputes and strife, or is it a sweet spirit that leads to righteousness, faith, love, and peace?"

We can hallow today, and every day, by setting ourselves apart for God to be used by Him. —JAL

Lord, may our lives be set apart
And useful in Your hands,
Pursuing righteousness and faith
As we fulfill Your plans. —Sper

A Christian's greatest joy is to be used by God.

An Urge to Be Anonymous

READ: Matthew 6:1–4

When you do a charitable deed, do not let your left hand know what your right hand is doing, that your . . . deed may be in secret.
—MATTHEW 6:3–4

The urge to misbehave and the desire to be anonymous always visit me together. Like partners making a sales call, they do their best to convince me that I can afford to do something wrong because I won't have to pay.

Human nature tells us to use the cover of anonymity to avoid taking the blame for the bad things we do. God, however, tells us something else. He wants us to use anonymity to avoid taking credit for the *good* that we do (Matthew 6:4). So why is it that the urge to remain anonymous seldom accompanies my desire to do good!

The Bible says we're not to let one hand know the good that the other is doing (vv. 3–4). In other words, within the body of Christ our deeds of charity should be done without calling attention to ourselves. This does not mean, however, that God wants good deeds to remain hidden; it just means that they should be done in a way that makes a good name for God, not ourselves (5:16).

When we volunteer our services or make donations to churches and organizations that do good work in the name of Jesus, we receive something much better than honor from our peers. We receive rewards from God, and God receives glory from others! (1 Peter 2:12).   —JAL

> *God bless you and keep you and give you His love;*
> *God prosper your labor with help from above.*
> *Be His strength in your arm and His love in your soul,*
> *His smile your reward and His glory your goal.* —Anonymous

When we serve in Jesus' name, He gets the glory.

Prisoners of Sin

READ: Galatians 3:19–29

The Scripture has confined all under sin, that the promise by faith in Jesus Christ might be given to those who believe. —GALATIANS 3:22

A 2008 report from the United Nations Office on Drugs and Crime said, "At any given time there are more than ten million people imprisoned worldwide." Since some prisoners are being released while new ones are being sentenced every day, there are more than thirty million total prisoners worldwide each year. Statistics like these have caused many people to work for prison reform and a reexamination of sentencing laws.

From a spiritual perspective, the Bible offers an even more staggering statistic: "The Scripture declares that the *whole world* is a prisoner of sin" (Galatians 3:22 NIV). In what is sometimes considered a difficult passage to understand, Paul says that although the Old Testament law could not impart life (v. 21), it was an effective teacher in showing us that we need a Savior who can give life (v. 24). The bad news is that "the Scripture has confined all under sin," and the good news is "that the promise by faith in Jesus Christ might be given to those who believe" (v. 22).

When we give our lives to Christ, who has fulfilled the requirements of the law, we are no longer imprisoned by sin. Instead, we enter a fellowship of people from every nationality and social status.

In Christ, we are free indeed! —DM

The law reveals the mind of God,
The prophets too made clear His will;
But Christ alone brings life and peace,
His words our deepest needs fulfill. —D. DeHaan

Deliverance from sin is the greatest of all freedoms.

Helped by Fear

READ: Proverbs 9:1–12

The fear of the Lord is the beginning of wisdom, and the knowledge of the Holy One is understanding. —PROVERBS 9:10

Fear means different things to different people. To professional golfer Padraig Harrington, it is a motivator to help him perform his very best. In 2008, when he won both the British Open and the PGA Championship, Harrington said, "Yes, fear is a big part of me. I'd like to say that I have all the trust and patience and I'm relaxed. No, that's not my makeup. [Fear] pushes me on. Keeps me getting to the gym. I have to work with it and use it."

Maybe it's the fear of failure, or the fear of losing his edge, but Harrington finds fear to be a useful thing in his professional life.

The follower of Christ can also be helped by fear. We are challenged in the Scriptures to a reverential fear of God, which is the best type of fear that there is. It causes us to be concerned about disobeying Him or living in opposition to His ways. It's being in awe of our great God, bowing to His perfect will, and seeking His wisdom for living. To that end, the proverb declares, "The fear of the Lord is the beginning of wisdom, and the knowledge of the Holy One is understanding" (Proverbs 9:10).

By fearing God rightly, we can live wisely in an uncertain world.
—BC

God dwells in light and holiness,
In splendor and in might;
And godly fear of His great power
Can help us do what's right. —D. DeHaan

Fear God, and you'll have nothing else to fear.

Seeds and Faith

READ: Galatians 6:7–10

Whatever a man sows, that he will also reap. —GALATIANS 6:7

I read a fable about a man who was browsing in a store when he made the shocking discovery that God was behind a sales counter. So the man walked over and asked, "What are You selling?"

God replied, "What does your heart desire?"

The man said, "I want happiness, peace of mind, and freedom from fear . . . for me and the whole world."

God smiled and said, "I don't sell fruit here. Only seeds."

In Galatians 6, Paul stresses the importance of sowing seeds of God-honoring behavior, for "whatever a man sows, that he will also reap" (v. 7). We can't expect to experience the fruit of God's blessings if we don't recognize the importance of doing our part.

It helps to follow the example of others who have sown good seed. Author Samuel Shoemaker said that a good example can either inspire us or cause us to say, "Oh yes, he (or she) is like that. He is not troubled by temper or nerves or impatience or worry as I am; he is just a happier temperament." Shoemaker continued, "It may not occur to us that perhaps he had to fight for his serenity, and that we might win if we would do the same."

Are you weary of the way you are? Ask God for His help and begin sowing seeds of new actions and responses today. In due season the Spirit will give the increase. —JY

We're always sowing seeds in life
By everything we do and say,
So let's make sure the fruit we reap
Comes from the good we do each day. —Hess

The seeds we sow today determine
the kind of fruit we'll reap tomorrow.

A Good Grooming

READ: Psalm 139:1–10, 23–24

Examine me, O Lord, and prove me; try my mind and my heart. For Your lovingkindness is before my eyes. —PSALM 26:2–3

Our dog, Dolly, is a seven-year-old West Highland Terrier. She loves to dig in the dirt, which means she gets very dirty. We bathe her every week or so at home, but occasionally she gets so grimy and tangled that we have to take her to a professional groomer.

She used to hate to go to the groomer because the woman was always in a rush and inclined to be bad-tempered and harsh. Getting Dolly through the door was a struggle. Just the sight of the shop made her want to run away.

So last year we decided to try another groomer and discovered that our dog, though not always overjoyed at the prospect, was less reluctant to go. That's because the groomer is kind to her, even though she must wash Dolly thoroughly, causing discomfort.

When sin and defilement accumulate in our hearts, we need to be cleansed. Like the psalmist David, we must ask God to "examine" and "try" our minds and hearts, and to point out our wicked thoughts, attitudes, and ways (Psalm 139:23–24). Our Lord may cause discomfort, for such exposure is often difficult, but we can approach Him without fear. The Lord's examination of us, though sometimes painful, is gentle and kind.   —DR

Search me, O God, and know my heart today;
Try me, O Savior, know my thoughts, I pray.
See if there be some wicked way in me;
Cleanse me from every sin and set me free. —Orr

Repentance is the hurt that leads to healing.

Where History Comes Alive

READ: Exodus 13:14–16

When your children say to you, "What do you mean by this service?" . . . you shall say, "It is the Passover."
—EXODUS 12:26–27

The movie *Night at the Museum* portrays the humorous experiences of a security guard at a natural history museum. The excitement begins for him when the displays come to life at night.

Inspired by this movie, directors of a real museum created a similar experience. The staff portrayed historic figures such as knights in armor, Victorian ladies, and Egyptian royalty. When children arrived at the museum, they were told that the people in the exhibits had come alive and needed to be led back to their proper place. As the children responded, history came alive for them.

Children need not be bored by history. This is especially true of Bible stories. Take Moses, for example. He escaped death as a child, was educated as a prince, worked miracles, and received the Ten Commandments on tablets. What exciting story elements that teach children about God!

Biblical stories have been shared with children for generations—all the way back to the times of Exodus (chapters 12–13) and Deuteronomy (chapter 6). Moses described times when children were retold vital stories from Jewish history.

Why not set a time to read Bible stories to the children in your life? Then watch their excitement as biblical history comes alive!   —DF

> *The stories in the Word of God*
> *Are there for us to see*
> *How God has worked in people's lives*
> *Throughout all history.* —*Sper*

The Bible's treasures are found by those who dig for them.

How Was I to Know?

READ: 1 Thessalonians 4:1–12

Do not grieve the Holy Spirit of God, by whom you were sealed for the day of redemption. —EPHESIANS 4:30

It was high-school concert season, and the music students were preparing for the big Christmas extravaganza. The teacher had clearly communicated every detail to the students and to the parents—on two different occasions—and the time for mandatory rehearsal was clearly spelled out.

But on rehearsal day one panicky mother called during practice to see what time her teenager was supposed to show up. Another called to say, "Oh, we're taking Tommy to Grandma's. It's okay if he misses rehearsal, right?" When the teacher reminded the parents that this required practice had already started, she heard, "Why didn't somebody tell me? How was I to know?"

Just as this teacher was troubled that her clear instructions were ignored, is it possible that God is troubled by our tendency to ignore His clear instructions? In 1 Thessalonians, Paul reminds us that his God-inspired message tells us "how to live in order to please God" and that those instructions have "the authority of the Lord Jesus" (4:1–2 NIV). The Lord is grieved, Paul explains, when we ignore His teaching and live our own way (Ephesians 4:30–5:2).

Let's make a point to read God's instructions and then live by them—with no excuses. —DB

> God's Word was given for our good
> And we are to obey,
> Not choose the parts that we like best,
> Then live in our own way. —Hess

There is no good excuse for ignoring God.

Humble Valor

READ: Philippians 2:19–30

*Receive him therefore in the Lord with all gladness,
and hold such men in esteem.* —PHILIPPIANS 2:29

A report by the *Chicago Tribune* said: "Scores of Americans, from clergymen to lawyers to CEOs, are claiming medals of valor they never earned." Fabrication of war records and bogus claims of bravery are becoming more widespread. One man, who falsely claimed a Navy Cross, later felt shame and said that real heroes rarely talk about what they've done.

Heroism is marked by an unselfish risking of life for the benefit of another. In Philippians, Paul commends two of his colleagues as true heroes of the faith. Timothy's unselfishness and proven character gained Paul's praise as a true son who had served with him in the gospel (2:22). And Paul described Epaphroditus as "my brother, fellow worker, and fellow soldier" who risked his life for the work of Christ (vv. 25, 30).

Paul told the believers in Philippi to "hold such men in esteem" (v. 29). Honoring fellow believers for their unselfish service to God is a biblical mandate. It is not hero worship, but an attitude of respect for a life well lived.

Through a word of encouragement or a tangible expression of appreciation, who can you honor today for their humble valor in serving the Lord and helping others in His name? —DM

*Heaven's heroes never carve their name
On marbled columns built for earthly fame;
They build instead a legacy that springs
From faithful service to the King of kings.* —Gustafson

Faith in Christ can make
extraordinary heroes out of ordinary people.

The Heat of Our Desire

READ: Psalm 42

*As the deer pants for the water brooks, so
pants my soul for You, O God.* —PSALM 42:1

Pastor A. W. Tozer (1897–1963) read the great Christian theologians until he could write about them with ease. He challenges us: "Come near to the holy men and women of the past and you will soon feel the heat of their desire after God. They mourned for Him, they prayed and wrestled and sought for Him day and night, in season and out, and when they had found Him the finding was all the sweeter for the long seeking."

The writer of Psalm 42 had the kind of longing for the Lord that Tozer spoke about. Feeling separated from God, the psalmist used the simile of a deer panting with thirst to express his deep yearning for a taste of the presence of God.

As the deer pants for the water brooks,

So pants my soul for You, O God.

My soul thirsts for God, for the living God. —Psalm 42:1–2

The heat of the psalmist's desire for the Lord was so great and his sorrow so intense that he did more weeping than eating (v. 3). But the psalmist's longing was satisfied when he placed his hope in God and praised Him for His presence and help (vv. 5–8).

May we have a longing and thirsting for Him that is so intense that others will feel the heat of our desire for Him! —MW

Only Jesus, the Living Water, can satisfy the thirsty soul.

God's Embrace

READ: Romans 12:3–11

*Be kindly affectionate to one another with brotherly love,
in honor giving preference to one another.* —ROMANS 12:10

Soon after her family left for the evening, Carol started to think that her hospital room must be the loneliest place in the world. Nighttime had fallen, her fears about her illness were back, and she felt overwhelming despair as she lay there alone.

Closing her eyes, she began to talk to God: "O Lord, I know I am not really alone. You are here with me. Please calm my heart and give me peace. Let me feel Your arms around me, holding me."

As she prayed, Carol felt her fears beginning to subside. And when she opened her eyes, she looked up to see the warm, sparkling eyes of her friend Marge, who reached out to encircle her in a big hug. Carol felt as if God himself were holding her tightly.

God often uses fellow believers to show us His love. "We, being many, are one body in Christ. . . . Having then gifts differing according to the grace that is given to us, let us use them" (Romans 12:5–6). We serve others "with the ability which God supplies, that in all things God may be glorified through Jesus Christ" (1 Peter 4:11).

When we show love and compassion in simple, practical ways, we are a part of God's ministry to His people.   —CHK

> *Teach me to love, this is my prayer—*
> *May the compassion of Thy heart I share;*
> *Ready a cup of water to give,*
> *May I unselfishly for others live.* —*Peterson*

We show our love for God when we love His family.

The Persecuted Church

READ: 1 Peter 4:12–19

*If anyone suffers as a Christian, let him not be ashamed,
but let him glorify God in this matter.* —1 PETER 4:16

One October morning in 2006, a woman and her six children were forced to witness an attack on her husband and their father. His assailants tried to force him to deny Jesus, but he refused. He continued to proclaim Christ as Lord and died praying for his family. The family is determined to follow Christ, even in their grief.

Another man was sentenced to three years in prison for allegedly insulting another religion. He's an outspoken Christian with a passion for Christ. He and his wife and children continue to be faithful and refuse to deny Him.

Persecution for the Christian faith is as real in our world as it was for the Jewish believers in the early church to whom Peter wrote. He prayed, "May the God of all grace, . . . after you have suffered a while, perfect, establish, strengthen, and settle you" (1 Peter 5:10).

Today is the International Day of Prayer for the Persecuted Church. These prayer points from Open Doors USA, a ministry that's committed to encouraging persecuted Christians, can help guide us as we pray:

- Pray for the safety and faith of the secret believers in countries where it is illegal to share about Christ.
- Pray for the health, perseverance, and encouragement of believers who are imprisoned for the gospel.
- Pray that those whose loved ones have died as martyrs will rely on God for their strength.

Together, let's bring our fellow believers before the Lord in prayer.
—AC

The blood of the martyrs is the seed of the church. —Tertullian

Fragile Existence

READ: Job 1:8–22

We should not trust in ourselves but in God.
—2 CORINTHIANS 1:9

The geological features at Yellowstone National Park fascinate me. But when I walk among the geysers, I'm aware of how close I am to danger. I am walking atop one of the largest, most active volcanoes in the world.

When I read the book of Job, I feel as if I'm walking through Yellowstone on a day when the volcano erupts, exploding the earth's fragile crust and bringing disaster.

Like tourists at Yellowstone, Job was enjoying life. He was unaware that only a hedge separated him from disaster (Job 1:9–10). When God removed that hedge and allowed Satan to test Job, his life exploded (vv. 13–19).

Many believers live in circumstances where it seems as if God, for some reason, has removed His hedge of protection. Others, also for reasons unknown, live in relative calm, seemingly unaware of their fragile existence. Like Job's friends, they assume that nothing bad will happen unless they do something to deserve it.

As we learn from Job, however, God sometimes allows bad things to happen to good people. Although disaster can strike at any moment, nothing has the power to destroy those who trust Christ (2 Corinthians 4:9). No disaster can separate us from God's love. —JAL

> *Though darker, rougher, grows the way*
> *And cares press harder day by day,*
> *With patience in His love I'll rest,*
> *And whisper that He knoweth best.* —Pentecost

God's love still stands when all else has fallen.

No Deal!

READ: Luke 4:1–13

*It is written, "Man shall not live by bread
alone, but by every word of God."* —LUKE 4:4

We've all seen and heard advertisements that entice us to take short-cuts to happiness: Buy our product and make no payments for one year! Instant gratification!

When the Devil tempted Jesus (Luke 4:1–13), he offered a shortcut to "satisfaction." He tried to tempt Jesus to take matters into His own hands rather than trust His Father.

When Jesus was hungry from forty days of fasting, Satan suggested that He use His power to turn stones into bread (vv. 2–3). Had the Lord done so, He would have been using His powers for His own benefit, and He refused.

Why didn't Jesus accept the Devil's offer of ruling all the kingdoms of the world right away (vv. 5–7)? He could have avoided the cross. But that would have gone against God's plan for Him—to give His life on the cross, to be resurrected, and to sit at the Father's right hand in His kingdom. Satan's offer of a shortcut was no deal at all.

Beware of enticements that seem to cost little for the present. Satan hopes to get you to do things his way. And he doesn't give up easily. Even after Jesus overcame a third temptation, Satan left only "until an opportune time" (v. 13).

Whenever you are offered a shortcut to happiness, watch out to see who's behind the cashier's counter! —CPH

*Lord, help me see the Devil's offers for what they are—enticements
to sin. Help me to keep my eyes focused on you and your Word, and
my ears attentive to you in prayer. Amen.*

The best way to escape temptation is to run to God.

Joy in the Midst of Grief

READ: Ezra 3:10–13

The people could not discern the noise of the shout of joy from the noise of the weeping. —EZRA 3:13

After only a few art lessons, ten-year-old Joel decided to try painting a flower. By looking at a color photograph of a Rose of Sharon, Joel was able to paint a beautiful mixture of blue, purple, red, green, and white. The flower had been photographed on the day Joel's aunt died, and Joel's painting made the flower seem to come to life. To the family, his painting symbolized a bittersweet mixture of feelings. While it provided a lasting reminder of the loss they had suffered, it also carried a celebration of Joel's newly discovered artistic gift. The painting gave joy in the midst of grief.

When the people of Judah returned to Jerusalem from captivity in Babylon, they too had a bittersweet experience. As they began rebuilding Solomon's temple, many in the crowd sang songs of praise. At the same time, some older people, who had seen the beauty of the original temple that had been destroyed by war, wept aloud. We are told that "the people could not discern the noise of the shout of joy from the noise of the weeping" (Ezra 3:13).

Grieving can be like that. While there is sadness in looking back, it also includes a promise of joy in trusting God for the future. Even in a devastating loss, we have this hope: The Lord provides joy in the midst of grief.   —DF

We sorrow not as others do,
Whose hopes fade like the flowers;
There is a hope that's born of God,
And such a hope is ours. —McNeil

Even in the bleakest times, Christians have the brightest hope.

Pleasing God

READ: Hebrews 11:1–6

We make it our aim . . . to be well pleasing to Him.
—2 CORINTHIANS 5:9

Andy Warhol, the pop-art painter of such American images as the Campbell's soup can, once said, "In the future everyone will be famous for fifteen minutes." But he was wrong. There are millions of people who will never grab their moment in the spotlight. Some of them are the men and women who spend their lives doing things like working hard, raising godly children, faithfully praying for others, sharing their faith with those who don't yet know Jesus. They teach Sunday school, bring meals to the sick, drive senior citizens to doctors' appointments, and do countless other kindnesses.

These people may never be recognized outside their circle of family and friends. Certainly, their names aren't well known. And although they willingly, and often sacrificially, give of themselves, they may not receive a whole lot of thanks or praise for their service. Yet God knows of their faithfulness and is pleased by their obedience.

Second Corinthians 5:9 teaches us to "make it our aim . . . to be well pleasing" to God. As we, by faith, believe in Him and give our lives in service to Him, He is pleased (Hebrews 11:6). That's our reward, because God's approval is always sweeter than the applause of the crowd. —CHK

Look not to the people around you,
Nor wait for their laurels of praise;
Enough that the Savior has found you
And calls you to serve all your days. —Hess

The deeds God finds pleasing are those done in service for Him.

The Problem with Self-Sufficiency

READ: Revelation 3:14–22

I know your works, that you are neither cold nor hot.
I could wish you were cold or hot. —REVELATION 3:15

The city of Laodicea had a water problem. One nearby town had fabulous hot springs and another had cold, clear water. Laodicea, however, was stuck with tepid, mineral-laden water that tasted like sulphur. Not hot. Not cold. Just gross.

Given those facts, the words of Jesus to the Laodicean believers in Revelation 3 must have stung. Jesus rebuked them for being "neither cold nor hot" (v. 15). And when He thought of them, He felt like vomiting (v. 16)—like the effect of their drinking water.

What was their problem? It was the sin of self-sufficiency. The Laodiceans had become so affluent that they had forgotten how much they needed Jesus (v. 17).

When we say we have everything we need, but Jesus isn't at the top of the list, He is deeply offended. Self-sufficiency distracts us from pursuing the things we really need that only He can give. If you'd rather have cash than character, if your credit cards are maximized and your righteousness is minimized, if you've become smart but aren't wise, then you've been shopping in all the wrong places. Jesus offers commodities that are far better (v. 18).

Jesus is knocking at your heart's door (v. 20). Let Him in. He will give you all you really need! —JS

We must be careful to avoid
All self-sufficiency;
If sinful pride gets in the way,
God's hand we will not see. —Sper

We always have enough when God is our supply.

Two Mites

READ: Mark 12:41–44

She out of her poverty put in all that she had, her whole livelihood. —MARK 12:44

Jesus sat in the temple near the treasury and watched as people walked by and deposited their gifts for the temple (Mark 12:41). Some made a show of it, perhaps so others could see how much they had given. Then a poor woman, a widow, came by and threw in two "mites."

A mite was the least valuable coin in circulation. Thus the widow's gift was very small, amounting to nothing in most folks' eyes. But our Lord saw what others did not see. She had given "all that she had" (12:44). The widow wasn't trying to draw attention to herself. She was simply doing what she was able to do. And Jesus noticed!

We mustn't forget that our Lord sees all that we do, though it may seem very small. It may be nothing more than showing a cheerful countenance in difficult times, or an unnoticed act of love and kindness to someone who happens to pass by. It may be a brief, silent prayer for a neighbor in need.

Jesus said, "Take heed that you do not do your charitable deeds before men, to be seen by them. Otherwise you have no reward from your Father in heaven. . . . But when you do a charitable deed, . . . may [it] be in secret; and your Father who sees in secret will Himself reward you openly" (Matthew 6:1–4). —DR

May our gifts be sacrificial,
From our hearts, and full of love;
Secretive and never showy,
Pleasing our great God above. —Sper

God looks at the heart, not the hand; at the giver, not the gift.

God Works in Mud

READ: Genesis 2:1–7

The Lord God formed man of the dust of the ground, and breathed into his nostrils the breath of life; and man became a living being.
—GENESIS 2:7

In a 1950s novel there is a scene in which four village men confess their sins to one another. One of the men, Michelis, cries out, "How can God let us live on the earth? Why doesn't He kill us to purify creation?"

"Because, Michelis," one of the men answers, "God is a potter; He works in mud."

This is literally what the Lord did in Genesis. The sovereign Creator formed and shaped humanity by unique design. This process involved fashioning a man from the dust of the ground.

The word *formed* in Genesis 2:7 describes the work of an artist. Like a potter, molding and fashioning mud into a pot or some other earthen vessel, so the Lord God formed humanity from clay.

God's work with dust and mud continued as He breathed into man the breath of life, changing his form into a living soul. This made man a spiritual being, with a capacity to serve and fellowship with the Lord.

After Adam and Eve sinned, God continued working in and with mud, sending His Son Jesus to die for humanity and then regenerating those who receive Him so that we can enjoy fellowship with Him. In gratitude, let's use our hands to do good works for His glory.   —MW

> *In His own image God created man,*
> *He formed his body from the dust of earth;*
> *But more than that, to all who are in Christ*
> *He gives eternal life by second birth.* —Hess

God is the only One who can make the dirty clean.

Precious Fruit

READ: Galatians 5:22–26

The fruit of the Spirit is love, joy, peace, longsuffering, kindness,
goodness, faithfulness, gentleness, self-control. —GALATIANS 5:22–23

How much would you be willing to pay for a piece of fruit? In Japan, someone paid more than $6,000 for one Densuke watermelon. Grown only on the northern Japanese island of Hokkaido, this beautiful dark-green sphere looks like a bowling ball. The nearly eighteen-pound watermelon was one of only a few thousand available that year. The fruit's rarity brought an astronomical price on the market.

Christians have fruit that is far more precious than the Densuke watermelon. It's called the fruit of the Spirit: "love, joy, peace, long-suffering, kindness, goodness, faithfulness, gentleness, self-control" (Galatians 5:22–23). Each "fruit" is a different aspect of Christlikeness. In the Gospels, we see how Christ exemplified these virtues. Now He wants to produce them in our hearts—in what we say, how we think, and how we respond to life (John 15:1–4).

A rare and delicious fruit may bring a premium price in the marketplace, but Christlike character is of far greater worth. As we confess all known sin and yield to God's indwelling Spirit, our lives will be transformed to the likeness of Christ (1 John 1:9; Ephesians 5:18). This spiritual fruit will fill our lives with joy, bless those around us, and last into eternity.   —DF

Think not alone of outward form;
Its beauty will depart;
But cultivate the Spirit's fruit
That grow within the heart. —D. DeHaan

Fruitfulness for Christ depends on fellowship with Christ.

Help with a Home Run

READ: 1 Peter 4:7–11

As each one has received a gift, minister it to one another,
as good stewards of the manifold grace of God. —1 PETER 4:10

Sara Tucholsky, a softball player for Western Oregon University, hit the first home run of her life in a game against Central Washington. But she nearly didn't get credit for it. As she rounded first base in excitement, she missed it! When she wheeled back to correct her mistake, she injured her knee. Crying, she crawled back to the base. By rule, she had to touch all four bases on her own for the home run to count. Her teammates could not assist her in any way.

Then Mallory Holtman, the first baseman for the opposing team, spoke up. "Would it be okay if we carried her around?" After conferring, the umpires agreed. So Mallory and another teammate made a chair of their hands and carted Sara around the bases. By the time they were through carrying her, many were crying at this selfless act of compassion, and Sara was awarded her home run.

The lesson for followers of Christ is clear: When fellow Christians stumble and fall, we need to follow the example of these ballplayers. Reach out. Lift them up and carry them along. It's a wonderful opportunity to "minister . . . to one another, as good stewards of the manifold grace of God" (1 Peter 4:10). —DE

When a fellow Christian stumbles
And he needs some help to stand;
Don't ignore his circumstances—
Offer him your outstretched hand. —Sper

No one is useless in this world who lightens
the burdens of another. —Charles Dickens

Beyond Imagination!

READ: Revelation 21:1–8

[It has not] entered into the heart of man the things which
God has prepared for those who love Him. —1 CORINTHIANS 2:9

A college professor at a Christian school perceived that his students held a distorted view of heaven; they considered it to be static and boring. So, to stir their imaginations, he asked them these questions:

"Do you wish you would wake up tomorrow morning to discover that the person you loved most passionately loved you even more? Wake up hearing music you have always loved but had never heard with such infinite joy before? Rise to the new day as if you were just discovering the Pacific Ocean? Wake up without feeling guilty about anything at all? See to the very core of yourself, and like everything you see? Wake up breathing God as if He were air? Loving to love Him? And loving everybody else in the bargain?"

In response to that professor's intriguing questions, the students all lifted their hands. If that's what heaven will be like, and even infinitely more so, they certainly wanted to be there.

"I go to prepare a place for you," Jesus told His disciples (John 14:2). We all share the desire—really a deep-down yearning—to be in that glorious home forever. It is a place of indescribable bliss. And the supreme blessing will be the presence of our Lord Jesus Christ himself!

—VG

When we all get to heaven,
What a day of rejoicing that will be!
When we all see Jesus,
We'll sing and shout the victory. —Hewitt

The greatest pleasures of earth
cannot be compared to the joys of heaven.

Confession and Thanksgiving

READ: Nehemiah 9:32–37

*They have not served You . . . in the many good
things that You gave them.* —NEHEMIAH 9:35

During a Sunday worship service, our congregation said this prayer
of confession in unison: "Gracious God, like many believers before
us, we complain when things do not go our way. We want abundance of
everything rather than what is sufficient to sustain us. We would rather
be elsewhere than where we are at the moment. We would rather have
the gifts You give to others than what You provide for us. We would
rather have You serve us than serve You. Forgive our lack of gratitude
for what You give."

Abundance is no guarantee of gratefulness or thanksgiving. Prosperity may even turn our hearts away from the Lord.

When a group of Jewish exiles returned from Babylon with Nehemiah to rebuild the walls of Jerusalem, they gathered to confess their
sins and those of their fathers. They prayed: "Neither our kings nor our
princes, our priests nor our fathers, have kept Your law. . . . For they
have not served You in their kingdom, or in the many good things that
You gave them, or in the large and rich land which You set before them,
nor did they turn from their wicked works" (Nehemiah 9:34–35).

Confession is a powerful prelude to a prayer of thanksgiving. Obedience is the Amen. —DM

Lord, before we come to ask Your blessing
On this special day we call Thanksgiving,
We would bow to You, our sins confessing,
Then we'll lift our praise in grateful living. —Hess

Confession opens the door to thanksgiving.

Called to Serve

READ: Mark 10:35–45

The Son of Man did not come to be served, but to serve.
—MARK 10:45

When George W. Bush was president, he made a surprise visit to serve Thanksgiving Day dinner to soldiers deployed overseas. One reporter covering the story thought that some might save their meal as a souvenir, explaining, "It's not often that anyone is served by the President."

All elected officials are public servants—in a global, symbolic way—so they are always serving. So it seems that an act of service should not have been one of the biggest news items of the day.

Many people have a genuine desire to serve others, but for some, service is really self-serving. This was true when Jesus was training His disciples. They were under the impression that following Him would make them great. But Jesus quickly set them straight: "Those who are considered rulers over the Gentiles lord it over them, and their great ones exercise authority over them. Yet it shall not be so among you" (Mark 10:42–43).

Jesus made it clear to His disciples that they were in training to become servants: "Whoever of you desires to be first shall be slave of all" (v. 44).

We can sign up for any number of leadership training seminars, but the only good leaders are those who are first and foremost good servants.   —JAL

> *They truly lead who lead by love,*
> *And humbly serve the Lord;*
> *Their lives will bear the Spirit's fruit*
> *And magnify His Word.* —D. DeHaan

A good leader is a good servant.

Loved Well

READ: Ephesians 3:14–21

That you . . . may be able to comprehend . . . what is the width and length and depth and height—to know the love of Christ.
—EPHESIANS 3:17-19

We were gathered with family for Thanksgiving dinner when someone asked if each person would share what he or she was thankful for. One by one we talked. Three-year-old Joshua was thankful for "music," and Nathan, aged four, for "horses." We were all silenced, though, when Stephen (who was soon to turn five) answered, "I'm thankful that Jesus loves me so well." In his simple faith, he understood and was grateful for the love of Jesus for him personally. He told us that Jesus showed His love by dying on a cross.

The apostle Paul wanted the believers in the church at Ephesus to understand how well God loved them, and that was his prayer: "That [they would] be able to comprehend with all the saints what is the width and length and depth and height—to know the love of Christ" (Ephesians 3:17–19). He prayed that they would be rooted and grounded in that love.

To ground ourselves in God's love, it would be helpful to review these verses frequently or even memorize them. We can also take a few minutes each day to thank the Lord for the specific ways He shows His love to us. This will help us to grow in our belief and be thankful—as Stephen is—that Jesus loves us "so well." —AC

O love of God, how rich and pure!
How measureless and strong!
It shall forevermore endure—
The saints' and angels' song. —Lehman

To renew your love for Christ, review Christ's love for you.

What a Ride!

READ: 1 Thessalonians 1

*The word of the Lord has sounded forth
. . . in every place.* —1 THESSALONIANS 1:8

Francis Asbury rode six thousand miles a year on horseback for nearly half a century. Despite ill health, he drove himself tirelessly. He sustained himself with venison jerky, a food that wouldn't spoil during his extended travels. Asbury is remembered for introducing the Methodist "circuit-riding preacher" as an effective way to capture the American frontier for Christ. Planting new churches in remote areas was central to his approach.

At the close of Asbury's ministry, he had recruited over seven hundred traveling preachers. In 1771, when Asbury arrived in the colonies, there were only about six hundred Methodists in America. Forty-five years later, there were 200,000!

In many ways, Asbury's strategy for planting churches reflects the approach of the apostle Paul. To the church he had planted in Thessalonica, Paul wrote: "From you the word of the Lord has sounded forth, not only in Macedonia and Achaia, but also in every place" (1 Thessalonians 1:8; see Acts 17:1–10).

The days of the circuit-riding preacher have come and gone. But each of us has a "frontier" where friends, relatives, and neighbors are our mission field. Can you think of someone today who needs to hear the good news?   —DF

> *Lord, lay some soul upon my heart,*
> *And love that soul through me;*
> *And may I nobly do my part*
> *To win that soul for Thee.* —Tucker

Those who love Christ have a love for the lost.

Preventing Regret

READ: 2 Samuel 18:31–19:4

The king was deeply moved, and went up to the chamber over the gate, and wept. —2 SAMUEL 18:33

In the 1980s, the British band Mike and the Mechanics recorded a powerful song titled, "The Living Years," in which the songwriter mourns his father's death because their relationship had been strained and marked by silence rather than sharing. The singer laments that he didn't get to tell his father "all the things I had to say." Struggling with regret over words unsaid and love unexpressed, he wishes that he could have told his father all this "in the living years."

King David similarly regretted his broken relationship with his son Absalom. Angered over David's refusal to punish Amnon for raping his sister Tamar, Absalom killed Amnon and fled (2 Samuel 13:21–34). David's servant Joab knew that he longed to go to his fugitive son, so he arranged for Absalom to be brought to David. But their relationship was never the same again. Absalom's bitterness sparked a conflict that ended with his death (18:14). It was a bitter victory for King David, causing him to lament his lost son and their failed relationship (18:33). No amount of grieving, however, could undo David's heartache.

We can learn from David's regret when dealing with broken relationships. The pain of trying to make things right can be hard. But it's much better to do what we can to make things right "in the living years."

—BC

A broken relationship can be repaired—but only if you're willing to try.

Heaven on Earth?

READ: Ecclesiastes 2:15–26

Set your mind on things above, not on things on the earth. —COLOSSIANS 3:2

The Singapore developer of an extravagant condominium advertised its new project as "Rediscover Heaven on Earth." I suppose it meant to convey to prospective buyers that their purchase would be so luxurious that it would be like living in heaven while here on earth.

Solomon, the writer of Ecclesiastes, was an extremely wealthy man (1:12). He tried to find heaven on earth and had the means to live as luxuriously as he desired (2:1–10). Yet he wasn't satisfied. So disillusioned was he with life, he described it with just one word—"vanity" (or "meaningless"). And he repeated the word eight times in chapter two alone. As long as he looked only at life "under the sun" (2:18), he felt hollow and dissatisfied. All of his striving was ultimately futile. There would come a day when he would have to relinquish his possessions and leave them to someone else (v. 18).

If you are a Christian, you can look to Christ's promise of a heavenly home He has gone to prepare (John 14:2). That's why Paul advised those who are enjoying what God has given: "Set your mind on things above, not on things on the earth" (Colossians 3:2).

Don't try to find heaven on earth. You won't—no matter how hard you look! —CPH

Lightly hold earth's joys so transient,
Loosely cling to things of clay,
Grasp perfections everlasting,
Where Christ dwells in heaven's day! —Bosch

Those who have their hearts fixed on
heaven will hold loosely the things of earth.

Delivering the Dirt

READ: Proverbs 26:20–28

Where there is no wood, the fire goes out; and where there is no talebearer, strife ceases. —PROVERBS 26:20

Christian industrialist and inventor R. G. LeTourneau is known for his enormous earth-moving machines. One of his products was known simply by the name "Model G."

A prospective buyer, hoping to stump a salesman, asked, "What does the G stand for?"

"I guess the G stands for gossip," was the salesman's quick reply. "Because, like gossip, this machine moves a lot of dirt, and moves it fast!"

The Proverbs have a lot to say about gossip: Those who gossip are untrustworthy (11:13) and should be avoided (20:19). Gossip separates the closest of friends (16:28) and keeps relational strife boiling (18:8). Gossip pours fuel on the coals of conflict, feeding the flames of hurt and misunderstanding (26:21–22).

The Hebrew word for *gossip* or *talebearing* actually means "whispering that is damaging." We fool ourselves into thinking that those juicy, whispered comments here and there are harmless. But gossip leaves behind a wide swath of destruction and is never a victimless crime. Someone is always hurt.

So here's a word to the wise: "Where there is no talebearer, strife ceases" (26:20). Let's leave the dirt-moving to big machines. Put the shovels away and revel in the joy of gossip-free relationships! —JS

> *Many things that others say*
> *Are not for us to tell;*
> *Help us, Lord, to watch our tongue—*
> *We need to guard it well.* —Branon

Destroy gossip by ignoring it.

The Galatia Church

READ: Galatians 3:1–12

Are you so foolish? Having begun in the Spirit, are you now being made perfect by the flesh? —GALATIANS 3:3

I was driving through the countryside when I spotted a church building whose name surprised me. It said, "The Galatia Church." The name caught my attention because I was certain no one would choose to name a church this unless it was a geographic necessity.

A study of the biblical book of Galatians reveals that it is Paul's most fiery letter—criticizing the people for legalism, self-effort, and the exchange of grace for a different gospel. Galatia was not exactly the kind of church that you would see as an example to be followed. The Galatians were trying to please God through their own efforts rather than by reliance on Him. Paul's charge against them was this: "Are you so foolish? Having begun in the Spirit, are you now being made perfect by the flesh?" (3:3).

Just as we cannot earn a relationship with God by our works, neither can we develop spiritually through our own strength. Paul's reminder to the Galatians (and us) is this: Dependence on God through the work of the Spirit in our lives is at the core of our walk with Christ.

If we think we can become like Jesus by our own efforts, we are, like the Galatians, fooling ourselves. —BC

> *Cast your futile efforts down,*
> *Down at Jesus' feet;*
> *Stand in Him, in Him alone,*
> *Gloriously complete.* —Proctor

The Holy Spirit is the Christian's power supply.

Nowhere Tickets

READ: John 14:1–6

Nor is there salvation in any other, for there is no other name under heaven given among men by which we must be saved. —ACTS 4:12

We kept getting tickets to nowhere. We had finished a missions trip to Jamaica and were trying to get home. However, our airline was having problems, and no matter what our tickets said, we couldn't leave Montego Bay. Over and over we heard, "Your flight has been canceled." Even though we had purchased our tickets in good faith, the airline could not back up its promise to transport us to the US. We had to stay an extra day before boarding a plane that could take us home.

Imagine thinking that you are headed for heaven, but discovering that your ticket is no good. It can happen. If you trust the wrong plan, you will get to the gate of eternity but be denied entrance into heaven to live with God forever.

The apostle Peter said there is salvation in no one else but Jesus (Acts 4:12). Jesus said, "I am the way, the truth, and the life. No one comes to the Father except through Me" (John 14:6). The only ticket to heaven goes to those who have put their faith in Jesus Christ and His death on the cross as payment for their sin.

Some offer other ways. But those tickets are worthless. To make sure you're going to heaven, trust Jesus. He's the only way. —DB

Lord, I know I'm a sinner and cannot save myself. I need you as my Savior. Thank you for dying in my place and rising again. I believe in you. Please forgive my sin. I want to live with you in heaven someday.

Jesus took my place on the cross and gave me a place in heaven.

The Best of Gifts

READ: John 1:10–13

Thanks be to God for His indescribable gift! —2 CORINTHIANS 9:15

Having trouble selecting that perfect gift for someone? A friend shared with me a few suggestions:

- The gift of listening. No interrupting, no planning your response. Just listening.
- The gift of affection. Being generous with appropriate hugs, kisses, and pats on the back.
- The gift of laughter. Sharing funny stories and jokes. Your gift will say, "I love to laugh with you."
- The gift of a written note. Expressing in a brief, handwritten note your appreciation or affection.
- The gift of a compliment. Sincerely saying, "You look great today" or "You are special" can bring a smile.

But as we begin this special month of celebration, why not pass on the best gift you've ever received? Share the fact that "the gift of God is eternal life in Christ Jesus" (Romans 6:23). Or share this verse from John 1:12: "As many as received Him, to them He gave the right to become children of God, to those who believe in His name." Remind others that "God so loved the world that He gave His only begotten Son, that whoever believes in Him should not perish but have everlasting life" (John 3:16).

The best gift of all is Jesus Christ. "Thanks be to God for His indescribable gift!" (2 Corinthians 9:15). —CHK

The greatest Gift that has ever been given
Is Jesus Christ who was sent down from heaven.
This Gift can be yours if you will believe;
Trust Him as Savior, and new life receive. —Hess

The best gift was found in a manger.

He Doesn't Stand a Chance

READ: Ephesians 6:10–18

He who is in you is greater than he who is in the world.
—1 JOHN 4:4

In 2004, Josh Hamilton was an outstanding pro baseball prospect, but he was suspended because of drug abuse. Then one night Josh had a life-changing dream. He was fighting the Devil. "I had a stick," he said, "and every time I hit him, he'd fall and get back up. I hit him until I was exhausted, and he was still standing."

After that nightmare, Hamilton vowed to stay clean. The dream returned, but with an important difference. "I would hit [the Devil] and he would bounce back," said Josh. But this time Josh was not alone. He said, "I turned my head and Jesus was battling alongside me. We kept fighting, and I was filled with strength. The Devil didn't stand a chance."

The Bible says that Devil doesn't stand a chance because the Spirit, who is in us, is greater than he is (1 John 4:4). Christ came to destroy the works of the Devil through His life, ministry, and sacrifice (3:8). At the cross, He disarmed and triumphed over the Devil (Colossians 1:13–14; 2:15).

Though defeated by the cross, the Devil remains active in this world. But his final defeat is certain (Revelation 20:7–10). Until then, we take up the whole armor of God (Ephesians 6:10–18), standing firm against him by Jesus' blood and His Word. He doesn't stand a chance.
—MW

And though this world, with devils filled,
Should threaten to undo us,
We will not fear, for God hath willed
His truth to triumph through us. —Luther

The Devil is a defeated foe.

Finding Jesus

READ: Romans 8:27–39

He who did not spare His own Son, but delivered Him up for us all, how shall He not with Him also freely give us all things?
—ROMANS 8:32

After someone stole a valuable ceramic figurine of baby Jesus from a nativity scene in Wellington, Florida, officials took action to keep thieves from succeeding again. An Associated Press report described how they placed a GPS tracking device inside the replacement figurine. When baby Jesus disappeared again the next Christmas, sheriff's deputies were led by the signal to the thief's apartment.

There are times when difficult circumstances or personal loss can cause us to feel that Christ has been stolen from our Christmas. How can we find Jesus when life seems to be working against us?

Like a spiritual GPS, Romans 8 guides us to God's never-failing love and presence with us. We read that the Holy Spirit helps us in our weaknesses and intercedes for us (v. 27). We know that God is for us (v. 31). And we have this grand assurance: "He who did not spare His own Son, but delivered Him up for us all, how shall He not with Him also freely give us all things?" (v. 32). Finally, we are reminded that nothing can separate us from God's love in Christ Jesus (vv. 38–39).

Look for Jesus in the manger, on the cross, risen from the dead, and in our hearts. That's where we can find Jesus at Christmas.   —DM

> *But what to those who find? Ah, this*
> *Nor tongue nor pen can show,*
> *The love of Jesus, what it is*
> *None but His loved ones know.* —*Bernard of Clairvaux*

If we focus only on Christmas, we might lose sight of Christ.

What You Can Do

READ: Ephesians 3:14–21

[I pray that] He would grant you . . . to be strengthened with might through His Spirit in the inner man. —EPHESIANS 3:16

Are you getting what you want out of life? Or do you feel that the economy, your government, your circumstances, or other outside factors are robbing you of value and joy?

Recently, a polling agency asked 1,000 people what they most desired in their lives. One fascinating result was that 90 percent of Bible-believing Christians said that they wanted these outcomes: a close relationship with God, a clear purpose in life, a high degree of integrity, and a deep commitment to the faith.

Notice that these heartfelt desires are all things we as individuals can do something about without outside human help. No government program will assist here, and tough economic times cannot steal these ideals. These life goals are achieved as we allow God's Word to rule in our hearts and as we receive the Spirit's strength to build up "the inner man" (Ephesians 3:16), resulting in true joy.

In our complicated world it's tempting to put our quest for what we desire into the hands of others—to expect an outside entity to fulfill our desires. While we sometimes need help, and we cannot live in isolation, it's not outside sources that provide true happiness. That comes from within—from letting Christ be at home in our hearts (v. 17).   —DB

> *Holy Spirit, all divine,*
> *Dwell within this heart of mine;*
> *Cast down every idol throne,*
> *Reign supreme and reign alone.*   —Reed

If a troubled world gets you down, look up to Jesus.

Presents or Presence?

READ: 1 John 2:24–29

In Your presence is fullness of joy; at Your right hand are pleasures forevermore. —PSALM 16:11

Oswald Chambers once wrote: "It is not God's promises we need, it is [God] Himself."

At Christmastime we often say, "God's presence is more important than presents." But the amount of time and effort we spend on shopping for gifts may indicate otherwise.

In certain parts of the world, people give gifts on December 6. By doing so, they have the rest of the month to focus on Jesus and the wonder of His birth, God's perfect gift to us.

When we say we want God's presence more than presents from others, perhaps we're being truthful. But how many of us can honestly say that we want God's presence more than His presents?

Often we want gifts from God more than we want God himself. We want health, wealth, knowledge, a better job, a better place to live. God may indeed want to give us these things, but we can't have them apart from Him. As David said, "In Your presence is fullness of joy" (Psalm 16:11). Presents may make us happy for a time; earthly gifts from God may make us happy temporarily; but fullness of joy comes only when we remain in a right relationship with God.

So, what would Christmas be like if we truly celebrated God's presence? —JAL

Lord, we want to remember you and your coming in special ways this Christmas. Give us creativity and thoughtfulness in our planning. Help us to focus on your presence and not on what we hope to give or receive.

God's presence with us is one of His greatest presents to us.

Advent Adventure

READ: Matthew 12:11–21

In His name Gentiles will trust.
—MATTHEW 12:21

During the season of Advent on the church calendar, Christians around the world light candles. The first candle symbolizes hope. The prophet Isaiah said that all nations will place their hope or trust in Christ, God's Chosen One (Isaiah 42:1–4; Matthew 12:21).

We think of Advent from the perspective of earthbound creatures who know nothing but this life. We rejoice that Jesus came to visit us on this beautiful planet that He made especially for us. But it's important to remember that Jesus came from a better place. He is first and foremost from heaven, a place more beautiful than we can imagine.

Whenever I think about Jesus coming to earth, I also consider that He had to leave heaven to get here. For Him, earth was hostile territory. Coming here was a dangerous venture (Matthew 12:14). Yet He came. Our just and compassionate God made himself vulnerable to human injustice. The Creator of the universe put on the garment of flesh and came to experience firsthand what life here is really like.

Jesus tasted death for everyone so that we can taste His goodness (Hebrews 2:9; 1 Peter 2:3). He left the splendor of heaven to bring us to glory (Hebrew 2:10). He gave His own life to give us hope for eternal life.   —JAL

The hope of Christmas is the song
Of angels in the sky,
And Christ within a manger laid
To bring salvation nigh. —Campbell

God broke into human history to offer us the gift of eternal life.

War ... Then Peace

READ: Luke 23:32–43

The peace of God, which surpasses all understanding, will guard your hearts and minds through Christ Jesus. —PHILIPPIANS 4:7

On December 7, 1941, a Japanese warplane piloted by Mitsuo Fuchida took off from the aircraft carrier Akagi. Fuchida led the surprise attack on the US Pacific Fleet at Pearl Harbor, Hawaii.

Through the war years to follow, Fuchida continued to fly—often narrowly escaping death. At the end of the war he was disillusioned and bitter.

A few years later, he heard a story that piqued his spiritual curiosity: A Christian young woman whose parents had been killed by the Japanese during the war decided to minister to Japanese prisoners. Impressed, Fuchida began reading the Bible.

As he read Jesus' words from the cross, "Father, forgive them, for they do not know what they do" (Luke 23:34), he understood how that woman could show kindness to her enemies. That day Fuchida gave his heart to Christ.

Becoming a lay preacher and evangelist to his fellow citizens, this former warrior demonstrated "the peace of God, which surpasses all understanding" (Philippians 4:7)—a peace enjoyed by those who have trusted Christ and who "let [their] requests be made known to God" (v. 6).

Have you found this peace? No matter what you have gone through, God makes it available to you.   —DF

> *There is peace in midst of turmoil,*
> *There is joy when eyes are dim,*
> *There is perfect understanding*
> *When we leave it all to Him.* —Brown

True peace is not the absence of war; it is the presence of God. —Loveless

Christmas Spirit

READ: Philippians 2:1–11

Let this mind be in you which was also in Christ Jesus.
—PHILIPPIANS 2:5

How would you define "the Christmas spirit"? Would it be a friendly smile between strangers, the sound of familiar carols, a tree with twinkling lights in a sea of brightly wrapped packages, or just that good feeling you get this time of the year?

Yet none of these captures the real meaning of the phrase. These represent feelings that may be a response to the commercialism that distorts the real spirit of Christmas.

J. I. Packer goes to the heart of this matter in his book *Knowing God*. He writes, "We talk glibly of the Christmas spirit, rarely meaning more by this than sentimental jollity. . . . It ought to mean the reproducing in human lives of the [temperament] of Him who for our sakes became poor, . . . the spirit of those who, like their Master, live their whole lives on the principle of making themselves poor—spending and being spent—to enrich their fellowmen, giving time, thought, care, and concern to do good to others . . . in whatever way there seems need."

In Philippians 2, Paul describes the God of heaven and earth as laying aside His divine glory and becoming our servant by dying on the cross for our sins. Then he urges us to duplicate that same mind of humble service to others. That's the true Christmas spirit.   —DD

> *If we look beyond the manger*
> *To the cross of Calvary,*
> *We will know the reason Christmas*
> *Brings such joy to you and me. —D. DeHaan*

The spirit of Christmas giving should be seen in all our living.

When Life Is Too Big

READ: 1 Kings 3:4–14

O Lord my God, You have made Your servant king instead of my father David, but I am a little child; I do not know how to go out or come in. —1 KINGS 3:7

As a young man, Jimmy Carter was a junior officer in the US Navy. He was deeply impacted by Admiral Hyman Rickover, the mastermind of the US nuclear submarine fleet.

Shortly after Carter's inauguration as president, he invited Rickover to the White House for lunch, where the admiral presented Carter with a plaque that read, "O, God, Thy sea is so great, and my boat is so small." That prayer is a useful perspective on the size and complexity of life and our inability to manage it on our own.

Solomon too knew that life could be overwhelming. When he succeeded his father, David, as king of Israel, he confessed his weakness to God, saying, "O Lord my God, You have made Your servant king instead of my father David, but I am a little child; I do not know how to go out or come in" (1 Kings 3:7). As a result, he asked for the wisdom to lead in a way that would please God and help others (v. 9).

Is life feeling too big for you? There may not be easy answers to the challenges you are facing, but God promises that if you ask for wisdom, He will grant it (James 1:5). You don't have to face the overwhelming challenges of life alone.   —BC

Each day we learn from yesterday
Of God's great love and care;
And every burden we must face
He'll surely help us bear. —D. DeHaan

Recognizing our own smallness can cause us to embrace God's greatness.

A Mere Happening?

READ: Ruth 2:1–12

In all your ways acknowledge Him, and
He shall direct your paths. —PROVERBS 3:6

Huang, a nonbeliever, was a visiting scientist at the University of Minnesota in 1994. While there, he met some Christians and enjoyed their fellowship. So when they learned he would be returning to Beijing, they gave him the name of a Christian to contact who was also moving there.

On the flight back to Beijing, the plane encountered engine trouble and stopped in Seattle overnight. The airline placed Huang in the same room with the very person he was to contact! Once they arrived in Beijing, the two began meeting weekly for a Bible study, and a year later Huang gave his life to Christ. This was not just a mere happening; it was by God's arrangement.

In Ruth 2, we read that Ruth came "to the part of the field belonging to Boaz" (v. 3). Boaz asked his servants who she was (v. 5), which prompted his special consideration toward her. When Ruth asked him the reason for such kindness, Boaz replied, "It has been fully reported to me, all that you have done for your mother-in-law. . . . The Lord repay your work, and a full reward be given you" (vv. 11–12).

Did the events in the lives of Ruth and Huang just happen? No, for none of God's people can escape God's plans to guide and to provide.
—AL

I know who holds the future,
And I know who holds my hand;
With God things don't just happen—
Everything by Him is planned. —Smith

A "mere happening" may be God's design.

Tears of Repentance

READ: Luke 22:54–62

Peter went out and wept bitterly.
—LUKE 22:62

My husband, a self-proclaimed computer illiterate, purchased a computer to help him with his business. After giving him a few pointers, I left him alone to do some experimenting. It wasn't long, however, before I heard a slightly panicked voice from the office: "Hey, where's that 'uh-oh' button?"

What he had been looking for, of course, was the "undo" key that lets you backtrack when you've made a mistake. Have you ever wished for one of those in life? A provision to reverse, repair, or restore what's been broken or damaged by sin?

After Jesus' arrest, Peter, one of His beloved disciples, denied three times that he knew Him. Then, we read, "the Lord turned" and simply "looked at" him. Peter "went out and wept bitterly" (Luke 22:61–62). His tears were most likely tears of shame and repentance. No doubt he wished he could undo his actions. But Peter wasn't left in his misery. After Jesus' resurrection, He restored Peter, giving him opportunity to reaffirm his love (John 21:15–17).

When you sorrow over sin in your life, remember that God has provided a method of restoration. "If we confess our sins," He will "forgive us" and "cleanse us from all unrighteousness" (1 John 1:9).   —CHK

We're thankful, Lord, that when we fall
We can begin anew
If humbly we confess our sin,
Then turn and follow You. —Sper

The way back to God begins with a broken heart.

Sowing Seed with Tears

READ: Ephesians 4:17–24

I have great sorrow and continual grief in my heart.
—ROMANS 9:2

In our Bible-study class, we were reading Ephesians 4:17–24 out loud when Alyssa began to cry. Most of us were wondering why, when she quietly said, "I'm crying because hearing this passage read out loud makes me see the condition that lost people are in. They're separated from God and are blind to it! That breaks my heart."

One person in the class admitted later that he was embarrassed he had never felt that sad about nonbelievers and had in the past even talked excitedly about the judgment they would receive one day from God.

The apostle Paul laid out the condition of the lost with these words: "[They have] their understanding darkened, being alienated from the life of God . . . because of the blindness of their heart" (Ephesians 4:18). He testified that he had "great sorrow and continual grief in [his] heart" because his fellow countrymen had not yet come to know the love of Christ (Romans 9:1–3).

As we think about the condition of nonbelievers, we can remember God's heart toward them: "The Lord is . . . longsuffering toward us, not willing that any should perish but that all should come to repentance" (2 Peter 3:9). When we share the Word of God and pray earnestly for others, eyes will be opened to His love.　　　　　　　　　　—AC

Oh, give me, Lord, Thy love for souls,
For lost and wandering sheep,
That I may see the multitudes
And weep as Thou didst weep.　—Harrison

Open your heart to the Lord, and He will open your eyes to the lost.

A Time for Readjustment

READ: Leviticus 25:1–7

*In the seventh year there shall be a sabbath
of solemn rest for the land.* —LEVITICUS 25:4

The earth's solar orbit takes 365 and a quarter days. Because of this, every four years an extra day is added to the calendar so we don't fall behind in the natural cycle of things. Each leap year we add that day onto the end of February. In this way, the calendar is readjusted to the astronomical timetable.

In the calendar of ancient Israel, God set up a remarkable means of readjusting things. Just as mankind was commanded to rest every seventh day (Exodus 20:8–10), so the land was to be allowed to rest during the seventh year (Leviticus 25:4). This sabbatical year allowed the farmland to replenish for greater fertility. In addition, debts were canceled and Hebrew slaves were set free (Deuteronomy 15:1–11; 12–18).

With our busy schedules and our hectic pace of life, we too need readjustment. Demands of work, family, and church can require reevaluation. One way we do that is by observing the Sabbath principle: making sure to set aside time to rest and prayerfully refocus our priorities. Jesus, for example, went "to a solitary place; and there He prayed" (Mark 1:35).

When can you pull aside from your activities and prayerfully ask God to reset your spiritual calendar to His Word and His will? Is it time for a readjustment? —DF

*To face life's many challenges
And overcome each test,
The Lord tells us to take the time
To stop, to pray, to rest.* —Sper

To make the most of your time, take time to pray.

Warning Lights

READ: Joel 2:12–17

*"Now, therefore," says the Lord, "turn to Me with all your heart,
with fasting, with weeping, and with mourning."* —JOEL 2:12

I didn't think that the hesitation in my car engine and that little yellow "check engine" light on my dashboard really needed my immediate attention. I would take care of it tomorrow. However, the next morning when I turned the key to start my car, it wouldn't start. My first reaction was frustration, knowing that this would mean money, time, and inconvenience. My second thought was more of a resolution: I need to pay attention to warning lights that are trying to get my attention— they can mean something is wrong.

In Joel 2:12–17 we read that God used the prophet Joel to encourage His people to pay attention to the warning light on their spiritual dashboard. Prosperity had caused them to become complacent and negligent in their commitment to the Lord. Their faith had degenerated into empty formalism and their lives into moral bankruptcy. So God sent a locust plague to ruin crops in order to get His people's attention, causing them to change their behavior and turn to Him with their whole heart.

What warning lights are flashing in your life? What needs to be tuned up or repaired through confession and repentance?   —MW

> *God's love is not some fuzzy thing*
> *That lets us do what we think best;*
> *It guides and warns, and shows the way,*
> *And always puts us to the test.* —D. DeHaan

Conviction is God's warning light.

God's Remarkable Word

READ: Psalm 119:89–96

Forever, O Lord, Your Word is settled in heaven. —PSALM 119:89

The discovery of the Dead Sea Scrolls in 1947 has been called the greatest archaeological find of the twentieth century. The ancient manuscripts found hidden in the caves near Qumran are the oldest known copies of key Old Testament books. In 2007, the San Diego Natural History Museum hosted an exhibition featuring twenty-four of these scrolls. One often-repeated theme in the exhibit was that during the past two thousand years the text of the Hebrew Bible (the Christian Old Testament) has remained virtually unchanged.

Followers of Christ who believe that the Bible is the eternal, unchanging Word of God find more than coincidence in this remarkable preservation. The psalmist wrote: "Forever, O Lord, Your Word is settled in heaven. Your faithfulness endures to all generations" (119:89–90). Jesus said: "My words will by no means pass away" (Matthew 24:35).

The Bible is more than a historical relic. It is the living, powerful Word of God (Hebrews 4:12), in which we encounter the Lord and discover how to live for Him and honor Him. "I will never forget Your precepts," the psalmist concluded, "for by them You have given me life" (119:93).

What a privilege we have each day to seek God in His remarkable Word! —DM

> *I have a companion, a wonderful guide,*
> *A solace and comfort whatever betide;*
> *A friend never-failing when others pass by,*
> *Oh, blessed communion, my Bible and I.* —*Knobloch*

To know Christ, the Living Word, is to love the Bible, the written Word.

Becoming Whole

READ: Romans 7:13–25

Work out your own salvation with fear and trembling; for it is God who works in you both to will and to do for His good pleasure.
—PHILIPPIANS 2:12–13

When a friend of mine fell off her bike and suffered a severe brain injury, doctors weren't sure she would survive. For several days she remained suspended between life and death.

The first good news came when she opened her eyes. Then she responded to simple voice commands. But with every small improvement, anxiety remained. How far would she progress?

After one difficult day of therapy, her husband was discouraged. But the very next morning he shared these welcome words: "Sandy's back!" Physically, emotionally, psychologically, and mentally, Sandy was becoming the "self" we knew and loved.

Sandy's fall reminds me of what theologians refer to as "the fall" of mankind (Genesis 3). And her struggle to recover parallels our struggle to overcome the brokenness of sin (Romans 7:18). If only her body healed, recovery would be incomplete. The same would be true if her brain worked but her body didn't. Wholeness means that all parts work together for one purpose.

God is the one healing Sandy, but she has to work hard in therapy to improve. The same is true of us spiritually. After God saves us through Christ, we must "work out" our salvation (Philippians 2:12)—not to earn it but to bring our thoughts and actions into agreement with His purpose.
—JAL

More like the Master I would ever be,
More of His meekness, more humility;
More zeal to labor, more courage to be true,
More consecration for work He bids me do. —Gabriel

To become whole, keep yielding to the Holy Spirit.

Giving Our Best

READ: Luke 19:12–26

Present your bodies a living sacrifice, . . .
which is your reasonable service. —ROMANS 12:1

The durian, a tropical fruit, is often called "the king of fruits." Either you love it or you hate it. Those who love it will do almost anything to get it. Those who hate it won't get near it because of its pungent smell. My wife loves it. Recently, a friend, who was grateful for what my wife had done for her, sent her a box of the finest quality durians. The friend took great pains to ensure that they were the best.

This gift caused me to ask myself, "If we can give the best to a friend, how can we do less for our Lord who gave His very life for us?"

The nobleman in Jesus' parable in Luke 19 wanted the best from ten servants to whom he gave money, saying, "Do business till I come" (v. 13). When he returned and asked for an account, he gave the same commendation—"Well done!"—to all those who had done what they could with the money entrusted to them. But he called "wicked" the one who did nothing with the money he had been given (v. 22).

The primary meaning of this story is stewardship of what we've been given. To be faithful with what God has given to us is to give Him our best in return. As the master gave money to the servants in the parable, so God has given us gifts to serve Him. It is we who will lose out if we fail to give Him our best. —CPH

> *Give of your best to the Master,*
> *Give Him first place in your heart;*
> *Give Him first place in your service,*
> *Consecrate every part.* —Grose

We are at our best when we serve God by serving others.

Jehovah-Jireh

READ: Matthew 6:5–15

Your Father knows the things you have
need of before you ask Him. —MATTHEW 6:8

In my early years as a pastor, I served in small churches where finances were often tight. Sometimes our family finances felt the weight of that pressure. On one occasion, we were down to the last of our food and payday was still several days away. While my wife and I fretted about how we would feed our kids in the next few days, our doorbell rang. When we opened the door, we discovered two bags of groceries. We had not told anyone of our plight, yet our provider God had led someone to meet that need.

This reminds me of the Old Testament account of Abraham when he was asked to sacrifice his son Isaac. At just the right moment, God provided a ram instead. Abraham called this place *Jehovah-Jireh,* meaning "The Lord Will Provide" (Genesis 22:14).

Jesus said, "Your Father knows the things you have need of before you ask Him" (Matthew 6:8). He is the One who is constantly caring for us and seeking the best for us—in times of hardship, need, and fear.

Peter wrote that we can cast all our cares upon Jesus, because He cares for us (1 Peter 5:7). We can turn to Him in our time of need.

—BC

I know not by what methods rare
The Lord provides for me;
I only know that all my needs
He meets so graciously. —Adams

What God promises, God will provide.

No Cause for Alarm

READ: Ephesians 4:25–32

"Be angry, and do not sin": do not let the sun go down on your wrath. —EPHESIANS 4:26

The sound of the alarm blaring from inside the church struck panic in my heart. I had arrived at church early one Sunday morning, planning to spend a little time in peace and quiet before the congregation arrived. But I forgot to disarm the burglar alarm. As I turned the key, the disruptive and annoying blasting of the alarm filled the building—and no doubt the bedrooms of sleeping neighbors.

Anger is a lot like that. In the midst of our peaceful lives, something turns a key in our spirit and triggers the alarm. And our internal peace—not to mention the tranquillity of those around us—is interrupted by the disruptive force of our exploding emotions.

Sometimes anger appropriately calls our attention to an injustice that needs to be addressed, and we are spurred to righteous action. Most of the time, however, our anger is selfishly ignited by the violation of our expectations, rights, and privileges. In any case, it's important to know why the alarm is sounding and to respond in a godly way. And one thing is sure: anger should never continue unchecked.

It's no wonder that Paul reminds us of the psalmist's warning: "'Be angry, and do not sin'; do not let the sun go down on your wrath" (Ephesians 4:26; Psalm 4:4). —JS

Spirit of God, please change my heart
And give me a new desire;
Help me to be a person of peace
Who's not controlled by anger's fire. —K. DeHaan

Anger left unchecked is cause for alarm.

Make a Joyful Shout

READ: Psalm 100

Make a joyful shout to the Lord, all you lands!
—PSALM 100:1

Duke University's basketball fans are known as "Cameron Crazies." When Duke plays archrival North Carolina, the Crazies are given these instructions: "This is the game you've been waiting for. No excuses. Give everything you've got. Cameron [Stadium] should never be less than painfully loud tonight." Clearly, Duke fans take allegiance seriously.

The songwriter of Psalm 100 took his allegiance to the Lord seriously and wanted others to do the same. "Make a joyful shout to the Lord!" he exclaimed (v. 1). God's people were to freely express their praise to Him because He was the covenant God of Israel, the God over all other so-called gods. They were called to focus all their energies on Him and His goodness.

God's goodness and grace should motivate us to freely express our love and allegiance to Him with shouts of joy. This may mean that those who are more reserved must push back the boundaries of restraint and learn what it means to be expressive in their praise to God. Those who are so expressive that they miss the beauty of silence may need to learn from those whose style is more reflective.

Worship is a time to focus on our Creator, Redeemer, and Shepherd, and celebrate what He has done.   —MW

Our thoughts about God should lead us to joyful praise.

God Alone

READ: 1 Corinthians 3:1–9

We are God's fellow workers. —1 CORINTHIANS 3:9

On May 29, 1953, New Zealander Edmund Hillary and his Sherpa guide, Tenzing Norgay, became the first people to reach the peak of Mount Everest, the highest mountain in the world. Since Tenzing did not know how to use the camera, Edmund took a photo of Tenzing as evidence that they did reach the top.

Later, journalists repeatedly asked who had reached the summit first. The expedition leader, John Hunt, replied, "They reached it together, as a team." They were united by a common goal, and neither was concerned who should get the greater credit.

It is counterproductive to try to determine who deserves the most credit when something is done well. The church at Corinth was split into two factions—those who followed Paul, and those who followed Apollos. The apostle Paul told them, "I planted, Apollos watered. . . . Neither he who plants is anything, nor he who waters" (1 Corinthians 3:7). He reminded them that they were "God's fellow workers" (v. 9), and it is God who gives the increase in ministry (v. 7).

Our concern about who deserves the credit serves only to take away the honor and glory that belong to the Lord Jesus alone.   —CPH

> *Let others have the honors,*
> *The glory, and the fame;*
> *I seek to follow Jesus*
> *And glory in His name.* —Horton

Jesus must increase; I must decrease.

The Star Shepherd

READ: Isaiah 40:25–27

Lift up your eyes on high, and see who has created these things. —ISAIAH 40:26

Some night when you're away from city lights, "lift up your eyes on high" (Isaiah 40:26). There in the heavens you'll see a luminous band of stars stretching from horizon to horizon—our galaxy.

If you have good eyes, you can see about five thousand stars, according to astronomer Simon Driver. There are, however, far more that you cannot see with the naked eye. In 1995, the Hubble Deep Field Study space probe concluded that there are billions of galaxies, each containing billions of stars. By one estimate, there are more than ten stars in the universe for every grain of sand on the earth.

Yet each night, without fail, God "brings out their host by number; . . . by the greatness of His might . . . ; not one is missing" (v. 26).

Why then do people say, "My way is hidden from the Lord"? (v. 27). Yes, billions of individuals inhabit this globe, but no one has been forgotten by God. He knows "those who are His" (2 Timothy 2:19). If He can bring out the incalculable hosts of heaven each night one by one, He can bring you into His light. He does so by "the strength of His power" (v. 26)—the power He showed when He raised Jesus from the dead.

Are the stars out tonight? Rejoice! God cares for you.   —DR

> *The God who made the firmament,*
> *Who made the deepest sea,*
> *The God who put the stars in place*
> *Is the God who cares for me.* —Berg

We see the power of God's creation; we feel the power of His love.

Can You Spare a Dime?

READ: 2 Corinthians 9:6–15

He who has mercy on the poor, happy is he. —PROVERBS 14:21

In her insightful book *The Forgotten Man,* Amity Shlaes provides fascinating stories about what life was like during the Great Depression in the US. At the center of that economic drama was "the forgotten man," a term used for the countless individuals who were thrown out of work.

A popular Depression-era song poignantly expresses their story:

> They used to tell me I was building a dream, with peace and glory ahead.
> Why should I be standing in line, just waiting for bread?
> Once I built a railroad, I made it run, made it race against time.
> Once I built a railroad; now it's done. Brother, can you spare a dime?

As these lyrics remind us, an economic downturn changes everything for hard-working people who lose their jobs. When that happens, we as Christians should do what we can for people in need.

In Galatians 2, Paul and Barnabas were reminded to evangelize and to "remember the poor" (v. 10). We can see that Paul did just that—preaching the gospel and encouraging believers to give financial aid to those in need (Acts 11:29–30; 1 Corinthians 16:1–3).

During tough economic times, we too should help people in need, spiritually and physically. A dime doesn't go far these days, but a generous attitude does. —DF

> The poor and needy everywhere
> Are objects of God's love and care,
> But they will always know despair
> Unless His love with them we share. —D. DeHaan

Good exercise for the heart is to bend down and help another person up.

God's Special Place

READ: Luke 2:1–7

[Mary] brought forth her firstborn Son, . . . and laid Him in a manger, because there was no room for them in the inn. —LUKE 2:7

As a young girl in the late 1920s, Grace Ditmanson Adams often traveled with her missionary parents through inland China. Later, she wrote about those trips and the crowded places where they stayed overnight—village inns full of people coughing, sneezing, and smoking, while babies cried and children complained. Her family put their bedrolls on board-covered trestles in a large room with everyone else.

One snowy night, they arrived at an inn to find it packed full. The innkeeper expressed his regret, then paused and said, "Follow me." He led them to a side room used to store straw and farm equipment. There they slept in a quiet place of their own.

After that, whenever Grace read that Mary "brought forth her firstborn Son, and wrapped Him in swaddling cloths, and laid Him in a manger, because there was no room for them in the inn" (Luke 2:7), she saw the event differently. While some described the innkeeper as an example of uncaring, sinful mankind who rejected the Savior, Grace said, "I truly believe that Almighty God used the innkeeper as the arranger for a healthier place than the crowded inn—a place of privacy."

Through eyes of faith, we see God's provision for Mary. Look for the ways He provides for you. —DM

> *Wait on the Lord from day to day,*
> *Strength He provides in His own way;*
> *There's no need for worry, no need to fear,*
> *He is our God who is always near.* —Fortna

Those who let God provide will be satisfied.

Mary's Christmas

READ: Luke 1:26–33; 2:4–7

Mary kept all these things and pondered them in her heart.
—LUKE 2:19

It was anything but an idyllic, silent night on that cool Bethlehem evening when a scared teenager gave birth to the King of Glory. Mary endured the pain of her baby's arrival without the aid of anything more than the carpentry-roughened hands of Joseph, her betrothed. Shepherds may have been serenaded in nearby fields by angels singing praises to the baby, but all Mary and Joseph heard were the sounds of animals, birth agony, and the first cries of God in baby form. A high-magnitude star shone in the night sky above the outbuilding, but the manger scene was a dreary place for these two out-of-town visitors.

As Joseph laid the infant in Mary's arms, a combination of wonder, pain, fear, and joy must have coursed through her heart. She knew, because of an angel's promise, that this tiny bundle was "the Son of the Highest" (Luke 1:32). As she peered through the semidarkness into His eyes and then into Joseph's, she must have wondered how she was going to mother this One whose kingdom would never end.

Mary had much to ponder in her heart on that special night. Now, over two thousand years later, each of us needs to consider the importance of Jesus' birth and His subsequent death, resurrection, and promise to return. —DB

> *Almighty God became a man*
> *By lowly, humble birth;*
> *And Mary treasured in her heart*
> *This Gift of boundless worth.* —Sper

God came to live with us so that we could live with Him.

The Hope That Banishes Hopelessness

READ: Philippians 2:5–11

God forbid that I should boast except in the cross of our Lord Jesus Christ. —GALATIANS 6:14

When atheistic communism was a world-menacing power, it proclaimed that there is no God and that faith in any future life is a deceptive illusion. Leonid Brezhnev had been the Soviet dictator, the embodiment of Marxist unbelief. But something happened at his funeral that contradicted atheism.

George H. W. Bush, then vice president of the US, was the country's official representative at the solemn, formal ceremony. He reported that while the casket was still open, Brezhnev's widow stared motionless at her husband's body. And just before the soldiers were about to close the lid, she reached inside and made the sign of the cross over his chest. What a desperate and significant gesture! That widow evidently hoped that what her husband had vehemently denied might somehow be true.

Thankfully, we can have hope beyond this earthly life. All we need to do is embrace by faith the saving message of the cross: Jesus died for our sins and rose again so that we might live eternally with Him. Do you believe? Then join with the apostle Paul in affirming that "we trust in the living God, who is the Savior of all men, especially of those who believe" (1 Timothy 4:10).   —VG

The cross is my hope for eternity—
No merit have I of my own;
The shed blood of Christ my only plea—
My trust is in Jesus alone. —Christiansen

Calvary's cross is the only bridge to eternal life.

Good Riddance!

READ: 2 Corinthians 12:7–10

My grace is sufficient for you. —2 CORINTHIANS 12:9

A shredder ate hundreds of pieces of paper and other items in New York City on December 28, 2008. Organizers of the second annual "Good Riddance Day" encouraged people to bring to Times Square their bad memories and suffering of 2008 and feed them into the industrial-strength shredder or toss them into an extra-large dumpster.

Some participants shredded pieces of paper with the words "the stock market" or "cancer." Others destroyed bank statements, and one person shredded a printed e-mail from a boyfriend who broke up with her.

We long to "shred" memories of bad things that others have done to us or difficult circumstances we're going through. Even the apostle Paul wanted relief from his present suffering, an infirmity that made him feel weak (2 Corinthians 12:7–10). But God said to him, "My grace is sufficient for you, for My strength is made perfect in weakness." God didn't take away the problem. Instead, He gave Paul the grace to live with it.

Difficulties burden us as we mull them over in our minds, affecting our relationships and our outlook on life. But believers in Christ have a place to take these burdens. First Peter 5:7 tells us, "[Cast] all your care upon [the Lord], for He cares for you." —AC

Whenever life's burdens oppress you
And trials seem too much to face,
Remember God's strength in your weakness;
He'll give you His power and grace. —Sper

God gives enough grace for whatever we face.

Power to Persevere

READ: James 5:1–11

You have heard of the perseverance of Job and seen the end intended by the Lord—that the Lord is very compassionate and merciful.
—JAMES 5:11

Professional golfer Paula Creamer had worked all year long to earn a berth in the 2008 ADT Championship, the year's final tournament on the LPGA tour. When the event began, however, Creamer was suffering from peritonitis, a painful inflammation of the abdominal wall. Throughout the four days of the tournament, she was in constant pain and unable to eat. She even spent a night in the hospital because of the condition. Still, she persevered to the end and, amazingly, she finished third. Her determination earned her many new fans.

The challenges and crises of life can tax us to the very end of our strength, and in such times it is easy to want to give up. But James offers followers of Christ another perspective. He says that while life is a battle, it is also a blessing: "Indeed we count them blessed who endure. You have heard of the perseverance of Job and seen the end intended by the Lord—that the Lord is very compassionate and merciful" (James 5:11).

In the example of "the perseverance of Job," we find encouragement and the power to persevere in life's darkest hours—power rooted in God, who is compassionate and merciful. Even when life is painful and hard, we can persevere because God is there. His mercy endures forever (Psalm 136).   —BC

I searched with all my heart to know
If God was really there;
He graciously revealed himself,
His mercy, love, and care. —Cetas

God provides the power we need to persevere.

In Which Realm Do You Live?

READ: Romans 8:1–10

*The law of the Spirit of life in Christ Jesus has made
me free from the law of sin and death.* —ROMANS 8:2

I was working with a petroleum company in Singapore when an inspector from another country visited. He came to check on a cargo of oil destined for his country, which was at war. When he heard the shriek of fighter planes overhead, he instinctively ran for cover. Embarrassed, he explained, "Sorry. I thought I was back home." He did what he would have done had he been in his war-torn country.

As I thought about this later, it reminded me of how easy it is for the Christian to dive back into old ways of sin out of sheer habit because of the many temptations in this world. Even though we are "in Christ Jesus" as Romans 8:1 says, we sometimes live as if we are "in sin."

God paid a very heavy price to take us out of the realm of sin. He did so by "sending His own Son in the likeness of sinful man to be a sin offering" (8:3 NIV). We are now to be governed by "the law of the Spirit of life," not by "the law of sin and death" (v. 2). The apostle Paul urges us to "set" our mind according to "the things of the Spirit" (v. 5). This means that we take our direction from God's Word as guided by His Spirit.

When you're tempted to dive back into old sinful ways, will you instead allow the Holy Spirit who resides in you to help you live more consistently with your standing "in Christ"? —CPH

*Born of the flesh, conceived in sin,
Then born of the Spirit, new life to begin;
I've been washed in Christ's blood and this will suffice;
Praise God I'm His child, I've been born twice! —Brandt*

When you are born again, you become a citizen of heaven.

Bad Idea?

READ: Hebrews 10:22–39

*Let us draw near with a true heart in
full assurance of faith.* —HEBREWS 10:22

The former athlete had neglected his body for too long, so he began an exercise routine. The first day, he did several push-ups and went for a light jog. The next day, more push-ups, a few sit-ups, and a longer run. The third day, he did exercises and a mile-and-a-half run. On the fourth day, our ex-athlete in re-training woke up with a sore throat.

Then he did one more exercise: He jumped to the conclusion that exercising was a bad idea. If all he got out of his huffing and puffing was sickness, it wasn't for him.

Let's examine another scenario. A Christian, realizing he has neglected his relationship with God, begins a new spiritual routine of Bible-reading and prayer. But after just a few days, some problems arise in his life. What does he conclude? Like the ex-athlete, should he decide that his spiritual quest is a bad idea and that it doesn't do any good? Certainly not.

We don't pray and read the Bible to get a perfect, trouble-free life. Pursuing God is not cause and effect. We do it because it draws us closer in our relationship with the One who is perfect. The pursuit of godliness will not exempt us from trouble (2 Timothy 3:12). But a life dedicated to loving and pursuing God (Hebrews 10:22) is always a good idea—no matter what happens. —DB

*The time we spend with God each day
Through prayer and reading of His Word
Will help us face what comes our way
And draw us closer to the Lord.* —Sper

The roots of stability come from being grounded in God's Word and prayer.

Point of No Return

READ: Deuteronomy 11:7–12

*The eyes of the Lord your God are always on [the land],
from the beginning of the year to the very end of the year.*
—DEUTERONOMY 11:12

Beloved pastor and Bible teacher Ray Stedman, who was pastor of a California church for forty years, once told his congregation: "On New Year's Eve we realize more than at any other time in our lives that we can never go back in time. . . . We can look back and remember, but we cannot retrace a single moment of the year that is past."

Stedman then referred to the Israelites as they stood on the edge of a new opportunity. After four decades of desert wanderings by their people, this new generation may have wondered if they had the faith and fortitude to possess the Promised Land.

Their leader, Moses, reminded them that they had seen "every great act of the Lord which He did" and that their destination was "a land for which the Lord your God cares; the eyes of the Lord your God are always on it, from the beginning of the year to the very end of the year" (Deuteronomy 11: 7, 12).

On New Year's Eve, we may fear the future because of events in the past. But we need not remain chained to our old memories. We can move ahead focused on God. Just as the Lord watched over the land and His people, so His eyes will be upon us.

God's faithful care will extend to every day of the new year. We can count on that promise.   —DM

> *God holds the future in His hands*
> *With grace sufficient day by day;*
> *Through good or ill He gently leads,*
> *If we but let Him have His way.* —Rohrs

The "what" of our future is determined by the "Who" of eternity.

The *Our Daily Bread* Writers

Dave Branon (DB), for eighteen years the managing editor of *Sports Spectrum* magazine, now is an editor for Discovery House Publishers and RBC Ministries. He has written over two thousand devotional articles and fourteen books. His most recent book is *Beyond the Valley*. Dave and his wife, Sue, love rollerblading and spending time with their children and grandchildren. Dave also enjoys traveling overseas with students on ministry trips.

Anne Cetas (AC), the managing editor of *Our Daily Bread* (ODB), has been on the editorial staff of ODB for over thirty years and began writing for ODB in September 2004. Anne and her husband, Carl, enjoy long walks and bicycling together, and they work as mentors in an inner-city ministry. Anne also teaches Sunday school and disciples new believers.

Bill Crowder (BC), who spent over twenty years in pastoral ministry, is an associate Bible teacher for RBC Ministries. Bill spends much of his time in Bible-teaching ministry for Christian leaders around the world. He is also the author of several books, including *The Path of His Passion* and *Singing the Songs of the Brokenhearted*. Bill and his wife, Marlene, have five children and several grandchildren.

Henry G. Bosch (HGB) served as the first editor of the daily devotional booklet that became *Our Daily Bread* and contributed many of the earliest articles. He was also one of the singers on the Radio Bible Class live broadcast.

Dennis DeHaan (DD) is a nephew of RBC founder Dr. M. R. DeHaan. He pastored two churches in Iowa and Michigan before joining the

RBC staff in 1971. He served as associate editor of ODB from 1973 until 1982, and then as editor until June 1995.

Mart DeHaan (MD) is the grandson of RBC founder, Dr. M. R. DeHaan, and the son of former president, Richard W. DeHaan. Mart is the president of RBC Ministries and is heard regularly on the *Discover the Word* radio program and is seen on *Day of Discovery* television. Mart and his wife, Diane, have two children.

Dr. M. R. DeHaan (MRD) was the founder of Radio Bible Class and one of the founders of *Our Daily Bread*. A physician who later in life became a pastor, he was well known for his gravelly voice and impassioned Bible teaching. His commitment to ministry was to lead people of all nations to personal faith and maturity in Christ. RBC Ministries continues to build upon the spiritual foundation of Dr. DeHaan's vision and work. A biography of Dr. DeHaan, *M. R. DeHaan: The Life Behind the Voice* by James R. Adair, is available from Discovery House Publishers.

Richard DeHaan (RD) was president of RBC Ministries and teacher on RBC programs for twenty years. He was the son of RBC founder, Dr. M. R. DeHaan, and wrote a number of full-length books and study booklets for RBC. Often called "the encourager," Richard was committed to faithfulness to God's Word and to integrity as a ministry. Richard went to be with the Lord in 2002.

David Egner (DE) is retired from RBC Ministries. During his years at RBC, Dave was editor of *Discovery Digest* and *Campus Journal* (now called *Our Daily Journey*). Dave still teaches English and writing at Cornerstone University and has enjoyed occasional guest-professor stints at Bible colleges in Russia. He and his wife, Shirley, live in Grand Rapids, Michigan.

Dennis Fisher (DF) was a professor of evangelism and discipleship at Moody Bible Institute for eight years. In 1998 he joined RBC Ministries, where he currently serves as managing editor of ChristianCourses.com. Dennis has two adult children and one grandson. He and his wife, Janet, live in DeWitt, Michigan.

Vernon C. Grounds (VG) went to be with the Lord on September 12, 2010, at the age of 96. He wrote over five hundred articles for ODB from 1993–2009. Former president of Denver Seminary and then chancellor, Dr. Grounds also had an extensive preaching, teaching, and counseling ministry. He will be deeply missed by many for his godly wisdom and example.

Tim Gustafson (TG) has worked with RBC Ministries for more than fifteen years and currently serves as Associate Director of Publications for RBC. Tim and his wife, Leisa, have one daughter and seven sons.

C. P. Hia (CPH) and his wife, Lin Choo, reside in the island nation of Singapore. C. P. has been a teaching leader for a men's Bible study for the past eighteen years. A retired businessman, he serves in the RBC Ministries Singapore office as Assistant International Director.

Cindy Hess Kasper (CHK) has served for more than thirty years at RBC, where she is now associate editor for *Our Daily Journey*. She is a daughter of Clair Hess, who for many years was RBC senior editor, from whom she learned a love for singing and working with words. Cindy and her husband, Tom, have three grown children and seven grandchildren, in whom they take great delight.

Albert Lee (AL) is Director of International Ministries for RBC and has the passion, vision, and energy to help expand the work of RBC Ministries. Albert grew up in Singapore, attended Singapore Bible College, and served with Singapore Youth for Christ from 1971 to 1999. Albert and his wife, Catherine, have two children and live in Singapore.

Julie Ackerman Link (JAL) is a founding partner of Blue Water Ink, a company that provides writing, editing, designing, and typesetting services. She has edited hundreds of books, including many for Discovery House Publishers. She has been writing for ODB since 2000 and is the author of *Above All, Love* and *A Heart for God*. Julie and her husband, Jay, are both involved in ministry at their church in Grand Rapids, Michigan.

David McCasland (DM) researches and helps develop biographical documentaries for *Day of Discovery* television. His books include the award-winning biography *Oswald Chambers: Abandoned to God* and

Eric Liddell: Pure Gold. David and his wife, Luann, have four grown children and live in Colorado Springs, Colorado.

Haddon Robinson (HR) is the discussion leader for RBC Ministries' *Discover the Word* radio program. Dr. Robinson teaches at Gordon-Conwell Theological Seminary, where he is the Harold J. Ockenga Distinguished Professor of Preaching, and has been recognized as one of the twelve most effective preachers in the English-speaking world. Dr. Robinson's articles have been published in many magazines, and he has authored several books, including *What Jesus Said about Successful Living* and *Decision Making by the Book.* He and his wife, Bonnie, live in Pennsylvania.

David Roper (DR) was a pastor for more than thirty years and now directs Idaho Mountain Ministries, a retreat dedicated to the encouragement of pastoral couples. David is the author of thirteen books, including *Psalm 23: The Song of a Passionate Heart* and *Teach Us to Number Our Days.* David enjoys fishing, hiking, and being streamside with his wife, Carolyn.

Joe Stowell (JS), former president of Moody Bible Institute, currently serves as president of Cornerstone University in Grand Rapids, Michigan. An internationally recognized speaker, Joe has also written numerous books, including *Radical Reliance, Eternity,* and *The Upside of Down.* He and his wife, Martie, have three children and ten grandchildren.

Herb Vander Lugt (HVL) remained a vital contributor to ODB up to the time he went to be with His Lord and Savior on December 2, 2006. Herb served as Senior Research Editor for RBC Ministries and had been with the ministry since 1966. Herb pastored six churches and, after retiring from the pastorate in 1989, held three interim ministerial positions.

Paul Van Gorder (PVG) began writing regularly for ODB in 1969 and continued until 1992. He also served as associate Bible teacher for the *Day of Discovery* television program and traveled extensively as a speaker for Radio Bible Class. He went home to be with the Lord in September 2009.

Marvin Williams (MW) has been writing for ODB since 2007 and also writes for *Our Daily Journey*. Marvin is senior teaching pastor at Trinity Church in Lansing, Michigan. He has also been associate pastor of youth at New Hope Baptist Church and assistant pastor at Calvary Church in Grand Rapids. Marvin and his wife, Tonia, have three children.

Joanie Yoder (JY), a favorite among ODB readers, went home to be with her Savior in 2004. She and her husband established a Christian rehabilitation center for drug addicts in England many years ago. Widowed in 1982, Joanie learned to rely on the Lord's help and strength. She wrote with hope about true dependence on God and His life-changing power.

Acknowledgments

January 16, lines from "So Send I You" by E. Margaret Clarkson, © 1968 Singspiration. Used by permission.

January 29, lines by Thomas O. Chisholm, © Renewal 1951 Hope Publishing Co. Used by permission.

February 13, lines from "When Love Is Found" by Brian Wren, © 1983 Hope Publishing Co., Carol Stream, Ill. All rights reserved. Used by permission.

February 15, lines by Haldor Lillenas, © Renewal 1945 Haldor Lillenas, assigned to Hope Publishing Co. Used by permission.

February 18, lines from "Be Thou My Vision," trans. by Mary E. Byrne, versified by Eleanor H. Hull, © Chatto and Windus, Ltd., London. Used by permission.

March 1, lines by Thomas O. Chisholm, © Renewal 1951 Hope Publishing Co. Used by permission.

March 4, June 26, November 24, lines from "The Love of God" by Frederick M. Lehman, © Renewal 1945, Nazarene Publishing.

April 8, lines by Julia Johnston, © Renewal 1939 Hope Publishing Co.

April 10, lines by Helen H. Lemmel, © Renewal 1950 H. H. Lemmel.

April 24, lines by Thomas Chisholm, © Renewal 1951 Hope Publishing Co.

May 4, lines by Baynard L. Fox, © 1963 Fox Music Publications. Used by permission.

May 27, lines by Amy Carmichael, © Dohnavur Fellowship.

Note to the Reader

The publisher invites you to share your response to the message of this book by writing Discovery House Publishers, P.O. Box 3566, Grand Rapids, MI 49501, U.S.A. For information about other Discovery House books, music, videos, or DVDs, contact us at the same address or call 1-800-653-8333. Find us on the Internet at http://www.dhp.org/ or send e-mail to books@dhp.org.